The Soviet Union in Transition

About the Book and Editor

Because of the recent transition in the Soviet Union's leadership, scholars worldwide have found it necessary to reevaluate Soviet domestic and foreign policy. In this volume, prominent Japanese, U.S., and European experts examine changes within the USSR as well as Soviet reactions to changes in the rest of the world. They assess the immediate implications of change for such areas as technology, energy policy, and economic reform and deliver commentaries on current policy directions and historical backgrounds of Soviet policies.

To commemorate its silver jubilee and to add the valuable perspective of Japanese Soviet-studies scholars to Western analyses, the Japan Institute of International Affairs held the symposium on which this volume is based.

Kinya Niiseki is director of the Japan Institute of International Affairs and the former Japanese ambassador to Austria, India, and the USSR.

Published in cooperation with the
Japan Institute of International Affairs

The Japan Institute of International Affairs, a central research institution, was founded in 1959 on the strong initiative of the late Prime Minister Shigeru Yoshida. In 1960 it was formally authorized by the Japanese Ministry of Foreign Affairs as a private, nonprofit, and independent organization. In commemoration of its twenty-fifth anniversary in 1985, the institute created the nation's first Center for Soviet Studies, aiming at enlarging and strengthening the study of the Soviet Union. At present, the institute's sphere of research covers a broad spectrum of issues ranging from international politics to international economics and law, thereby reflecting the enhanced position of Japan in the world community.

The Soviet Union in Transition

edited by Kinya Niiseki

Contributors

Seweryn Bialer
Sir James Eberle
Marshall I. Goldman
Tsuyoshi Hasegawa
Kenichi Ito
Young C. Kim
Hiroshi Kimura
Kazuyuki Kinbara
Peter Knirsch
Boris Meissner
Tsuneaki Sato
Donald S. Zagoria

Routledge
Taylor & Francis Group
LONDON AND NEW YORK

First published 1987 by Westview Press

Published 2019 by Routledge
52 Vanderbilt Avenue, New York, NY 10017
2 Park Square, Milton Park, Abingdon, Oxon OX14 4RN

Routledge is an imprint of the Taylor & Francis Group, an informa business

Library of Congress Cataloging-in-Publication Data
The Soviet Union in transition.
(Westview special studies on the Soviet Union and Eastern Europe)
1. Soviet Union—Foreign relations—1975-
2. Soviet Union—Economic policy—1981-
3. Soviet Union—Politics and government—1953-
4. Soviet Union—Foreign relations—Asia. 5. Asia—Foreign relations—Soviet Union. I. Niiseki, Kinya, 1916- . II. Series.
DK289.S686 1987 327.47 86-32611

British Library Cataloguing-in-Publication Data
The Soviet Union in transition.—(Westview special studies on the Soviet Union and Eastern Europe).
1. Soviet Union—Foreign relations —1975-
I. Niiseki, Kinya
327.47 PK289

ISBN 13: 978-0-367-29618-6 (hbk)

ISBN 13: 978-0-367-31164-3 (pbk)

Contents

Preface

I would like to express my sincere gratitude to the participants from the United States, Europe, and Japan. Their participation has enabled us to reach our objectives, and I believe that the presentations and opinions of these participants resulted in suggestions that will be extremely useful in analyzing Soviet policies under Gorbachev's leadership.

Finally, on behalf of the Japan Institute of International Affairs, I wish to acknowledge the assistance of the Ministry of Foreign Affairs, the Kajima Institute of International Peace, the Japan Foundation, the Tokyo Club, and the Asia Foundation for meeting part of the obligations for the symposium.

Kinya Niiseki

Introduction

Owing to geographical proximity and the complexity of Japanese-Soviet relations, the USSR has always been of intense interest to Japanese scholars and the Japanese public. The recent changes in the USSR's leadership following a prolonged period of succession crises have further enhanced Japan's interest in Soviet affairs, and Japanese experts on the Soviet Union have begun to seek closer contacts with U.S. and European researchers. In turn, steady advances in Soviet studies in Japan have motivated scholars in the United States and Europe to seek the fresh insights that the Japanese view offers them.

With this in mind, and in commemoration of its silver jubilee, the Japan Institute of International Affairs brought together several prominent Soviet-affairs experts from the United States, Europe, and Japan at the Tokyo International Symposium on the Soviet Union in Transition. The objectives of the symposium were to evaluate the new Soviet leadership under Gorbachev, to assess the immediate implications of Soviet policy orientation, and to envision the character of Soviet society in the coming decade.

As an open field for debate, the exchange promoted by this symposium broke fertile ground for cultivating, comparing, and synthesizing ideas.

The symposium succeeded in fulfilling its mandate. In particular, its international composition revealed the processes by which geographical and national concerns influence perceptions of the USSR and determine the ways in which scholars from different parts of the world analyze the Soviets.

For instance, the Europeans at the symposium viewed the Soviets as posing a lesser threat than that perceived by the U.S. scholars. In addition, the Europeans suggested that by maintaining diplomatic pressure while promoting constructive dialogue and cultural exchanges, the West could encourage the USSR to make changes it might not be willing to undertake if it felt pressured by outside interests. By contrast, some U.S. experts sensed that the Soviets might resort to foreign expansion to divert the tension among the populace that has resulted from domestic decline. Others expressed the belief that economic problems would constrain Soviet expansionism.

Some of the Japanese participants felt that the economic importance of their country might move the USSR to take Japan more seriously. They also surmised that as the Soviet leadership begins to recognize the Japanese influence, the USSR might actually attempt to undermine Western solidarity by seeking closer ties with Japan and Western Europe.

In the realm of domestic policy, the Japanese, U.S., and European assessments of Gorbachev's goals and limitations were in general agreement: Significant reforms will be very difficult for Gorbachev to accomplish; in fact, the only conceivable reforms will occur within the system, perhaps including some highly visible but essentially token changes.

A consensus was also reached with regard to the Soviet economy: Although Gorbachev will try to improve economic performance by overhauling current organizations and practices, no fundamental economic reform will occur given the underlying immobility of the Soviet system.

Along the way to that conclusion, the exchange of perspectives among participants was particularly fruitful. A Japanese participant who noted the parallels between Chinese economic reform and Eastern European experiences shed new light on recent developments in the USSR. Then, the European perspective disclosed a similarity in the trade relations between Japan and the Soviet Union and those between Eastern and Western Europe: In both relationships, political constraints emerged during the 1970s as trade volumes increased, and trade relations were complicated by the general fear of becoming too dependent on Western countries. Finally, an American interpretation of the economic impact of Soviet energy policies revealed that the USSR has much to learn from Japanese conservation practices if it is to meet its own energy needs.

The participants also generally agreed that the influence of the USSR's military sector will continue to be strong. Because the military is faced with a great need for advanced technology, it is not likely to resist a certain amount of economic reform and even some improvement in relations with the West.

To the Japanese, it appears that the Soviets have three policy options: (1) to ease international tension as a means of obtaining new technology on credit from the West, (2) to restrict military expenditure and avoid increased investment in the military sector, and (3) to embark on reform from above. From the European perspective, on the other hand, the Soviet Union's main problem with high technology is not access or invention, but implementation: The centralized socialist system discourages the introduction of new technology into everyday practice, regardless of whether the technology has been domestically developed or imported from abroad.

The most important overall conclusion reached was that the confrontational stance of the two superpowers is unlikely to change and will continue to influence the course of international politics. The current period of transition in the Soviet Union offers General Secretary Gorbachev an opportunity to improve the world climate by improving relations with the United States through continued arms control negotiations. Quite apart from national or geographical concerns, all of the symposium participants recognized the importance of continued efforts by the two superpowers to reach an understanding and maintain world peace.

The Japan Institute of International Affairs sought to introduce to foreign participants the present level of Soviet studies in Japan. We hope that we succeeded in fulfilling this aim and that the symposium facilitated future cooperative research among Japanese and foreign researchers and institutions.

1

The Soviet Union in a Changing World

Seweryn Bialer

The title of this chapter defines the problem for the Soviets and for us: The world is changing very rapidly and the situation in the 1980s is very different from that in the 1970s, when the Soviet Union was changing very slowly. Until recently, there had been a gap in many respects between what was happening in the Soviet Union and what was happening in the rest of the world. But the traditional Soviet slogan, "to catch up with and surpass the industrial countries of the world" in economic or military power, has now been replaced in practice if not in words by the desire to keep up with the industrial democracies in technology and to some extent in military matters as well.

I have divided this chapter into two parts. The first will deal with the changing world and the second with the Soviet Union. Without an understanding of what has changed in the world, one cannot really understand the major dilemma in which the Soviet Union finds itself today and which, in my opinion, will continue throughout the 1980s and beyond. Of course, the subject matter—a changing world—is enormous; accordingly, I shall provide some very brief comments and then concentrate on one element of the changing world—namely, the correlation of forces, both political and military, in the international arena.

The underlying change in the world over the past ten years was the technological revolution. The third industrial revolution into which many countries, almost all industrial democracies, entered has been a revolution of communications, information, and services, and we only vaguely understand it. The question of how far this revolution will go has not yet been fully analyzed. When Andropov noted in one of his articles that the Soviet people really do not know the society in which they live—that their images are based on the past—I realized that one could say the same about Western societies with regard to the technological revolution. We are too preoccupied with its immediate development, but we really have not studied deeply what the consequences of this revolution will be for all the countries of the world.

There is a new factor to consider now, an element that we all regarded in the 1950s and 1960s as being in decline in the industrial democracies—namely, the question of nationalism. In my opinion, an upsurge of nationalism has occurred in the industrial democracies. It is largely related to the issue of protectionism.

Another factor we did not expect has been the rise of fundamentalism. Fundamentalism can be understood as pertaining not only to religion but to ideology as well. I am referring here to both Islamic fundamentalism and the upsurge of ideological fundamentalism occurring in the United States.

A third factor is the increased polarization occurring in almost all dimensions of international affairs. There is no doubt that after a period of fifteen years of improvement in U.S.-Soviet relations (or, let's say, at least the absence of a decline), we now see a period in which the polarization between the democratic countries and the Soviet Union has increased, especially with regard to relations between the Soviet Union and the United States. It is not a cold war like the one we remember from the first ten years after World War II, a period without any communication and without any recognition, either by the Soviet Union or by the United States, that a conflict had to be managed. The rules of the game, and some kind of minimal accommodation to prevent confrontation, simply had to be defined. But this is not the case today. I think that even during the most tense moments of U.S.-Soviet relations in the past few years—in the middle of the Reagan administration, for instance—the world was not close to a war; and I do not believe that we have a cold war now. One reason we cannot speak about cold war is that, although détente has been nearly destroyed, the damage has occurred primarily in the relations between the Soviet Union and the United States. But détente is still alive—maybe not so vibrant as in the past, but still very much alive in Europe. Nevertheless, I must stress that the changes occurring in the world have resulted in a greater polarization between the two superpowers—a polarization that, in my opinion, will continue for a very long time regardless of the achievements gained in the summit meeting or in arms negotiations after that.

Another great polarization exists between the north and the south. The illusion that developing countries can industrialize and develop—and especially the illusion that the Soviet model provides a road, a map of how to change, of how to become industrial—has been abandoned not only in Africa, which is faced with a tragic economic situation, but also in countries in Central and South America. Moreover, the gap between the north and the south in international relations has grown rather than contracted. At the same time, the idea of socialism in those countries has declined enormously (albeit with some exceptions).

A still greater polarization exists within the alliance of free nations: Western Europe, Japan, and the United States. Differences of opinion and policy are inevitable between sovereign bodies, but I think that the level of polarization among these nations today is much greater than it has been in the past.

Let me now point to a potential source of trouble that is difficult to analyze: For the first time in Western Europe there are two parties out of power (one in Germany and one in Great Britain) that have programs of military security and foreign policy that in many respects are at variance with the consensus of the nations of the Atlantic Alliance. Of course, one can always say that parties out of power change when they come to power—and this often is the case. But in my opinion the variance here is so great that even if there is movement closer to the center, some basic military and political differences will remain. Three years ago I wouldn't have thought that the Labour party (because of its movement to the Left) or the German Socialist party would come to power; but it is still possible that within the next five years those parties will come into power. This very possibility is a symbol, in a way, of the differences between the United States and Western Europe, both in their approach to the Soviet Union and in general policy.

Polarization also exists within the Soviet empire—that is, within the "Soviet alliance." Never before have we seen both the population and the communist elites of Eastern European countries fighting for greater independence from the Soviet Union; nor have the differences between the Soviet Union and almost all Eastern European countries been so great. I am speaking, of course, about the whole area, not about specific countries; and the situation is new precisely because, despite the occurrence of rebellions, uprisings, and unionism such as Solidarity in Poland, there has never before been such a combination of public dissatisfaction and dissatisfaction of the elite with relations with the Soviet Union.

We also see a new situation in the arms race, particularly with regard to the use of space. Both the concept of defensive versus offensive weapons and the philosophy of arms deployment are of crucial importance and great complexity. The question of verification may very well be the stumbling block that makes impossible a comprehensive arms agreement. In this age of missiles, nobody can know whether a warhead is nuclear or conventional; hence there must be some verification of the destruction, production, and deployment of weapons—verification that is impossible in space (that is, by means of satellites).

The arms control talks of the 1960s and 1970s represented gradual steps—very minimal steps in many respects—in the effort to move forward the idea of arms control. The SALT type of arms control agreement has completely lost its constituency, on both the Right and the Left in the United States. The Right was always against it, and the Left has become disillusioned with it because during the time it lasted, the number of warheads in the arsenals of the great powers nearly tripled. So what we are now facing is a struggle, a negotiation for an agreement with the Soviet Union that will become comprehensive, that *must* become comprehensive—an agreement that will have to take into consideration all types of weapons and other countries, not only the Soviet Union and the United States, but, for example, England, France, and China as well. This is a very difficult proposition, and we have clearly entered a period of arms control and arms race quite different from that of the past.

In speaking about the changing world, I would now like to concentrate on one point—namely, on the *correlation of forces.* The term itself originated in the Soviet Union, and its meaning is much broader than that of *military balance.* It includes economic equilibrium, social stability, and even psychological balance. I think it is important to speak in such terms—that is, in terms that go beyond the military question within the correlation of forces—not only because this perspective is valuable in itself but also because it reflects the way in which the Soviet leaders themselves analyze the West. This is the first question they ask themselves when they are deciding on long-term or middle-range strategies: What is the correlation of forces?

The general conclusion, in my opinion, should be that the correlation of forces in the 1980s, in comparison especially to the early 1970s, a ten-year difference, has shifted dramatically against the Soviet Union. Yet no real change has occurred in military balance over the past five or six years. Every step we have taken has also been taken by the Soviet Union—and vice versa. So the military balance, as such, is not different. Nevertheless, the man in the street would say otherwise—and he would be right in a sense, because the military balance has changed dramatically in a psychological way. The image of power, and of who holds that power, *has* changed. But the actual military balance has not.

What has changed in the military realm, however, is the direction in which the military balance is moving. The present trend started in the late 1970s under President Carter and sped up under President Reagan. It is now headed either toward a new arms race that neither superpower could win or toward a comprehensive arms control agreement that will be equitable, symmetrical, and just for both countries, one that will provide for common security instead of security for individual nations.

With regard to nonmilitary factors, there is no doubt that the Soviet Union currently faces many dilemmas and crises. The crises are not solely economic but have social, political, cultural, ideological, and psychological dimensions as well. Indeed, given the increased difficulties in the Soviet Union along all such dimensions (relative to the past), we would have to describe the crisis as systemic.

The Soviet Union's crisis can also be viewed from a completely different perspective—namely, in comparison to other countries, both democratic and nondemocratic. Until the early 1970s, the gap between the Soviet Union and its adversaries had closed (for instance, its GNP had improved significantly relative to other countries, especially the United States). But this relative improvement has ceased, and there is no sign that the Soviet Union's weakening will be reversed. Evidence of this crisis can be seen clearly in the realm of technology as well as in the military field. In short, the gap, far from being closed, is now actually widening.

A change in Soviet foreign policy is also evident. Over the past six or seven years, the Soviets have lost the initiative in the international arena. They have been reactive in their policy, reacting to what other countries did or wanted to do. They clearly have been and still are in a period of retrenchment in which they cannot expand as they had done in the 1970s. They will have to continue to concentrate on fewer targets of opportunities for gaining influence and power than they had in the 1970s.

In my opinion, the Soviets' foreign policy has no central concept. Those who think that détente with Western Europe is a substitute for détente with the United States are, I believe, in great error. In the Soviet Union the distinction is not whether détente—good relations with the United States—should exist or be restored, and whether one should concentrate on the Western Europeans as the other partner for détente; rather, the issue is how to use Western Europe in reaching détente with the United States. At a time when the relations between the United States and the Soviet Union are poor, Western Europe provides a target of opportunity that the Soviet Union used very clumsily in the last German elections but one probably being employed now in a much more imaginative way: pressure on the United States to make concessions to the Soviet Union in arms control negotiations.

Soviet policy is fraught with many dilemmas that show no sign of being resolved. The dilemma in the Soviets' internal situation is that they are weaker than before but still have high aspirations, and in their relations with Third World countries the Soviets are unclear in their goals and very dissatisfied with the present situation.

To illustrate the problems in Soviet foreign policy one need only mention the situation in Africa, where more so-called national liberation movements are fighting against the Soviets and Soviet friends than against the United States or Western Europe and their friends. This situation represents a major change.

A major change is also under way in Eastern Europe. At present, this region could best be described, I believe, as the "Greater Eastern European Co-Stagnation Sphere." The economic, political, and military situation there has clearly entered a period of decline.

Of course, the most obvious symbol of this decline is Poland. And it is rightly so considered—not only because of its importance as the larger and most strategically located country (and with the largest army) in the Warsaw Pact, but also because its stability has not been restored. (In other words, the unrest in this Eastern European country did not, after it was quashed, lead to normalization as had happened in Hungary in 1956 and in Czechoslovakia after 1968.) Indeed, the Polish situation has not been resolved. By the same token, one should not mistake the apathy and fatigue of the Polish workers for signs that Poland has stabilized. It has not.

The central dilemma is one between cohesion and viability—between stability and orthodoxy. Let me say a few words on this question of stability and orthodoxy. The Soviet Union has learned from the Polish example. In its hopes to bring about political orthodoxy in Eastern Europe, it is pursuing, I would say, a very hard line in Eastern Europe. But the Soviet Union also wants the Eastern European nations of its empire to be stable. And to be stable those nations must have closer relations with Western Europe. They must not only open up trade relations but also acquire credit. Hence the clash of two different Soviet desires: the desire for political orthodoxy so as not to encourage a situation akin to Solidarity, and the desire for social and political stability, which requires Western help.

There is no way in which this dilemma can be resolved. I think that Gorbachev made a short-run decision for orthodoxy, for a hard policy. But what will happen in the longer run cannot be foreseen. As the Soviet Union itself cannot pay for development in Eastern Europe, its policy will continue along the same lines as before—and the stability of Eastern Europe, which is based on the performance of the regimes involved, not on nationalism or tradition, will be endangered. Moreover, the social instability in Eastern Europe will lead to political instability.

We must now return to our discussion of correlation of forces and military balance. A major element in the change related to the former is the movement of the center of gravity of economic and military matters to Asia. This is an extremely important trend, a trend visible along many dimensions. Inside the Soviet Union, the question pertains to Siberia. The Soviet Union cannot survive as a global economic and military power if the development of Siberia is not achieved, regardless of the cost. From a military point of view, it is clear that the arms race in the Pacific has grown relative to the situation in Europe. Consider, for example, the following questions: "When you speak about global parity with the United States, do you speak about parity only in the global sense (meaning that disparities within areas are not important so long as parity is achieved overall)? Or do you see the necessity of parity within every area itself?" Until three years ago the Soviet military would have answered that global parity is essential and that regional parity would be required only in Europe. Two years ago the military would have specified two areas—the Western Pacific in addition to Europe. In short, Soviet military expenditures in the Pacific are greater now and, in fact, are increasing more rapidly than expenditures relative to the central theater in Europe.

The movement of the aforementioned center of gravity toward Asia can also be seen in the fact that Japan, which until recently had been primarily interested in economic questions and was "only" a great economic power, has decided to become a great political power as well. Indeed, Japan is currently strengthening its political ties with various countries, and its political influence has grown immensely in many areas—especially the Middle East and Brazil. Needless to say, this development is regarded by the Soviet Union as a major blow to its position in Asia.

A related phenomenon is China's modernization. I cannot predict whether the Chinese will achieve all they want to achieve. I must simply say that what is happening in China is potentially the third most important event of the twentieth century following World War I and the development of nuclear weapons. The modernization of 1,300,000,000 Chinese over the next forty or fifty years is a very unlikely scenario. However, it is possible—given a good agricultural base that would provide food for the cities—that some regions near Shanghai, Beijing, and Canton will develop modern industry and, consequently, corporate arrangements with Japan, West Germany, and the United States. Therefore, even if China fulfills only 10 percent of its goals, we will see another Japan on the globe.

Another element in the change of the correlation of forces concerns the movement of continental Europe away from the notion of One

Europe—that is, away from the idea of a unified Western Europe. This can be seen in the relative economic decline of Western Europe, where the whole bureaucratic structure of major industrial organizations—so perfectly suited to the second industrial revolution—has proved quite unsuitable for the third industrial revolution. Hence the gap between the United States and Japan on the one hand and Western Europe on the other will likely increase.

One can see in Western Europe a growing difference in the approach to the Soviet Union displayed by that region and the United States. In some respects, Europeans judge the Soviets by the behavior they display within their region. They therefore view the Soviet Union as a very troublesome neighbor. But the United States, which views the Soviet Union from a global perspective—and in a more ideological way than does Western Europe—views the Soviet Union as an adversary.

Major changes in the Middle East are contributing, as well, to the change in the correlation of forces. The Arab-Israeli conflict there, which has been central to the conflict in the Middle East, has declined in relative importance; at the same time, the conflict within the Arab world—the Muslim world—has increased in importance. It is also there that the Soviet influence has reached a new low—the lowest point ever, in fact.

Finally, we come to the change in the United States. The decade of the late 1960s and 1970s was a terrible one for this country. It was a decade of the Vietnam War, a decade of retreat from its leadership role, a decade of neo-isolationism (or at least a lack of activism) in the international arena. And Watergate, which represented a major crisis—and ultimately a victory—for the democratic institutions of the United States, left a scar of disunity and doubt in the United States that has healed at last only in the past few years. Yet because of its economic performance and its recent surge of technology, the United States is in a better position now than before to use its power as a foreign policy resource.

This combination of factors leads me to conclude that a massive change (rather than a cyclical one) has occurred over the past six or seven years. This change will be considered one of the major political and military developments of the twentieth century. The nations that can adjust to that change will prevail in the 1980s and 1990s; those that do not adjust will defer.

How has the Soviet Union adjusted to the new international situation, to the changing world? In answering this question, we must point to the Soviet paradox. The Soviet Union is a country with enormous military power, but one that is also declining domestically and losing its "empire." At the same time its aspirations for international dominance, for equality with the United States, and for greater influence and power in the Third World have not declined. I do not believe that the Soviet Union will become the dominant international power because it simply does not have the resources. (Its military power alone is not a sufficient resource.) The real danger lies in its aspirations to become such a power.

How can such a paradox continue to exist? My answer is very simple: It has survived because of nuclear weapons. The Soviet Union and the United States are *not* equal powers. The latter is far superior in military, economic, and technological potential; without nuclear power the Soviet Union would today be in a militarily worse situation than it was in 1940. Nuclear weapons have equalized unequal powers—namely, the democratic nations and the Soviet Union. And nuclear weapons have proven useful to the Soviet Union in other respects as well. In particular, they have led to a decline in conventional military expenditures for both sides—in the case of the West, to probably one of the lowest levels in the twentieth century. At the same time, the growth of strategic potential in the Soviet Union has been paralleled by the development of conventional weaponry.

In addition, of course, the Soviets can use nuclear weapons to manipulate the legitimate fears of people in other countries. By contrast, such fears cannot be created or manipulated by the West in a country as closed as the Soviet Union.

As I noted earlier, the dimensions of the crisis that forms one side of the Soviet paradox are many. Politically, this crisis has manifested itself in the paralysis of leadership evident throughout the past five years. Socially, it has been expressed in terms of alcoholism, absenteeism, corruption, and thievery—social phenomena that Gorbachev is now trying to fight but that cannot be conquered simply by coercion. Other steps, such as social reforms, are needed. Culturally, the crisis has been reflected (even given the practice of censorship) in books recently published in the Soviet Union. Previously, books were characterized by Hollywood-style happy endings; now the futility and the emptiness of life is often presented. Depicted in one work are the efforts of a factory director to prevent the pollution of a river. He wins his battle and is promoted to a higher post. However, the director who succeeds him pollutes the river himself.

The Soviet Union's crisis has revealed a pessimism that was merely interrupted by Andropov and Gorbachev. The prevailing attitude stands in contrast to the optimism of the past, when people believed that the future belonged to communism, that the Soviet Union was catching up, that there were no fortresses the Bolsheviks could not conquer.

The very basis of the crisis, however, is economic in nature. The Soviet Union's current difficulties in this area have reached crisis proportions primarily because they cannot be neutralized or even partly overcome by the methods used previously. In the past the Soviets threw capital and human resources toward development, but without paying sufficient attention to other elements such as technology.

The problems of the past were partly neutralized by a high level of growth that provided for investments and the ability to employ almost 3 million new people every year in the labor force. But this is no longer possible. The increase in the labor force has declined to less than 300,000 people a year, and the investment resources are therefore small.

The issue of investments is, indeed, an important one. The concern is not guns versus butter but guns versus investments and butter versus investments. Moreover, the factor of infrastructure plays an enormous role. The Soviet Union can be likened to a giant with huge muscles and a minuscule circulation system, given that the quantity and quality of its railroads, storage places, and so on, are insufficient relative to the enormous economy of the country. The amount of waste involved is thus incredible (e.g., about 20 percent of harvested crops are wasted).

Finally, I must mention from this economic point of view the idea of the fitness of the system to particular tasks. The Soviet system has certainly succeeded in some economic tasks. It was successful in building its steel industry and in mobilizing its vast resources for the development of smokestack industries. It was very successful in military development and mildly successful in the mass production of consumer goods. But it has been quite unsuccessful with regard to agriculture.

We turn once again to the third industrial revolution, a revolution of information and communications. The fit of the Soviet system to this type of technological development has been even worse than that for agriculture. This is the case not because the Soviet Union's computers are outdated (in fact, they *are* a generation or two behind), but primarily because its social and political systems simply do not provide the adaptability, exchange of information, and equipment sufficient to maximize productivity. Therefore, in my opinion, even if the Soviet Union increased its computer production by ten times, it will remain unable to use those machines productively (as they are used in the West) unless it changes some basic rules of planning.

The crisis I have described thus far is a crisis of effectiveness, then—not a crisis of survival. Those who expect the Soviet Union to disintegrate because of its nationality problems, who believe that the Soviet Union is politically unstable, who think that there is a new arms race and that we can push and push until it explodes—such people are, in my opinion, very much in error. This crisis of effectiveness has no precedent in the history of the Soviet Union. If it is not overcome, if the trend is not reversed, the Soviet Union, in the words of Gorbachev, will not enter the twenty-first century as a respected great power.

How can the new Soviet general secretary make his way out of this crisis? Those who think in terms of a Hungarian reform or a Chinese revolution are simply mistaken. The Soviet Union's primary goal was best described by Shevardnadze before he became foreign minister (i.e., while he was still the boss of Georgia): "to improve the economic mechanism based on the existing economic mechanism." In other words, the economic mechanism must be improved without fundamental (i.e., structural) reform.

Gorbachev wants to increase social and managerial discipline, to bring science and technology closer to industry, to fight and finally abolish all the accumulated irrationalities that resulted from the idiosyncrasies of the leadership over the past five years. By doing so, Gorbachev would change the trend and slightly improve the Soviet performance. (For instance, between a quarter and a half of a point could be added to the country's GNP, which has recently grown at the rate of 2 percent a year.) Whether he will succeed in this partial improvement I cannot say for certain, of course. But my opinion is that he will succeed in some respects; if nothing else, his personnel policy will yield some positive effects.

I have no doubt at all, however, that the improvements brought about by Gorbachev's policy—a policy that does not include structural reform—will be small. Moreover, they will be exhausted by the end of this decade.

Soviet policy can be broken down into four key objectives. The first is to improve the Soviet image in the international arena—that is, to regain the fear and respect commanded by the Soviet Union in the 1970s. In my opinion, the USSR's image can be improved primarily by means of a hard-line stance. (Such a stance is apparently being taken in Afghanistan, given the intensification of fighting, the greater pressure being placed on Pakistan, and the increased intrusion into Pakistani airspace. We also see evidence of this stance in the Soviet Union's relations with Eastern Europe, where the countries of the region are being pressed to contribute more to the Soviet Union's buildup and at the same time to be politically orthodox.) The main instrument of the Soviet Union's improved image may well be Gorbachev himself. But I do not know how long this image will last.

A second goal of Soviet foreign policy is to tarnish the United States' image of invincibility—specifically, by revealing and exploiting its vulnerabilities. I think it was Adam Ulam who developed the idea that one can divide Soviet policy within every period into two types: as either the policy of a speculator or the policy of a rentier. For the speculator, the risk is high but the return is large. The rentier, on the other hand, has a slow return but perfect security. I think that, at present, the Soviet Union's policy with regard to the United States is that of a rentier.

The Soviet Union does not have to make trouble for the United States; it can simply exploit the troubles that already exist. I am speaking here primarily about such regional danger spots as the Philippines, Pakistan, the Korean peninsula, and, of course, Central America. The Soviet investment has increased, but not to the point where a confrontation with the United States is imminent; yet the level of investment is sufficient to ensure that the United States' anti-Sandinista policy will not go beyond the arming of the Contra army and that the Sandinista government will survive.

A third goal of Soviet policy pertains to Western Europe and, in my opinion, will be directed toward Japan. It involves an attempt to start a peace offensive. (The summit meeting is one such beginning, I believe.)

The fourth and final goal is arms control. I believe that the Soviet Union now really wants such control. Whether it will agree to the steps that would make possible a comprehensive arms control agreement in the negotiations between the United States and the Soviet Union, nobody knows. But given the international and domestic position of the Soviet Union, one can clearly see why it would choose to avoid an arms race that could prove very costly. Such an arms race could actually provide the United States with a first-strike capability against the Soviet Union that would not be reciprocated—particularly in the event that the United States develops a form of space defense that would defend existing U.S. ballistic missiles. At any rate, I think there is a chance that the Soviet Union is sufficiently interested in arms control to agree to a program that would be acceptable to both sides.

In conclusion, I see neither a peaceful period in front of us nor an apocalypse. I think that in order to anticipate what will happen, one has to learn the lessons implicit in what has already happened. Here are four of the most important lessons.

First, regardless of atmospherics, regardless of various hopes, the political differences between the United States and the Soviet Union are so large and go so deeply into history, into the mindsets and objective interests of the leaders, that conflict—not cooperation—will for the foreseeable future be the dominant element in U.S.-Soviet relations.

Second, I see a lesson in the fact that nuclear deterrence as the key concept of the atomic era really did work throughout the past forty years. Even after the Soviet Union achieved parity, deterrence worked quite well. We should try not to move away from the idea of deterrence. Indeed, we must rely on that idea. Of course, we would prefer a deterrence that hinges on a basic equilibrium—a stability—between the two great powers. But the main point to be made is that deterrence works.

Third, there is the lesson of prudence. Despite all the tension between the United States and the Soviet Union, there was never, in my opinion, a moment of danger of war by accident or by deliberation—either regionally or globally. The reason is that both countries followed a course of unwritten agreement to the effect that certain lines would never be crossed. I could list many such lessons of prudence, among them the situation in Lebanon. An unwritten agreement came into effect there when the Soviets brought in their officers, their technicians, and their most sophisticated anti-aircraft systems, and when the U.S. Marines landed in Lebanon and two task forces of Americans came close to the shores of Lebanon. In short, the Soviets let us know that they would use their SAM-5s only in the event of an Israeli air force attack on Damascus. (It is interesting that they specified the air force of Israel, not that of the United States—and that we looked for the first face-saving opportunity to withdraw from Lebanon.)

Another lesson of prudence: Never try to push a defeated ally too far. In 1973, for example, during the Yom Kippur War between Israel and Egypt, U.S. pressure prevented the Israelis from destroying the Egyptian army on the bank of the Suez Canal.

Finally, there is a very important lesson that I hope the Soviets have learned but one I am not sure we have learned. The lesson is very simple: Don't try to take short-term advantage of your opponent or enemy, thereby sacrificing long-range goals. Put more simply: Don't kick a superpower. In the 1970s, the United States was beset by weakness and tragedy. The Soviet Union exploited this weakness and this tragedy. By doing so, of course, it brought about a turn in the U.S. atmosphere, a change in its policy, and a completely new situation. There is no doubt that the United States is currently prevailing. But let us not be arrogant about that. And let us not imitate the Soviet error. In other words, let us try to agree with the Soviet Union on arms control negotiations that will provide equal safety for the Soviet Union and the United States.

There are two options open to the United States in an arms control agreement. The first is to develop strategic defenses, and the second is to achieve a comprehensive agreement on radical cuts in offensive weapons. I prefer the second option. I prefer it primarily because I think that it can be achieved. (The antiballistic-missile aspect of SDI can also be achieved in about fifteen to twenty years, but only as the result of an arms race in offensive weapons.) A comprehensive arms agreement on offensive weapons cannot be combined with testing and development of segments of the space defenses because the best defense for the Soviet Union would then be to increase its offensive forces.

The United States and its allies must begin to think about their relationship with the Soviet Union not as one in which the conflict can be solved—it cannot be solved because deep differences of ideology are involved—but as a relationship in which the conflict can be *managed.* Indeed, we *must* manage it—but without betraying our values and interests. At the same time, we must be able to prevent confrontations that, in going against the lessons of prudence, lead to conflict. I really do hope that we can approach the management of confict in this way; we have certainly reached a point where such management can be more successful precisely because of our great power.

2

East-West Relations: A European Perspective

Sir James Eberle

I have spent most of my adult life being concerned with the Soviet Union. I speak not as a scholar but as one occupied with the practical effects of Soviet security policy. My principal interests during my early years were narrowly based, concerned with matters of the sea and of navies. But in the latter part of my naval career, as one of NATO's three Supreme Commanders, and responsible to fifteen governments for maritime affairs in the eastern Atlantic and most of the waters of northwestern Europe, I was much more broadly concerned with the wider aspects of Soviet foreign policy. For senior military officers today need to be as much the "managers of peace" as they are the "captains of war."

My view of the Soviet Union and of its people was generally an uncomplicated one. During my naval career I had been taught the basic tenets of Marxist-Leninist faith—in not too different a way from that in which, during my school days, I had been instructed in the Christian faith and, briefly, in the other great religions of the world. But just as reading the stories of the prophets in the Bible gave me little insight into how Christians lived their lives in the modern world, so Marxism-Leninism provided me with all too little real idea of how people in the Soviet Union thought and acted on a day-to-day basis. I was, of course, aware that they had a different "framework" in which their thoughts were set—but I had little or no direct contact with the Soviets that would have enabled me to relate that framework to the practical problems that governed their lives and mine. I felt a degree of isolation from them that set "Russians" and "Russian Communists" in a quite different category from people in all other areas of the world—in Japan and China, in whose waters I spent much of my early naval career, or in

Africa, or the Middle East, or the Mediterranean and the United States, where I was fortunate to be carried in my naval duties. As a NATO commander-in-chief, I set up a skeleton "Soviet staff" in my headquarters to enable me to understand better my potential adversary, the commander-in-chief of the Soviet Northern Fleet, and his problems. But for myself, I was aware that I was able to do little more than think as an Englishman in the shoes of a Soviet admiral rather than as a Soviet admiral himself.

It was thus of very great interest to me when, having retired from the active list of the Royal Navy, I had the opportunity to visit the Soviet Union and to meet and talk with senior Soviet officials in London and Moscow and those from East European bloc countries. This brought a level of personal contact that I had never been able to achieve before. My view of the Soviet Union, previously remote and uncomplicated, now became personal and very complex. I was brought quickly to an understanding of the comment of an experienced Sovietologist who had once remarked to me, "I have come to realize that the more I know about Russia, the less I understand."

I recall listening in Moscow last year to a general of the Soviet General Staff describe why the Soviet Union felt threatened by the United States. While listening to the general, I realized as I closed my eyes that I could hear almost the same speech, almost exactly the same words, being spoken by any NATO general or admiral in Brussels about the Soviet Union. Here was a classic case of "mirror imaging," with each side describing intentions and capabilities and motives to the other that were scarcely recognizable in one's own experience. Here were the seeds of suspicion, mistrust, and fear that so easily flourish in the fertile soil of isolation and imagination. But aside from the formal level of Marxist monologue, there emerged a more personal level of contact in which the individual reaction of a Soviet colleague seemed to fit readily into my own store of human experience. Immediately I was faced with the problem of deciding whether that reaction was a genuine expression of his personal view or a conditioned response aimed at misleading and misinforming. Because of this difficulty, it tends to be the accepted Western view that all such Soviet responses are to be disbelieved and mistrusted as rhetoric and disinformation—and, in particular, that we should disregard the strong message frequently sent from Soviet bloc countries that we in the West overestimate the effect of ideology in the day-to-day process of decision making in Communist societies.

But it is doubtless far too simplistic to assume that there is little or nothing in the responses of those in official positions in the Soviet Union that is "genuine," in our normal understanding of the meaning of that word. There is an element of truth in Mr. Gorbachev's question in a recent *Time* magazine interview: Why was it that all Soviet efforts to escape from the vicious circle of the arms race and mutual suspicion were described only as "propaganda"? Yet we know that certain Soviet statements are gross distortions of the facts as we observe them. When one is told, as in the apocryphal naval story, that certain spare parts are crated in boxes in which the Top is marked Bottom and the Bottom is marked Top, it is inevitable that there is some confusion as to which way the box should be placed.

I have dwelt at some length on these rather personal reminiscences because I believe that they illustrate at an individual level some of the dilemmas that we, the democracies, face in dealing with the Soviet state. Ever since the Russian Revolution, the countries of Europe have faced the dilemma of trying to decide whether the Soviet Union is an opportunist, expansionist, and totalitarian state intent on world domination and the revolutionary introduction of international communism, or whether it is an oppressive, authoritarian, Marxist regime obsessed with its own ideology and survival. In more practical terms, can we treat the Soviet Union as one of two equal superpowers whose reaction to the Western democracies is predictable by the established norms of international behavior? Or are we to believe that the fruits of détente, seen so widely during the 1970s as a more constructive and less confrontational relationship between the two superpowers, are not borne on the tree of U.S.-Soviet relations because, in the words of Georgi Arbatov,

> bourgeois theoreticians are totally unwilling to understand that the "rules of the game" which determine the "unequal" positions of capitalism and socialism on the world arena are laid down not by communists but by history itself. Its laws dictate the steady development of society towards socialism, towards the collapse of the capitalist system. This is something to which the critics of the Marxist-Leninist conception of peaceful co-existence are unable to reconcile themselves. . . . The laws of history, according to the convictions of communists, lead capitalist society—sooner or later—to revolution; and . . . a reverse development is simply impossible. Here the question of "equality" between the two sides can no longer arise.[1]

I referred earlier to the "isolation" of Soviet society, an isolation that applies almost equally to Soviet bureaucracy. It is an isolation whose effects apply in both directions. It affects both the view of the Soviet Union by the West and that of the West by the Soviet Union. It is perhaps the basis upon which the word "perceptions" has gained so much currency in the language of international relations during the last decade. In Moscow there can be little doubt that the 1970s were perceived as a period of Soviet gain during which the "correlation of forces" moved in favor of the Soviet Union. The United States' attempt to stem the advance of communism in Southeast Asia by military action in Vietnam had failed. In the aftermath, the Nixon administration in its negotiations over SALT I and the era of détente appeared to concede the recognition, so earnestly sought by the Soviet Union, of its full status as a superpower and an equal of the United States. As the growth of U.S. military power faltered, that of the Soviet Union went from strength to strength, as emphasized in the nuclear field by the deployment of the SS-20 missile and in the conventional field by the expansion of the Soviet Navy and Air Force.

It was this perceived decline in U.S. power and influence that the new president, Ronald Reagan, set out to arrest. Through rhetoric, and by increasing military expenditure and stimulating U.S. economic growth, Mr. Reagan restored in generous measure the self-confidence of the people of the United States. At the same time, the saga of the succession of aging Soviet leaders, increasing internal economic problems, difficulties in Afghanistan, a growing sense of separate national interest among the countries of Eastern Europe, and the political failure to prevent the deployment of Cruise and Pershing II missiles in Europe indicated that, in the early 1980s, the shift in the correlation of forces that had previously been in favor of the Soviet Union was now reversed.

But perceptions are not only about what is past. They concern the present and the future as well. And it is in the field of present and future perceptions, the perceptions not only of what the Soviet Union is but also of how the West should deal with it, that we begin to see significant differences of approach between Europe and the United States.

Whether people in Europe see the Soviet Union as a "revolutionary" power or as a "status quo" power, most Europeans believe that the risks to the Soviet Union of starting a war in central Europe are immeasurably greater than the possible threats to their way of life. They still believe in deterrence, despite warnings by Henry Kissinger and others that NATO strategy is no longer credible because it relies on the threats of U.S. nuclear retaliation. Thus, unlike many Americans, they do not view the Soviet Union as an immediate military threat. Of course, they recognize the potential of Soviet military power should the Western democracies drop their guard—and there is widespread recognition of the need for strong NATO conventional forces. But Europeans increasingly see that the Soviet Union, like the United States, has much difficulty in turning its military power into political influence. There is now much less talk of the dangers of the "Finlandization" of Western Europe, not least because the Finnish people are seen to be doing very nicely in terms of their freedom to pursue their own way of life.

Thus people in Europe tend to see threats to their security in much more subtle tones of national interest than do people in the United States, in ways more related to the political challenge of the terrorists, to the social challenges of restructuring society to deal with today's technologies, and to the economic challenges of international trade competition and protectionism. There is movement toward the importance of "economic security" rather than of "territorial security," in which Japanese concepts of comprehensive security are beginning to be taken as "read," even if not "for granted"; this is only because of the underlying final sanction in the use of nuclear weapons possessed by the United States, Britain, and France. Thus when President Reagan declared the objective of his Strategic Defense Initiative (SDI) as making nuclear weapons "impotent and obsolete," it was not received with great acclaim in Europe. For if the price of making nuclear weapons impotent and obsolete was to be an increased risk of conventional war, then that price was too high to pay. Europe must not be made a haven, safe for conventional war. In two world wars with conventional weapons, more than 50 million people have been killed.

Let me immediately acknowledge the danger of suggesting that there is a single and agreed European view on the answer to the question, "What is the Soviet Union, and how do we best deal with it?" There are differences of national interest, as well as perception, among the countries of Western Europe; and, of course, there are differences of view across the political spectrum of each of the individual countries, as indeed there are in the United States. But these differences are a privilege and a right for our democracies.

Nevertheless, it would be equally wrong for me to suggest that there is no general thrust of a "prevailing view" in Western Europe. Such a view prevails because it is based upon the experiences of European history and culture, upon geopolitical factors, and, to some extent, upon a growing sense of European identity. Although the steps along the path to European unity have been long and tortuous, and although progress is likely to continue to be characterized by the process of two paces forward and one pace back, I believe that real progress has been made toward a more coherent European identity in the realms of economics, foreign policy, and European security. Western European governments have committed themselves to a full examination of a possible new treaty of Political and Security Cooperation in Europe—now going on at the Inter-Governmental Conference in Luxembourg—which was agreed by the Heads of the European Community governments at their council meeting in Milan in July. Such commitments are, I believe, helping to lead to a new and broadly accepted framework in which Western European relations with both Eastern Europe and the Soviet Union can be conducted. This framework constitutes a four-cornered structure in which a "macro" dialogue is conducted at the superpower level between Washington and Moscow—and at a parallel "micro" level there is a growing dialogue between Western and Eastern European countries. There are then, of course, the vital "end" links of relations between Western Europe and the United States, and between the Soviet Union and Eastern Europe; there are also cross-linkages between Washington and Eastern Europe, and between Western Europe and Moscow.

As a matter of more limited interest, I have been struck in my own talks with Soviet officials by the dichotomy in the Soviet view of where their principal lines of contact should lie. In one sense, the Soviet Union, as befits a superpower, wishes only to talk seriously with another superpower—which essentially excludes the Europeans. And yet the Russians also see themselves as "Europeans" and thus feel frustrated that other Europeans listen so little to the messages they are trying to convey.

I have spoken thus far in the most general terms about some of the European background to East-West relations. I would now like to turn in more specific terms to some of the issues of today. I had hoped to arrive at this conference fresh from two separate series of high-level meetings in Britain with Soviet officials. Unfortunately, the defection of the Soviet KGB chief in London, Mr. Gordievsky, and the resulting expulsion of Soviet and British diplomats led to the postponement of both sets of talks. Insofar as these talks involved the relationship between my own institute, the Royal Institute of International Affairs, and our sister institute in Moscow, IMEMO (the Institute of World Economy and International Relations), there were indications that, in private at least, the Russians shared in some measure the British government's wish to resume a more normal relationship at an early stage.

The postponement of these talks was a particular disappointment to me because I believe that we stand at a moment of great importance in the field of East-West relations—an importance that, at least until very recently, did not appear to be appreciated by the Reagan administration in Washington.

Let us go back to the turn of the year. Mr. Gorbachev, not yet the elected leader of the Politburo and the Soviet Communist party, visited Britain. He and his wife Raisa made an immediate public impact. Here was a Soviet leader with a style that was very different from that of the stereotype of the senior Soviet *apparatchik*—slow, stolid, and unsmiling. Mrs. Thatcher commented that this was a man with whom she could do business.

Very shortly afterward came the death of Mr. Chernenko and the rapid announcement of Mr. Gorbachev's election to the leadership. We then knew that this was a Soviet leader with a new and refreshing style. Here was a new communicator, able to discuss and argue on his feet, and to whom ordinary citizens in Western countries felt that they could relate. What we did not know was whether this change of style in Soviet leadership might also represent a change of substance in Soviet policy. The signs that might be an indicator of the future were eagerly awaited from Mr. Gorbachev's first speech to the Central Committee meeting in March. In the Soviet version of this story, Mr. Gorbachev's advisers carefully examined every phrase of that speech to make it as conciliatory as they were able, so as to indicate a wish for a new and less confrontational relationship with the United States. And, indeed, the press of Western Europe widely interpreted it in this way. But, again according to the Soviet story, the reaction of the U.S. administration was seen in Moscow to have been negative—and it was reported that Mr. Gorbachev himself felt deeply hurt by American accusations of the "hypocrisy" of Soviet leaders. In the Soviet view, an olive branch that had been offered was thrown back in their faces. Relations between the U.S. administration and the new Soviet leadership had gotten off to a poor start. By May there were statements that U.S.-Soviet relations were as bad as they had been for a number of years.

On the other hand, there were increasing signs of a more positive approach to the Soviet relationship with the countries of Western Europe. These overtures, later described by Mrs. Thatcher as a "peace offensive," were to a large extent interpreted as a replay of previous Soviet efforts, as in the case of the debate over deployment of Cruise and Pershing missiles in Europe, to divide the European allies in NATO from the United States. But if I am correct in recognizing a conscious effort to improve Soviet–Western European relations, then I believe that there may have been a more positive aspect of the policy than merely a matter of wedge-driving between Europe and the United States.

Moscow had begun to appreciate the extent of change in Eastern Europe. In almost all the Eastern European countries there is a growing recognition that socialist countries need to develop their economies, and thus their societies, in a way that is best suited to their own individual historical, geographical, and industrial needs and aspirations.

Of course, there are limits to such change, as the previous thirty years in the DDR, Czechoslovakia, Hungary, and Poland had tragically revealed; although events in China are beginning to challenge the conventional wisdom concerning where those limits may lie. But small, incremental changes are much more difficult to forbid or to resist. The course of change away from the central control enshrined in communist dogma can be seen in external as well as internal factors. The growing trade links between Eastern and Western Europe, the growing communication across the Iron Curtain such as the reception of West German television, and the worldwide flow of capital funds, all add to an increasing awareness of the need for economic reform if the socialist bloc countries are not to drop further and further behind the living standards of the West. Gone are the heady days of Mr. Khrushchev's claim that the Soviet economy would effectively bury that of the United States by the next century. Thus, if the Soviet Union is to find itself increasingly unable to control incremental economic change in Eastern Europe, then perhaps it should try to get on better terms with Western Europe, which is, in part at least, an engine of such change.

A consequence of the Soviet desire for better relations with Western Europe is to place limitations on Soviet behavior toward Eastern Europe. For Western Europe would certainly be significantly less willing to listen to a Soviet Union that was being overtly oppressive toward Eastern Europe than to a Soviet Union that appeared to be pursuing a more benign relationship.

Furthermore, there are narrower considerations of Soviet interest. Mr. Gorbachev has shown himself to be acutely aware of the economic deficiencies of the existing Soviet economic system. If these are to be corrected, there is a need both for internal change and for access to more advanced technology. If Mr. Gorbachev is forced to rule out any relationship with Mr. Reagan that might allow the Soviets to have easier access to U.S. technology, then perhaps he might try to gain access to Western European technology—an action that could be in the best interests of both sides.

But not all the indicators of U.S.-Soviet relations have been set to "stormy." In the wings, discussions have been moving ahead on regional issues; and even if the meeting on the Middle East did little more than provide the opportunity for both sides to set out their individual positions, it appears to have made possible the recognition that it was in the mutual interests of both sides to show restraint in their own Middle East involvement. Talks have also taken place behind the scenes, in due course resulting in agreement for a summit meeting between Mr. Gorbachev and Mr. Reagan.

This agreement, characterized in Soviet statements as representing "an encouraging, positive development" in U.S.-Soviet relations, seemed to give rise to early disagreements. In Washington, the impression was given that the U.S. administration saw the summit as a welcome "getting to know you" arrangement, but not as an opportunity for substantive negotiation or agreement. In Moscow, it became clear that Mr. Gorbachev was likely to challenge Mr. Reagan strongly on matters of substance, particularly in relation to Star Wars.

But such a challenge should not be seen as arising from Soviet economic weakness and decline. Mr. Gorbachev's current perception of the world may be much less favorable toward the West than we are ready to acknowledge. The Soviet government may genuinely see the Western economies as struggling to cope with the problems of industrial transition and massive unemployment. It may not unreasonably view the huge problems of international debt, with its serious political, social, and economic consequences for the Third World, as a millstone hanging around the neck of the capitalist system.

The Soviet government sees the United States as facing serious problems resulting from Reaganomics, which have more than doubled the U.S. national debt. It sees rising pressures for trade protectionism and hears of the dangers to the West of a trade war. It observes the ending of the postwar consensus on security policy in a number of Western European countries. It sees the Atlantic Alliance facing the most potentially divisive issue of its history in the Strategic Defense Initiative. And it has a new, young, vigorous leader who, for the first time, has seemingly gained the initiative in determining the attitudes of Western Europeans toward arms control—in particular, through his announcements of unilateral decisions to halt further deployments of SS-20 missiles and the testing of ASAT weapons and nuclear warheads. Mr. Shultz may, and perhaps rightly, wish to disregard Mr. Shevardnadze's UN proposals for "Star Peace" as propaganda. Western European public opinion is unlikely to do so.

The fundamental choice that faces Mr. Gorbachev, following the summit, is whether to make the improvement of U.S.-Soviet relations the focus of his foreign policy, or whether to put U.S.-Soviet relations on ice for at least the duration of the Reagan administration. His choice should logically depend on an appreciation of the likely course of U.S. foreign policy during the next two years. However, it is more likely to rest on a more narrow judgment as to whether Mr. Reagan is so committed to SDI that he is unlikely to be willing even to trade some short-term restraint on ABM testing and development in return for significant reductions in long- and intermediate-range missiles. In this case, the Soviet Union has little option but to "put the shutters up" at Geneva and to allow Soviet propaganda, pressure from Europe, and constraints on the U.S. budget to limit the development of SDI beyond the research phase.

If he decides that progress is not possible on the central nuclear issues, then Mr. Gorbachev is likely to conclude that progress in other areas of U.S.-Soviet policy—such as regional issues, trade and technology, and confidence building—will be similarly unproductive. He would then be free to allow Soviet diplomacy to play a more active role in Western Europe and Asia.

The West continually underestimates Soviet concern for the security of its eastern borders. The Soviet Union might well consider that it would have considerable potential political leverage in Japan if it was willing to consider a change in the status of the Northern Islands. Mr. Gorbachev would almost surely like to withdraw militarily from Afghanistan if he could only find a political solution that would offer a compliant Afghan government in Khabul. Such withdrawal would also open possibilities for the normalization of relations with China.

The opportunities for Soviet diplomacy in Western Europe offer many tempting potential rewards. It is significant, perhaps, that Mr. Gorbachev made his first major visit abroad as general secretary—to France—only six weeks before the U.S.-Soviet summit meeting. This could have been an indication of the importance Mr. Gorbachev attaches to Western Europe in the overall contrast of East-West relations, and of an attempt to break away from the Gromyko myopia of U.S.-Soviet dialogue, even though the superpower relationship must remain a central issue for the Soviet Union.

These are all important foreign policy objectives for the Soviet Union that could receive considerably higher priority.

In my final remarks, let me return to a more general theme—the future and long-term interests of the democracies. Looking into the next century, I consider it very unlikely that the Soviet Union will have anything to offer to the world in terms of ideology or social and economic management. It is likely to remain a global power by virtue of its military strength and its capability for destroying the world. It will inevitably be subject to the historical process of change. The direction of that change does not seem likely to follow the path of international communism. It is thus the task of the democracies to so conduct their affairs that inevitable change, to which they also will be subjected, can take place gradually and peaceably. Against this background there are two alternatives for the thrust of Western policy vis-à-vis the Soviet Union. The first is a policy of forcing change upon the Soviet Union by keeping pressure upon it in every field—by maintaining military competition, by applying economic pressure, by enforcing a rigid regime against transfers of technology, and by keeping too high the political price that Mr. Gorbachev would have to pay to gain a breathing space in which he could overhaul the Soviet economic system. This policy may be characterized by the expression "The Squeeze."

The alternative is a policy of "constructive engagement." This policy reflects the idea that change can best be encouraged by contact, that the revitalization of existing economic systems is largely dependent on the use of new technology, and that the spread of information technology in a closed political system will make that system less closed. It also recognizes mutual benefit in trade. This policy may be characterized by the expression "The Hug."

Of course, the two policies represent theoretical, simplistic polarities of thought. In practical terms, policy making must involve a judicious mixture of both. In Europe, however, there is little doubt that the resulting balance will be a good deal closer to the policy of "Hug" than to that of "Squeeze"—if for no other reason than that a cooperative relationship with the Soviet Union provides the only hope of diminishing the barriers that divide Europe into East and West. It is not clear what balance the people of the United States will wish to choose for the longer term. We can, however, expect that the results of the summit meeting will largely determine what the U.S. administration is able to choose for the next two or three years.

Notes

1. Georgi Arbatov, *The Ideological Struggle in Contemporary Ideological Relations* (1970).

3

"Gorbachevism"—Simply Old Wine in a New Bottle?

Hiroshi Kimura

Setting

Does change in leadership make a difference in Soviet policy?[1] This is a pivotal question and one that almost all specialists on Soviet affairs must consider, given Mikhail S. Gorbachev's succession to the USSR's top leadership post in March 1985. Gorbachev is young, dynamic, and fast-moving—so different from previous incumbents of the general secretaryship. The CPSU's new general secretary has raised expectations among peoples within and outside the Soviet Union to such a level that it is not an overstatement to speak of what might be called "Gorbachev fever." Nevertheless, it is still too early to assess whether Gorbachev will bring any significant, meaningful changes to the Soviet Union.

To begin with, we are not yet certain about either the personality or the political orientation of the new general secretary. The most recent edition of the *Soviet Great Encyclopedia,* published in 1972 (the third edition), did not carry even his name. *The 1984 Soviet Encyclopedia* (Volume 1) devotes only six lines to describing Gorbachev.[2] There is no hard evidence to prove that the new leader is really reform oriented, as has been often reported in the Western media. Gorbachev may well be an authoritarian-type politician (in the Stalinist sense) who likes to see discipline and rigorously executed law and order.[3]

Furthermore, even if we can assume that Gorbachev intends to change the Soviet Union, we cannot be certain that he will succeed in doing so. Whether the new Soviet general secretary will successfully initiate and implement his policies depends upon the environment surrounding him and situations in which he finds himself. Among the "environment and situations" that Gorbachev must reckon with, three stand out.

The first is the *human environment*. There are at least three layers of people with whom the new general secretary must deal. First, he must play a complex power game with his colleagues on the CPSU's Politburo and Central Committee. To be sure, the power and position of the CPSU's general secretary in the Soviet system and practice are quite powerful, far more so than is generally recognized. Yet, the power of the general secretary is not unlimited. Since the demise of Stalin, the general secretary (or the first secretary) of the CPSU has been only one of *primus inter pares*, ruling the Soviet Union largely on the principle of collective leadership. Unless Gorbachev intends to become a second Stalin, he will need to obtain endorsement or support, whether positive or passive, from his colleagues.

The second element in Gorbachev's human environment is the Soviet bureaucracy. Of particular importance is the middle-layer people of Soviet bureaucracy and management; these middlemen strongly oppose any radical changes (e.g., economic "reform") that might deprive them of their vested interests. If Gorbachev wants to do something innovative, he must be prepared to undertake a battle with the entrenched and conservative middle level of the party—the government bureaucracts, and factory and *kolkhoz* managers.

The third element in the human environment that the new general secretary ought to take into consideration is the Soviet populace in general. Soviet citizens currently appear to have ambivalent feelings and expectations toward the leadership under Gorbachev. On the one hand, they certainly have the strong expectation that the new general secretary will do something to break the stalemated deadlock (as best illustrated by the stagnating economy) in which they have found themselves, especially since the late Brezhnev period. On the other hand, most are unwilling to pay the cost of rejuvenation. For example, the Soviet citizen who would like to see his boss fired for corruption may not want to be forced to work harder himself. The Soviet public, accustomed after more than six decades to living within a system that discourages incentive and initiative, cannot be awakened overnight. It has been observed that Gorbachev "does not smoke, and drinks sparingly" and that he "limits himself to a glass or two of wine with his meal" when traveling abroad as a guest.[4] Such a leader may be tempted to mistakenly assume that his fellow citizens have the same kind of willpower and self-restraint.

The second environment that Gorbachev must reckon with is the Soviet *system*. The new general secretary ought to bring changes and conduct reforms within the framework of Soviet-style socialism. Soviet socialism is based on such principles as public ownership of the means of production, centralized planning of production and distribution (i.e., rejection of the market economy), and a one-party political system, to mention only a few of its most important characteristics. It is hard to know whether Gorbachev is willing to undertake the bold, revolutionary reforms necessary given these principles of socialism.

Last but not least, the environment facing Gorbachev in his conduct of both domestic and foreign affairs includes the *international* environment. It goes without saying that the domestic matters of any given country cannot be isolated from international circumstances. Just as China's "modernization" drive requires peace and security in its surrounding environments, so the Soviet Union's attempt for economic reform will need a reduction of tensions in the international arena. Slowing the arms race with the United States will be of particular importance.

The advent of Mikhail Gorbachev seems thus to necessitate discussion of the following questions: (1) Does the change in the guard at the Kremlin make a difference in the policy of the Soviet Union? (2) If so, on which level (e.g., style, personnel, policy, system) and to what extent can we expect those changes to occur? (3) What are the priorities of the Gorbachev leadership? Do we agree with the standard view that "house cleaning" (e.g., rejuvenating the sluggish Soviet economy, consolidating Gorbachev's own power base, managing complaints and pressure in Eastern Europe) is a more urgent task for the new leadership than improving U.S.-Soviet relations? Or should we view domestic and foreign affairs as inseparably intertwined to such an extent that we cannot identify which is important? These questions will be discussed and partially answered in this chapter.

Change in Style and Personnel: De-Brezhnevization?

Before we proceed to an examination of whether the Gorbachev leadership will bring about change in the Soviet Union—and, concomitantly, in the world—we should define "change." In my view, we should differentiate between four kinds of changes: (1) change in *style,* (2) change in *personnel,* (3) change in *policy,* and (4) change in the *system.*

"Very young, energetic, intelligent, prudent, yet pragmatic. Soft, elegant, but prestigious"—this is the description of Mikhail Gorbachev made by Japanese Prime Minister Yasuhiro Nakasone, after he met the new Soviet leader in Moscow at Chernenko's funeral. Many share the observation that Gorbachev differs from his predecessors in terms of *style.* For instance, the general secretary has eschewed the development of a "cult of the personal leader." Soviet newspapers including the party organ *Pravda* have called him simply "Mr. Gorbachev." Instead, Gorbachev seems eager to cultivate the image that he is a populist type of political leader. By paying energetic visits to plants in Moscow, Leningrad, Kiev, Dniepropetrovsk, and Minsk, he has tried hard to generate a direct dialogue with the people on a "grass-roots" level. Moreover, the new general secretary is not very secretive about his family life. On the contrary, Gorbachev appears to be demonstrating intentionally what an open, humane, familiar political leader he is. He has not hesitated to subject his stylish wife, daughter, and granddaughter to public scrutiny.

The *speed* with which the Gorbachev leadership has moved since assuming office has been remarkable. When Gorbachev came to power, almost all international observers expected the new leader to move slowly, biding his time as he consolidated his power. But Gorbachev is moving very quickly, indeed—particularly in his drive to replace aging officials with younger men in the party, the government, and the military. As early as April, for example, the new party chief elevated three Central Committee Politburo members, one candidate member of the same body, and one secretary of the Central Committee (CC). The two new full members of the Politburo (Egor Ligachev, 63, and Nikolai Ryzhkov, 55) were promoted without passing through the stage of candidate membership. On June 1, Gorbachev appointed another full member of the Politburo (Edward Shevardnadze, 57), who replaced Romanov, 61, and on the following day appointed the newcomer in the Politburo foreign minister, replacing A. Gromyko, 77. Anatolii Dobrynin, 65, Soviet ambassador to the United States for two decades, is said to have been abruptly replaced by Yurii Vorontsov, 55, former ambassador to France.

The CPSU has 157 posts of first secretary of the *oblast'* and *raion;* of these Gorbachev has already reshuffled 21 posts, fewer than in the reshuffle under Andropov (34 posts) but more than in that under Chernenko (15 posts). Gorbachev has done all this in five months or so. The Soviet Union has about 105 government ministers, and Gorbachev has thus far changed 14 of them. Although this number is smaller than the number of replacements under Andropov (25), it already exceeds that relating to the replacement of ministers under Chernenko (9). These figures show how fast Gorbachev has been moving, compared with even Andropov.

Without hesitation, the new party chief launched a shake-up in the upper echelons of the Soviet armed forces. He replaced veteran Marshal Alexei Yefishev, 77, with General Alexei Lizichev, 57, as head of the political directorate of the Soviet armed forces. The shake-up of the armed forces also included the retirement of Marshal Vladimin Tolubko, 70, the commander of Soviet strategic rocket forces; and Viktor Kulikov, 63, the current Warsaw Pact commander. Although the event was unconfirmed as of this writing, Marshall Nikolai Orgakov, 67, is said to have made a spectacular comeback as first deputy defense minister and Warsaw Pact commander.

Domestic Policy: Systemic Change or Within-System Change?

Why has Gorbachev moved so rapidly in carrying out the reshuffling of his personnel? By appointing those who are loyal to him, he undoubtedly aims to consolidate his power base. But this does not seem to be the only reason behind the shake-up. Gorbachev also intends to replace aging, inefficient officials with younger and more efficient ones. His personnel changes may indicate that he intends to reshape the current situation of the Soviet Union. In other words, leadership change in the Kremlin this time may accompany more than a change in personal *style*. This being the case, to what extent will changes in *substance* take place under Gorbachev? Will the changes be simply cosmetic, or will they be of a more drastic, profound nature? To put it differently, does Gorbachev intend to bring about *systemic* change or simply *within-system* change? With these questions in mind, let us examine the domestic and foreign policies being conducted under the new Soviet leader.

"Economic Reform": Squaring the Circle

Among Western Sovietologists, and even among some Soviet politicians and specialists, the consensus is that the Soviet Union has been suffering from a sluggish economy urgently in need of bold reform measures. Gorbachev has two options if he intends to prevent the Soviet economy from getting worse.[5] One is what can be termed "systemic" reform, requiring fundamental changes in the Soviet "socialist" type of economic system. Gorbachev has yet to clearly articulate what he intends to do with the stagnating Soviet economy, partly because he does not want to give potential rivals an opportunity to criticize him.[6] In his speech at the plenum of the CPSU's Central Committee in April 1985, Gorbachev called for a "revolutionary transformation" of the Soviet economic mechanism (*khoziastvennyi mekhanizm*) to help it shift to a "fundamentally new technological system."[7] But change in the economic *mechanism* differs from change in the economic system, because the latter includes, in addition to the former, the arrangements for the ownership of the means of production and the organizational structure to administer and conduct economic activity.[8] In this and other speeches Gorbachev has made it clear that he has no intention of revamping the socialist character of the economy by lessening the "social ownership of the means of production and central planning."[9] Judging from his speeches, it seems possible that the economic restructuring the new general secretary envisages entails streamlining the socialist economy or, in his words, "further perfecting the entire economic system of socialism."[10] Thus, it seems unlikely that Gorbachev will opt for "systemic" reform of the Soviet economy.

Gorbachev's second option is "within-system" reform—organizational and institutional changes that stop short of changing the entire Soviet socialist system. This is the option chosen by Gorbachev since he came to power. As already noted, he has energetically conducted extensive personnel changes in the party, government fields, and elsewhere. This personnel shuffle reflects not only Gorbachev's desire to consolidate his power base but also his intention to change policy and its implementation. Particularly noteworthy in this regard is Gorbachev's rapid promotion of Nikolai Ryzhkov, the head of the Economic Department of the Central Committee of the CPSU. In Gorbachev's first major personnel shuffle, which took place at the plenum of the Central Committee in April 1985, Ryzhkov, as noted above, was directly promoted to full member of the Politburo, by passing nonvoting candidate membership. Not a great deal is known about Ryzhkov. He does not seem to be a strong advocate either for consumers or for the Soviet military-industrial complex. So far he has echoed Andropov's and Gorbachev's calls for greater "discipline," "socialist competition," and "the creativity of the masses." Time will tell whether Ryzhkov is a real reformist. But it is certain that Gorbachev will rely on Ryzhkov as his chief executive if he chooses to embark upon a reform of the Soviet economy.[11]

Second, Gorbachev has continued his predecessors' policy of letting the Soviet people work harder, combining spiritual and material incentives. He has campaigned against corruption, tightened labor discipline and morale, promised more material incentives, and urged more independent decision making in enterprises and collective farms. What, if anything, is new about Gorbachev's way of conducting these campaigns is that he does so in a slightly bolder manner than his predecessors. This is best illustrated by his anti-alcohol campaign and the legalization of small-scale, private enterprise in the agricultural and service spheres.

It is no secret that Soviet technological backwardness is the most serious problem faced by the Soviet leadership.[12] In his letter addressed to the Brezhnev leadership fifteen years ago, Andrei Sakharov warned that "in the 'second industrial revolution' the Soviet Union lags behind the United States."[13] Sakharov's warning may not have been headed by the Soviet leadership, but the Soviet's technological problems are more serious than they were fifteen years ago. Here again Gorbachev faces a familiar dilemma: How can he encourage the worker and managerial initiative that is essential to making full use of the new high technology (particularly computers, microprocessors, and copying machines) while maintaining the central planning and information controls inherent in Soviet socialism? This task is as difficult as squaring a circle. Gorbachev's proposal for wider "publicity (*glasnost'*) in work" of the party, Supreme Soviet, government, and social organizations[14] illustrates this dilemma. On the one hand, if the Soviet general public is provided full information on what is going on within and outside the USSR, the stability of the Soviet regime might be threatened. On the other hand, the Soviet people have reached the stage where, unless they are better informed, they cannot work efficiently.

Foreign Policy: "De-Gromykoization"?

Gromyko's Departure from the Foreign Ministry

In early July 1985, CPSU General Secretary Mikhail Gorbachev stunned the world with the sudden nomination of Shevardnadze as the new Soviet foreign minister.[15] Andrei Gromyko, veteran diplomat with twenty-eight years of experience in foreign affairs, seems to have been sidelined or even "kicked upstairs" to be chairman of the Presidium of the Supreme Soviet (president of the USSR). What motivated the new Soviet general secretary to dare to make such an extraordinary move? The key seems to be Gromyko's replacement, 57-year-old Edward Shevardnadze. Shevardnadze is a Georgian who was elevated to a CPSU Politburo position only a day before his appointment as foreign minister. In foreign affairs, he was virtually a blank slate, completely unknown on the international scene. It is probable that in deliberately choosing someone with little foreign policy background, Gorbachev intends to handle foreign affairs himself.

The next question to be raised is how Gorbachev intends to change the traditional "Gromyko" diplomacy. And to what extent will we see a shift in Soviet foreign policy?

There seem to be at least two positions within the Kremlin with regard to the Soviet foreign policy orientation.[16] Proponents of the first position regard U.S.-Soviet relations as still the most important and fundamental in current international affairs. Those adhering to this point of view include the late Brezhnev, Chernenko, and Ustinov, as well as certain professional Americanologists such as Georgii Arbatov, director of the Institute of U.S.A. and Canada. Gromyko has faithfully accepted and implemented this "United States–first" policy.

Proponents of the "United States–first" position believe that the role of military strength—above all, a powerful nuclear arsenal—is of prime importance in assessing the "correlation of world forces." The United

States and the USSR are the only nuclear superpowers that have the capability of destroying each other (i.e., they both have second-strike capability). These proponents, while insisting on Soviet dominance of Eastern Europe, concede Western Europe and Japan to the United States. In a list of Soviet foreign policy priorities, global confrontation with the United States occupies the primary place from the viewpoint of this position. In contrast, relations with Western Europe, Japan, and other countries are of secondary importance, subordinate to the primary objective of struggle with the United States. This concept of "bipolar world" was particularly strong during the cold war period. For example, in 1959, the heyday of the cold war, Nikita S. Khrushchev remarked: "The case of international tension is like a cabbage. If you tear off the leaves one by one you come to the heart. And the heart of this matter is relations between the Soviet Union and the United States."[17] A quarter-century later, one architect of Soviet foreign policy was still assigning U.S.-Soviet relations the central and pivotal place, upon which quadrilateral relations in Asia among the Soviet Union, United States, People's Republic of China, and Japan depend. In his keynote speech given at the annual gala convocation on the eve of Revolution Day on November 6, 1984, marking the Bolshevik Revolution of 1917, then Soviet Foreign Minister Andrei A. Gromyko said: "The International situation depends in many respects on the state of relations between the Soviet Union and the United States."[18]

The Soviet proponents of this first position appear to believe that the USSR's dealings with the United States on the global level will determine its interactions with countries in other regions. Hence the basic strategy of Soviet foreign policy seems to be "let us do business or struggle with the United States first, leaving a short while for the others at the later stage." More concretely, if the USSR happens to lose the battle with its major adversary, the United States, it might not be of any use for the Soviets to make much effort elsewhere. Conversely, if it could win its battle with the United States, the USSR would find its victory or success in other areas much easier—perhaps even automatic. This framework of Soviet perception of current world situations—and the Soviet Union's concomitant strategy in international affairs—helps us understand why the Soviet Union has continued to follow counter-productive policies, for example, toward Japan. Because they firmly believe in final victory over their arch-opponent, the United States, Soviet leaders do not care much in the meantime about their temporary losses or failures in their counterproductive conduct of foreign affairs toward Japan.

Third, some of advocates of the first position have gone even so far as to consider it expedient to control Western Europe and Japan through the United States. They seem to regard it as a "lesser evil" to put Tokyo under the Pentagon's military control rather than to let Japan become independent and rearm itself.

The second position is an anti-U.S., pro–Western Europe, pro-Japan view, given its strong tactical emphasis on a division within the West. First, proponents of this view do not regard the contemporary world as simply bipolar; rather, they embrace an idea that more nearly resembles what some American specialists on international affairs call a "pyramidal multilayer world order."[19] Second, proponents of this view are concerned about what the Soviet Union may lose with regard to its relations with Western Europe and Japan while it is engaged in a major battle with its arch-opponent, the United States. Third, they regard it as more advisable for the Soviet Union to exploit "rifts" (Lenin's term)[20]—that is, differences in views and interests within Western countries. In short, the second position advocates a strategy of launching attacks first upon the more vulnerable spots (i.e., Western Europe and Japan) and leaving the more powerful and harder spots (i.e., the United States) for the later stage.

Proponents of this position appear to include the late Andropov, Boris Ponomarev, the late N. N. Inozemtsev, and Alexander Yakovlev. For example, Ponomarev, head of the International Department of the CPSU's Central Committee, believes that "the contradictions between the United States, Western Europe and Japan continue to intensify."[21] Inozemtsev, former director of the Institute of World Economics and International Relations (IMEMO), has asserted that "the real correlation of forces in the capitalist world is characterized by the relative weakening of the U.S. position, the growth of economic and financial power of Western Europe and Japan."[22] Yakovlev, appointed by Andropov as a successor to Inozemtsev and by Gorbachev as head of the CC's propaganda department, has written of a "relative levelling in the strength of the three centers of power: the USA, Western Europe and Japan," and has argued that "in the historically foreseeable future the centrifugal tendency in the capitalist world will grow."[23]

Gorbachev's position is yet to be confirmed. But it is true that he has placed deliberate stress on the Soviet Union's desire to improve its relations with other nations as well as with the United States. In an election speech delivered on February 20, 1985, Gorbachev called for "political dialogue" between the USSR and West European countries.[24] On July 2, as already noted, Gorbachev appointed Shevardnadze the new Soviet foreign minister, kicking Gromyko upstairs to titular head of the state—that is, president of the USSR. This replacement was shortly followed by another important one, that of the Soviet ambassador to the United States: Anatolii Dobrynin, a veteran Soviet diplomat, who served in Washington for more than twenty-three years, was replaced by Yurii Vorontsov, Soviet ambassador to France. These major foreign policy personnel changes took place even prior to the general secretary's visit to France and the summit meeting with the U.S. president. About the same time, Gorbachev appointed Yakovlev to head of the propaganda department of the CPSU's Central Committee. These appointments indicate, first, that Gorbachev himself intends to be in charge of conducting Soviet foreign affairs; and, second, that he intends to pursue the "de-Gromykoization" of Soviet foreign policy.

Policy Toward Asia

Assuming Gorbachev wants to change Soviet foreign policy, to what extent have Soviet policies toward Asia and Japan changed since his succession to power? This is the major question I would like to address in the remainder of the chapter.

In his welcome speech addressed to Indian Prime Minister Rajiv Gandhi at a dinner party on May 21, Gorbachev proposed a conference of all-Asian countries on security.[25] He hopes to have bilateral talks with Asian countries as a first step toward the conference. This proposal seems to reveal that the Gorbachev government has not yet developed an original scheme for dealing with Asia. Gorbachev's proposal is reminiscent of Brezhnev's proposal for an Asian collective security system, first announced in 1969.[26] Faced with indifference, coolness, and even suspicion in Asia, the idea of establishing an Asian collective security system has fallen gradually into oblivion and been quietly dropped.[27] Instead, the Kremlin has shifted to a strategy of accumulating a series of selective *bilateral* treaty arrangements between the USSR and the various Asian states as building blocks for an eventual edifice of *collective* security embracing all of the states in the continent.[28] Has anything recently happened that urges the Gorbachev leadership to revive the earlier Brezhnev proposal? The Soviet Union's limited rapprochement with the PRC and expansion in Indochina are regarded as recent gains and achievements for the USSR in Asia. The normalization of Sino-Soviet relations is particularly important given that the Brezhnev proposal was regarded as an anti-Chinese ploy.[29] Yet the rapprochement of Sino-Soviet relations remains limited; indeed, the response of China to Gorbachev's proposal was again indifferent and cool. The New China News Agency simply reported two days later that "observers have pointed out that the [Gorbachev's] proposal is similar to Brezhnev's scheme in 1969, in which Asian nations scarcely showed an interest."[30]

In fact, Gorbachev's proposal is not so original as Brezhnev's scheme. Both clearly share one tendency to apply to Asia the European collective security system agreed upon at Helsinki in 1975. In his speech to Indian Prime Minister Gandhi, Gorbachev asked, "Is it not advisable, considering *Europe's* experience, to think of a common, comprehensive approach to the problem of security in Asia?" (emphasis added).[31] "Of course, the way to this is a complicated one," Gorbachev continued; "however, the road to *Helsinki* was not smooth and even, either." (emphasis added).[32] These statements suggest that, like Brezhnev and other Soviet leaders before him, Gorbachev naively believes that he can apply the same policies, methods, and tactics that succeeded in Europe to vastly different situations in Asia. So long as Gorbachev remains so naive and fails to appreciate the complexities in Asia, his foreign policy toward Asia will not be of much success.

Another unchanged aspect of Soviet foreign policy under Gorbachev toward Asia is the Soviet effort to prevent Western countries from forming a quasi-military alliance against the Soviet Union there. It is quite natural for the Kremlin to strongly oppose increases in the military capacity of its arch-opponent, the United States, in Asia. Particularly noteworthy of late is the Soviet concern about the increasing role that Japan and other countries, such as Republic of Korea (ROK), are expected to play in "U.S. global and regional strategy against the USSR." For example, a *Red Star* article entitled "Dangerous Partnership: What Japan's 'Involvement' in NATO Entails" sets forth the following criticism: "The United States is encouraging in every possible way the strengthening and expansion of ties between its West European and Far Eastern partners and between NATO and Japan under the banner of ensuring the West's 'security' and the defense of the values of 'Western civilization.'"[33] The article goes on to say that "Japan is fulfilling the role of a U.S. rear base."[34] Moreover, "the all-around support of the United States and Japan for such a 'bastion of Western democracy' in Asia as the bloody dictatorial regime in South Korea should be particularly mentioned."[35] In criticizing the "anti-Soviet military alliance of the USA, Japan and ROK," Gorbachev has not distinguished himself from his predecessors. In his speech at the dinner party to welcome the Vietnamese delegation headed by Le Duan on June 28, for instance, Gorbachev stated: "One cannot but see that the United States of late has visibly stepped up its military preparations in that region [Asia and Pacific basin]. It is encouraging revanchist trends in the policy of the ruling quarters and pressing on with the forging of a militarist alliance of Washington, Tokyo, and Seoul."[36]

But while heavily criticizing the security arrangements of the United States and its allies, the Soviet Union has not restrained itself from increasing its own military capabilities and those of its allies. The increased number of SS-20 mobile medium-range missiles deployed beyond the Urals provides a good example. As of the beginning of 1984, the total number of SS-20s deployed by the USSR in its Asian territory was 135; this number was recently reported to be approximately 200. It became evident in July that the Soviet Union is providing the Democratic People's Republic of Korea (DPRK) with MIG-23 warplanes, which will eventually number between 45 and 50.[37] The supply of this third-generation aircraft to the DPRK may significantly affect the existing military balance not only on the Korean peninsula but also in the Far East in general.[38] According to Dr. Amos Jordan, director of the Center for Strategic and International Studies at Georgetown University, this decision was made by Gorbachev himself.[39]

Since Gorbachev assumed office, Sino-Soviet relations have been steadily improving, and yet they have not made any great political diplomatic breakthrough. In his inaugural speech to the extraordinary plenum of the CPSU Central Committee on March 11, Gorbachev made a new overture to the People's Republic of China, stating that "we would like to see a serious improvement in relations with the P.R.C. and consider that given reciprocity this is fully possible."[40] The Soviet Union and China seemed willing to work out an implicit modus vivendi whereby the two states would push ahead in developing economic, cultural, and other links with each other. In particular, contacts and ties in trade and economic affairs have been making rapid progress in recent months. The visit to Moscow of Chinese Vice-Premier Yao Yilin to meet Soviet First Deputy Premier Ivan Arkhipov in July 1985 to sign an accord on economic and technological cooperation indicated that both "communist" countries need each other economically given their current level of economic development.[41] By 1990, bilateral trade between these two countries is expected to be double what it was in 1985.[42] It is obvious, however, that neither the Soviet Union nor China can get along without technology and know-how from the advanced industrial countries. In this regard, the Sino-Soviet rapprochement is of limited value.

Another, and related, constraint is of a politico-diplomatic nature. The Chinese seem unwilling to drop the three "obstacles" that must be cleared before Beijing's relations with Moscow can be normalized. It is highly improbable that the Soviet Union will fulfill any one of these preconditions in the foreseeable future. In his inaugural speech, for instance, the new Soviet leader emphasized that it is the duty of the Soviet government "to preserve and strengthen in every way the fraternal friendship of our closest friends and allies," thus implicitly reiterating that Moscow cannot be expected to sacrifice the interests of clients such as Afghanistan, Vietnam, and Mongolia, in pursuit of accommodation with Beijing.[43] In short, the Gorbachev government is trying to negotiate with the Chinese on its own terms. Despite repeated calls by the new Soviet leader for better ties with the PRC, Gorbachev did not dare to meet the Chinese vice-premier this time.[44] In this regard, one is unable to find much difference between Gorbachev and his predecessors.

Policy Toward Japan

Soviet perception is one (though not the only one) of the most important determinants of Soviet foreign policy.[45] To put it in a very simple way, the Soviet perception of Japan is a fusion of two somewhat opposing images. The Soviets see Japan as an economic and technological giant on the one hand, but as a military dwarf on the other. Although in recent days the Soviets have vigorously criticized "the resurgence of Japanese militarism," in fact, they still have a very low opinion of Japan in the military field. For example, in an article entitled "Militarization of Japan—Threat to Peace in Asia," Dmitrii Petrov, head of Japan's section of the Institute for Far Eastern Studies in Moscow, remarked in 1981: "Today and in the near future Japan will be unable independently to resolve strategic problems and offensive large-scale operations. Japan's military doctrine envisages the use of the American 'nuclear umbrella' and every kind of cooperation with the military forces of the United States and its Asian allies."[46] As long as Soviet foreign policy makers continue to regard military strength as the most important component in their concept of "correlation of forces," Japan will not rank high in their list of foreign policy priorities. In contrast, however, the more weight Soviet leaders attach to economic and technological elements, the higher the position occupied by Japan becomes in their priority list. The remark made by Vitalii Kobysh, chief of the U.S. section of the International Department of the CPSU's Central Committee, provides a good example. In a report on his visit to Japan in 1982, Kobysh wrote:

> Although Japan does not belong to the category of great power, her weight in the contemporary world is very significant and is constantly growing. Toward the end of this century Japan's GNP will constitute 12 percent of that of the whole world. It is unrealistic not to take this into consideration when analyzing the correlation of forces in the whole area. As demonstrated by the experience of this country, today the influence of a state is not determined by its military potential.[47]

Of course, it is premature to interpret this remark as indicating any significant change in the Soviet assessment of relative weight of variables. But it is worth bearing in mind that a change in Soviet thinking may be under way. In place of the traditional assessment of Japan, a new mix with more emphasis upon non military, and above all economic and technological, factors may be gradually emerging.[48]

Furthermore, the realization that a new era regarding the Asia-Pacific region is drawing near has contributed to the change in Soviet perceptions of Japan. As noted at the outset of this chapter, the Soviet Union has been called a Eurasian country but essentially a European power. This European-oriented attitude has begun to change as the weight of world economic activities has shifted from Europe to the Asia-Pacific region. How much significance the Soviet Union has attached to this region can best be illustrated by the fact that in recent years the Soviet Pacific Fleet, with its headquarters at Vladivostok, has suddenly grown into the largest of the USSR's four fleets. Despite its strong desires and claims to be a major Asia-Pacific power, however, the Soviet Union has not yet acquired either the prestige or the influence to be allowed membership in the community. There may be many reasons for this failure, but no one can deny that one of the obvious ones is the poor record of Soviet foreign policy toward Japan, one of the most important countries in the region.[49] Geopolitically speaking, the bow-shaped Japanese archipelago lies in the way of Soviet access to the Pacific Ocean. From the diplomatic perspective, not to mention from the economic point of view, Japan also occupies a significant position, and its voice has become more and more audible and influential in the region. It may be no exaggeration to say that until it improves relations with Japan, the USSR will not be a full-fledged member of the Asia-Pacific community. In spite of the vital role that Japan plays in Soviet strategy in the region, Soviet diplomacy with regard to Japan has been almost a total disaster. There is a marked gap between Japan's significance for Moscow's objectives in the Asia-Pacific region and Moscow's conduct toward Tokyo. One cannot completely rule out the possibility that Soviet leaders will come to realize the foolishness of their past policies toward Japan and the need to redress them even from a tactical point of view.

In sum, the Kremlin's recent foreign policy toward Japan is based on a mix of the two perceptions described above: the traditional view of underestimation of—and even contempt for—Japan, on the one hand, and the reassessment of Japan as an increasingly important independent actor, particularly in the Asia-Pacific region, on the other. Those holding the former perception are content with a Soviet-Japanese policy that is more or less an extension of U.S.-Soviet strategy. The latter urges the formation of a distinct foreign policy toward Japan *per se* that is independent enough to be distinguishable from U.S.-Soviet policy and takes full account of specific conditions of Japanese-Soviet relations.

Soviet leadership under Gorbachev has thus far displayed to Japan a mix of attitudes and measures stemming from these two perceptions.

On the one hand, Soviet attempts to pay more attention to Japan than before and to woo the Japanese to the Soviet Union are becoming evident. Calling Japan "the land of the rising sun,"[50] Soviet newspapers have recently carried numerous articles emphasizing the Soviets' need to learn from the "Japanese people's unique capability to creatively master technology."[51] Ever since Gorbachev's meeting with Japanese Prime Minister Yasuhiro Nakasone at Chernenko's funeral, the Soviets have refrained from mentioning the "Northern Territories" issue, which never fails to stir up Japanese nationalism. Instead, they have referred to the problem only indirectly with expressions such as "hardships and obstacles artificially fabricated by the Japanese side in the way of the development of relations between the two countries."[52] The Soviet government under Gorbachev permitted Yasue Kotori, the Japanese ambassador to the USSR, to deliver a speech to the Soviet people via Moscow television on Japan's national day (April 29). In that speech he emphasized that "the two countries [Japan and the Soviet Union] should embark on dealing with the main task—that of concluding a peace treaty—after settling those questions, the solution of which was envisaged at the time diplomatic relations were normalized between our countries."[53] It was crystal clear that Kotori was advocating the solution of the Northern Territories question. As mentioned before, Masuo Takashima, former Japanese ambassador to Moscow, was not permitted by the Chernenko government to read the same text to the Soviet audience, although he had been able to do so during the Andropov era.[54] Chernenko's toleration of the Kotori speech may indicate that he is more flexible toward Japan than was Chernenko. Still, it would be premature to say that the Gorbachev government will be more flexible than the Andropov government with regard to Japan.

On the other hand, the Soviet's traditional contempt for militarily weak Japan remains firmly rooted in the Soviet leadership under Gorbachev. The Soviet proposal to Japan on confidence-building measures (CBMs) in the Far East provides a good example.[55] Japan does not want to conclude any treaty or agreement with the Soviet Union until it settles the territorial question in the peace treaty. With the aim of shelving the peace treaty and hence the territorial issue, the Soviet Union has tenaciously proposed an agreement that might serve as a substitute for a peace treaty. The Soviet-proposed CBMs in the Far East constitute a typical example. Frustrated by Japan's negative reaction to the CBMs, the Gorbachev leadership threatened Japan in *Pravda,* stating that if Japan will not consider the CBMs seriously, then the chances are that Japan's sea-lane security might not be guaranteed. The CPSU's major organ argued: "Japan greatly depends upon imported resources. Accordingly, Japan must be well aware of the fact that escalation of the arms race in sea-lane communication only increases her vulnerability. The Soviet Union is ready to apply the proposed CBMs to the sea-lanes such as the Indian Ocean and the Pacific Ocean. If Japan accepts the Soviet proposal, it will fit well in with her vital interests."[56]

Gromyko's departure from the Foreign Ministry seems to the author of this paper to help enhance a more moderate attitude, thereby weakening toward Japan. It is well known that the former foreign minister's diplomatic attitude and stance toward Japan were negative. No one regards his nickname "Mr. Nyet" as more appropriate than do the Japanese. Of course, the change in foreign ministers this time was not made primarily with an aim toward redressing Soviet foreign policy regarding Japan. But it was not wrong to speculate that, as long as Gromyko remained foreign minister of the Soviet Union, Soviet-Japanese relations would not change much. All of sudden, however, one of the constraints has been taken away. In that sense, the new Soviet team in charge of foreign affairs provides both opportunities and challenges for Japan—opportunities that might be used in Japan's favor and challenges that might be exploited by the Soviets at Japan's expense. Whichever is the case, Japan's foreign policy toward the Soviet Union stands at a crossroads as well.

Notes

1. Valerie Bunce, *Do New Leaders Make a Difference? Executive Succession and Public Policy Under Capitalism and Socialism* (Princeton, N.J.: Princeton University Press, 1981), esp. 140ff.

2. *Bolshaia Sovetskaia Ensiklopia,* Vol. 7 (Moscow: Izdatek'stvo Sovetskaia ensiklopedia, 1982), p. 75; *Sovetskii ensiklopedicheskii slovar* (Moscow: Sovetskaia ensiklopedia, 1984), p. 322.

3. See, for example, Hidetake Sawa, "Kremurin-no Kenryoku-gunzo," *Sankei Shimbun,* No. 69 (August 19, 1985). See also Gorbachev's speech, "40th Anniversary of the Soviet People's Victory in the Great Patriotic War," *Pravda* (May 9, 1985).

4. Thos. G. Bustson, *Gorbachev: A Biography* (New York: Stein and Day, 1985), pp. 16, 85.

5. For a discussion of two similar alternatives, see Alec Nove, *Political Economy and Soviet Socialism* (London: George Allen & Unwin, 1979), pp. 156–157. Joseph S. Berliner, a professor at Brandeis University, has proposed four alternatives: the "conservative," the "reactionary," the "radical," and the "liberal" models. See Berliner, "Managing the USSR Economy: Alternative Models," *Problems of Communism,* Vol. 32 (January/February 1983), p. 40.

6. Elizabeth Teague, "Gorbachev Picks Up Where Andropov Left Off," *Radio Liberty Research Bulletin* (March 14, 1985), p. 3.

7. *Pravda* (April 24, 1985).

8. Morris Bornstein, "Improving the Soviet Economic Mechanism," *Soviet Studies*, Vol. 37, No. 1 (January 1985), p. 1.

9. *Pravda* (April 24, 1985); M. C. Gorbachev, *Zhivoe tvorchestvo naroda* (Moscow: Politizdat, 1984), p. 14; *Material'i vneochered-nogo plenuma Tsentral'nogo komiteta KPCC* (March 11, 1985 goda) (Moscow: Politizdat, 1985), p. 10.

10. Gorbachev, *Zhivoe*, p. 12; *Material'i*, p. 10.

11. Terry McNeill, "Nikolai Ryzhkov—Gorbachev's New Economic Overload," *Radio Liberty Research Bulletin* (May 8, 1985), p. 1.

12. Marshall I. Goldman, "Gorbachev and Economic Reform," *Foreign Affairs* (Fall 1985), pp. 57–58; Jerry F. Hough, "Gorbachev's Strategy," *Foreign Affairs* (Fall 1985), pp. 8–9.

13. A. D. Sakharov et al., "Appeal to the Party-Government Leaders of the USSR (March 10, 1970)," *Survey*, No. 76 (Summer 1970), p. 162.

14. Gorbachev, *Zhivoe*, p. 30; *Pravda* (March 12, 1985); *Material'i*, p. 11.

15. *Pravda* (July 3, 1985).

16. Regarding the classification of these two positions, I am grateful for the positions classified by Jerry Hough (although my classification is slightly different from his). See Hough, "Russia's Technology Gap: A Prod to Dynamic Reform?" "Debate on Detente: Four Kremlin Positions," and "Going with the Flow Inside the Kremlin," *International Herald Tribune* (January 15–17, 1985).

17. *New York Times* (May 11, 1959), cited by Dan Caldwell, *America-Soviet Relations: From 1947 to the Nixon-Kissinger Grand Design* (Westport, Conn.: Greenwood Press, 1981), p. 3.

18. *Pravda* (November 7, 1984).

19. For example, see Stanley Hoffmann, *Gulliver's Troubles, or The Setting of American Foreign Policy* (New York: McGraw-Hill, 1968), pp. 21–46.

20. V.I. Lenin, *Polnoe cobranie sochinenii*, Vol. 41, 5th ed. (Moscow: Politizdat, 1963), p. 55.

21. *Pravda* (April 23, 1974).

22. Ibid. (August 20, 1974).

23. See the titles by Hough cited in Note 16.

24. *Pravda* (February 21, 1985).

25. Ibid. (May 22, 1985).

26. Ibid. (June 8, 1969).

27. Robert A. Scalapino, "The Political Influence of the USSR in Asia," in Donald S. Zagoria, ed., *Soviet Policy in East Asia* (New Haven, Conn.: Yale University Press, 1982), p. 87.

28. Arnold L. Horelick, "The Soviet Union's Asian Collective Security Proposal: A Club in Search of Members," *Pacific Affairs*, Vol. 47 (Fall 1974), p. 274; Horelick, "Soviet Policy Dilemma in Asia," *Asian Survey*, Vol. 17 (June 1977), p. 511.

29. Victor Zorza, "Collective Security," *Survival*, Vol. 11 (August 1969), p. 248; Peter Howard, "A System of Collective Security," *Mizan*, Vol. 11 (July-August 1969), pp. 199–201, 203; Hemem Ray, "Soviet Diplomacy in Asia, *Problems of Communism* (March-April 1970), p. 46; Ian Clark, "Collective Security in Asia," *The Round Table*, No. 252 (October 1973), pp. 477–478; Alexander O.

Ghebhardt, "The Soviet System of Collective Security in Asia," *Asian Survey,* Vol. 13 (December 1973), p. 1076; Horelick, "The Soviet Union's Asian Collective Security Proposal," p. 269; Howard M. Hensel, "Asian Collective Security: The Soviet View," *Orbis,* Vol. 19 (Winter 1976), pp. 1564, 1579; Alfred Biegel, "Moscow's Concept for Collective Security in Asia," *Military Review,* Vol. 57 (February 1977), pp. 3, 7, 11.

30. *Yomiuri Shimbun, Mainichi Shimbun,* and *Nihon Keizai Shimbun* (May 23, 1985).

31. *Pravda* (May 22, 1985).

32. Ibid.

33. *Krasnaia zvezda* (June 5, 1985).

34. Ibid.

35. Ibid.

36. *Pravda* (June 29, 1985).

37. *Sankei Shimbun* (June 28, 1985); *Asahi Shimbun* (July 2, 1985); *Yomiuri Shimbun* (July 6, 1985); *Asahi Shimbun* (July 20, 1985); *Sankei Shimbun* (July 30, 1985).

38. See the counterargument made by Paul D. Wolfowitz, U.S. assistant secretary of state, on August 12, 1985, that "despite North Korea's acquisition of MIG-23 warplanes from the Soviet Union, the United States and South Korea's combined forces will maintain a qualitative edge," in the *Japan Times* (August 16, 1985).

39. *Yomiuri Shimbun* (July 6, 1985).

40. *Material'i,* p. 11.

41. *Pravda* (July 11, 1985).

42. TASS (July 10, 1985).

43. *Material'i,* p. 11.

44. *Sankei Shimbun* and *Nihon Keizai Shimbun* (July 13, 1985).

45. Seweryn Bialer, "Soviet Foreign Policy: Sources, Perceptions, Trends," in Bailer, ed., *The Domestic Context of Soviet Foreign Policy* (Boulder, Colo.: Westview Press, 1981), pp. 409–441.

46. D. V. Petrov, "Militarizatsia Yaponii—ugroza miru v Azii," *Problem'i dal'nego vostoka,* No. 1 (1981), p. 51.

47. Vitalii Kobum, "Est' vichod iz tupika," *Literaturnaia gazeta,* No. 51 [4909] (December 22, 1982).

48. Hiroshi Kimura, "Soviet Policy Toward Japan," in Dan Caldwell, ed., *Soviet International Behavior and U.S. Policy Options* (Lexington, Mass.: Lexington Press, 1985), pp. 122–123.

49. Hiroshi Kimura, "Failure of Soviet Policies Toward Japan," *Asia Pacific Community,* No. 16 (Spring 1982), pp. 1–16.

50. *Krasnaia zvezda* (March 28, 1985); *Pravda* (April 3, 1985).

51. *Literaturnaia gazeta* (June 19, 1985).

52. *Krasnaia zvezda* (March 15, 1985); *Pravda* (April 29, 1985).

53. *Foreign Broadcasting Information Service* (Soviet Union) (May 2, 1985), p. c1; *Yomiuri Shimbun* (evening edition), April 30, 1985.

54. See the evening edition of *Asahi Shimbun* (April 30, 1983); *Foreign Broadcasting Information Service* (Soviet Union), p. c1; *Sankei Shimbun, Yomiuri Shimbun,* and *Nihon Keizai Shimbun* (April 30, 1984); *Japan Times* (May 1, 1984).

55. Hiroshi Kimura, "The Soviet Proposal on Confidence-Building Measures and the Japanese Responses," in Joshua D. Katz and Tilly C. Friedman-Lichstschein, eds., *Japan's New World Role* (Boulder, Colo.: Westview Press, 1985), pp. 81–104.

56. *Pravda* (June 22, 1985).

4

Implications of Leadership and Social Change for Soviet Policies

Boris Meissner

The Leadership of the Soviet One-Party State

The distinctive nature of the Soviet Union lies less in its external appearance as a federally structured Soviet republic than in its organization as a one-party State. One-party rule emerged in Russia in 1918 as a result of a particular historical constellation. It took on greater shape in the course of the civil war waged between the Whites and the Reds until 1921. The ideological justification and hence legitimation of a permanent dictatorship by the Communist party established by Lenin derived from his party and State doctrine, which greatly fostered the transformation of Marxism into Leninism.

The monopoly of power wielded by the CPSU was codified in the USSR constitution of 1936. The party's legal status, not only its political power position, is expressed even more clearly in the 1977 constitution. The CPSU is now described in Article 6 as "the leading and controlling force of Soviet society, the core of its political system and of its State and social organizations." It lays down not only the "general direction of social development" but also "the course of the domestic and foreign policies of the USSR." This means, first, that the party is the core of the entire State structure and not only of the social order; and, second, that it alone has the authority to decide on government policy. Basic domestic and foreign policy decisions, which are binding on the actual government organs, are taken by the leading bodies of the party and not those of the Soviets. This constitutional framework indicates the CPSU's claim to total power, which can be met only through a totalitarian form of one-party rule.

The new constitution is based on the concept of the "people's State" developed by Khrushchev, according to which the CPSU is regarded as the "vanguard of the whole people" and no longer merely as the "vanguard of the proletariat." This does not constitute a decisive move away from Lenin's political and party doctrine. Now that the CPSU represents the whole people, it continues to be a social force ranking above the State in the narrow sense, the latter being primarily of instrumental significance.

Deriving from this dominance of the unitary, centralistic party is its precedence over the other institutions that, together with the party, constitute the political system of the Soviet Union. Governmental and organizational power is thus exercised primarily by the party's permanent leading bodies and not by the highest State organs—namely, the Presidium of the Supreme Soviet of the USSR and the Council of Ministers of the USSR. Owing to the centralistic structure of the party, as laid down in its statutes, the Politburo is the de facto government and hence the central political decision maker. In the exercise of this function it enjoys unlimited power inasmuch as it is not subject to any control from below. The only institution, apart from the Party Congress, that can take a decision differing from that of the Politburo is the Central Committee of the CPSU, which in formal terms ranks higher than the Politburo.

The Politburo is not a monolithic entity. To a certain extent it is a coalition of the ruling institutions and apparatus united in it. The greater the number of these institutions, the more difficult it becomes to reconcile their often divergent interests. On the other hand, greater integration of the individual institutions is achieved in this manner.

The general secretary, who heads the Central Committee's Secretariat and hence its entire machinery, occupies a key position. However, as he is not a party chairman, he is unable to circumvent the Politburo in basic domestic and foreign policy decisions as long as the principle of "collective leadership" is applied.

The power of the general secretary (or first secretary) has always largely depended on the relationship between the Politburo and the Secretariat of the Central Committee, and on whether it was the monocratic element represented by the general secretary and his close adherents or the oligarchic element in the shape of the "rule by Bojars" that predominated in the "collective leadership" formed by the full members of the Politburo.

Given the ideologically determined precedence of the party machinery over the State machinery and its individual components, the general secretary always has good prospects of consolidating in the overall political framework the leading role devolving upon him by virtue of his office and of developing it gradually into genuine supremacy. His power may then range from a position of dominance, as reflected in the titles "Master" (*khozyain*) used by Stalin in 1929, "Chief" (*rukovoditel*) used by Khrushchev in 1961, and the title "Leader" (*vozhd*) in the sense of an autocratic dictator. Although Stalin was designated "Leader" in 1934, he did not fully achieve autocracy until after the great purge in 1939. At any rate, in view of the specific nature of the Soviet Union as a one-party State, the general secretary represents, irrespective of the actual power he wields, not only the party but also the entire State. It therefore appears expedient to divide the history of the Soviet Union since Lenin, who ruled for almost seven years, into the period of rule of the respective party chiefs and hence State leaders: Stalin (twenty-nine years), Khrushchev (eleven years) and Brezhnev (eighteen years).

Despite the changes that occurred, each period shaped by these leaders had certain characteristic features; thus, notwithstanding the individual personalities and the different degrees of power enjoyed by them, one can speak of a specific era in each case. It is therefore justifiable to refer not only to a "Stalin era" and a "Khrushchev era" (including Malenkov) but also to a "Brezhnev era"—even though Leonid Ilyich Brezhnev, who died on November 10, 1982, shortly before hs 76th birthday, did not have the same formative power as either Stalin or Khrushchev.

Three men followed Brezhnev in swift succession. At 79 and 82 years of age, respectively, upon their elections, Andropov and Chernenko were the oldest party functionaries to assume the post of general secretary. However, it was due less to their age than to serious illness that their leaderships were of very limited duration. Gorbachev, who was 54 years old upon his election, is the youngest among the Kremlin leaders, but not the youngest incumbent ever of the post of general secretary. Stalin was only 43 years old when he rose to this position.

In view of Gorbachev's age, a lengthy period bearing his name is likely to occur, barring any unforeseen events. It is certainly possible that the brief periods under the leadership of Andropov and Chernenko, which Gorbachev helped to shape, will eventually be regarded as belonging to a single "Gorbachev era." Nonetheless, it would appear appropriate to view each of these changes of leadership separately. Not only was power assumed differently in each of the three cases, but different impulses also emanated from each of the new leaders. Whether these impulses contain the beginning of a new development can best be established by means of a comparison with the situation existing at the end of the "Brezhnev era."

The Changes of Leadership Since Brezhnev

After Khrushchev's fall in October 1964, the repeal of his administrative reform led to the restoration of the dualistic structure of the Soviet one-party State. By restoring a relative balance between the individual institutions making up the Soviet Union's system of political rule, the State machinery was considerably strengthened in comparison with the party machinery. Consequently, it was a long time before Brezhnev was able to acquire a dominant position in the Kremlin leadership in the face of considerable opposition, which also delayed the adoption of the new USSR constitution. This endeavor was greatly facilitated by incorporating KGB Chief Andropov, Defense Minister Grechko, who was replaced by Marshal Ustinov after his death, and Foreign Minister Gromyko into the "collective leadership" in 1973. Thus three people became Politburo members who were to play an important role after Brezhnev's death. Furthermore, this permitted representation of the State security service, the armed forces, and the foreign service alongside the government machinery, to which the economic administration was in turn linked.

Brezhnev was able to strengthen his position not only by assuming the post of chairman of the Defense Council of the USSR, reaching the rank of marshal of the Soviet Union, but also by acquiring in 1977 the position of chairman of the Presidium of the Supreme Soviet of the USSR—that is, the nominal head of state (*glava gosudarstva*). Owing to his changeable health and his advanced age, it was not possible for Brezhnev, despite this acquisition of power, to achieve the desired monocracy, which would have been the logical outcome of the hierarchical structure of a totalitarian one-party system. The more he loosened the reins, the more he was drawn into the "collective leadership." Thus he was prompted at the 26th CPSU Congress in February–March 1981 to profess his commitment to "collective leadership" and to refrain from changing the membership of the Politburo, whose role he particularly emphasized, and that of the Secretariat of the Central Committee.

The crisis of successorship and thus the appearance of an interregnum started even while Brezhnev was still alive. The three changes of leadership in rapid succession after his death heightened this impression of an interregnum.

By virtue of the resultant appointments, the manner in which these changes of leadership occurred revealed certain structural weaknesses in the totalitarian one-party system. The strength of the Soviet one-party State lies in the enormous concentration of power in the hands of the rulers—a power that can be exploited for achieving specific political objectives. Given firm leadership, the one-party system permits extensive mobilization of the masses if exceptional circumstances so require. On the other hand, the one-party system has a number of weaknesses caused mainly by inadequate legal limitation of State omnipotence, the elimination of any organized opposition, and the resultant lack of democratic consensus. A growing gulf between State and society as well as a declining efficiency in the overall system are the outcome. The Soviet centrally planned economy, too, has fostered this development to a considerable degree.

The more fragile the Marxist-Leninist doctrine became in the course of time as an ideological basis of legitimation, the more these weaknesses were bound to emerge in the Soviet one-party State. Two other specific deficiencies of one-party rule became evident with the changes of leadership in the Kremlin. First, as no formal arrangement exists for succession to the post of general secretary, difficuties are caused if there are two equally strong candidates or if there is only one candidate who does not have an adequate majority of supporters in the Central Committee. As a "regency council," the Politburo performs the de facto function of an electoral body. However, its decisions require formal confirmation by the Central Committee. As a result, the candidate may have to make certain concessions for his election to the leading oligarchs in the Politburo.

Second, unlike democratic heads of government, the new general secretary is not able to compile his cabinet largely as he likes. Instead, he is forced to retain the existing members of the Politburo, the Central Committee's Secretariat, and the highest State organs, including his opponents. He can thus charge the composition of the top echelons of the party and State leadership only gradually. Additional difficulties occur if the new general secretary has only a narrow power base or if his health deteriorates more quickly than anticipated, as was the case with Andropov and Chernenko. All these factors forced Andropov, after his controversial election, to place special emphasis on balanced "collective leadership"—especially since the oligarchic element had been further strengthened by the change of leadership. This strengthening is evidenced by the fact that the proceedings of the Politburo's weekly meetings have since then been covered by the Soviet press, unlike previous practice.

Andropov owed his election as general secretary primarily to Ustinov and Gromyko. However, because of the power political situation, he was equally dependent on an alliance with Chernenko, who had been the losing candidate in the election, and with Prime Minister Tikhonov and Grishin, head of the large Moscow party organization. Both were supporters of Chernenko. Andropov also had to show consideration for that part of the "Brezhnev faction," including Shcherbitsky, who had voted for him. Later on, he was likewise intent on offsetting the appointment of Romanov, head of the Leningrad party organization, as one of the leading secretaries of the Central Committee by ensuring the advancement of Gorbachev.

It was necessary to preserve this balance for two reasons. Ustinov and Gromyko, in addition to Romanov as their adherent, favored a tougher course in domestic policy and priority being given to the heavy-goods and military industries. On the other hand, Chernenko, Tikhonov, and Gorbachev attached particular value to the simultaneous development of the consumer-goods industry and the services sector. They advocated reforms, albeit in different fashions. These opposing domestic positions, which were also discernible at the time of the second change of leadership after Andropov's death on February 12, 1984, made themselves felt in different stances on East-West détente and arms control policy.

The tougher course in domestic and foreign policy under Andropov was fostered by the increase in political influence enjoyed by the armed forces, which had already grown under Brezhnev because of the accelerated arms buildup. This increased influence became particularly evident when a South Korean airliner was shot down on September 1, 1983, and Chief of General Staff Marshal Ogarkov and his first deputy, Marshal Akhromeev, justified this action. The decision to discontinue arms control talks with the United States at the end of 1983 was probably also determined to a considerable extent by the military leaders at the time. The influence of the KGB, which Andropov himself had headed for fifteen years, also increased.

By developing a team of his own, Andropov tried to reduce his reliance on the old members of the Politburo, irrespective of the faction they belonged to. This course of action was subsequently continued by Gorbachev.

One of Andropov's first decisions in this connection was to promote Aliev, the party leader from Azerbaijan, whom he trusted on account of his previous service with the KGB, from a candidate to a full member of the Politburo. He then sought to draw on leading Great Russian functionaries, most of whom had previously belonged to Kirilenko's group but, because of his demise, had lost their patron. To start with, Ryzhkov was made a secretary of the Central Committee and head of a new economic department in it; this was followed by the appointment of Ligachev as a secretary of the Central Committee entrusted with the important department for party organization. Upon Pelshe's death, Solomentsev, for many years prime minister of the Russian Soviet Federal Socialism Republic (RSFSR), was made new chairman of the Commission of Party Control and a member of the Politburo. Vorotnikov, who succeeded Solomentsev as prime minister of the RSFSR, became first a candidate and then a member of the Politburo under Andropov. Chebrikov also became a new candidate of the Politburo, succeeding Fedorchuk as head of the KGB; the latter assumed the post of USSR minister of the interior. Chebrikov belonged to the "Brezhnev faction" but had already held a leading position in the KGB under Andropov.

Despite assertions to the contrary, the reappointments effected in the central party and government machinery under Andropov were only of a limited nature. Chernenko's influence on the Central Committee remained largely intact, as did that of Tikhonov on the USSR Council of Ministers. However, through the appointment of Aliev and Gromyko as his first deputies, Tikhonov had to accept a limitation of his position as de jure head of government.

After the second change of leadership, Chernenko was able to rely on this support in the party and government machinery. The fact that the leading functionaries sponsored by Andropov came to an accommodation with him was illustrated by the assumption by Ryabov, another member of Kirilenko's "team," of the post of deputy prime minister of the USSR in September 1984.

Andropov followed the example set by Brezhnev. After biding his time and assuming the post of chairman of the Defense Council of the USSR, which the general secretary is entitled to by virtue of his office, he had himself elected chairman of the Presidium of the Supreme Soviet of the USSR in June 1983. Chernenko was able to acquire the two government posts much more quickly. However, like Andropov, due to changeable health he was unable to make use of the concentration of power achieved by this accumulation of offices. Moreover, the latter did not offset the strengthened position of Gromyko and Ustinov within the "collective leadership." They were initially able to prevent Gorbachev, who under Chernenko had advanced to the position of second secretary of the Central Committee, from being incorporated into the top echelon of the Kremlin leadership.

In the spring of 1985, a shift of power occurred to the benefit of the Politburo's orthodox wing, which was supported by the proponents of priority being given to the heavy-goods and armaments industries and to an improvement of the military arsenal. This led to a zigzag course in Soviet policy that was particularly noticeable in foreign policy.

This development was fostered by the deterioration of Chernenko's health. Like Brezhnev, he was forced to take lengthy breaks, during which Gorbachev deputized for him. It was only after his return to Moscow from a long summer holiday (a return connected with the demotion of Chief of General Staff Marshal Ogarkov) that a shift of power occurred in the opposite direction. This shift was assisted not least by Ustinov's ill health, which led to his death in December 1984. It permitted Chernenko, backed by Gorbachev, to adopt a more flexible course in foreign policy as a means of bolstering the domestic projects envisaged by him. The changed constellation of power also permitted Gorbachev to move up to the top level of leadership.

Starting in the autumn of 1984, Chernenko became surprisingly active. In his activities he relied mainly on Gorbachev, with whom he was in agreement on most substantive issues. On the other hand, like the older members of the Politburo, he was interested in maintaining a certain balance within the "collective leadership." Consequently, it was Gromyko, who had adapted himself to the changed power political position, and not Gorbachev, who held the speech on November 6, 1984, commemorating the sixty-seventh anniversary of the October Revolution. This outlook also prompted Chernenko to refrain from enlarging the Politburo.

Chernenko's hope of experiencing the 27th Party Congress, which was to be brought forward to the end of 1985, was not fulfilled. The renewed deterioration of his health in the second half of December led to his death on March 10, 1985.

In this period of transition, Gorbachev was able to expand his power. His successful visit to Britain enhanced his personal prestige. He was generally regarded as the heir apparent to Chernenko. The third change of leadership thus took place much more quickly than the previous ones. In order to gain time, Romanov, his rival, apparently advocated the candidacy of Grishin. But even if such efforts had in fact been made, they proved futile.

It is hard to assess the role played by Gromyko in the period leading up to the change of leadership. Although Gromyko announced to the Central Committee on March 11, 1985, the Politburo's proposal that Gorbachev be elected as new general secretary, it cannot automatically be assumed that he acted as king-maker. Subsequent developments also ran counter to this point of view. After all, Chernenko supported the candidacy of Andropov before the Central Committee, although he had initially been defeated. The arguments used by Gromyko in his speech were simply not couched in terms favorable to Gorbachev. The speech was thus not published until a week later in a small brochure issued by the State publishers, and it did not appear in the Soviet press.

Gromyko's main aim was to reaffirm the cohesion of the Kremlin leadership in connection with Gorbachev's candidacy. He stated that the "cracks" spoken of abroad had existed "neither today nor yesterday." But he also added that, owing to his long-standing service, he was perhaps able to see "slightly more clearly than some comrades" that Gorbachev, whose qualities he particularly praised, was the right man.

With his words of support, Gromyko wanted to instill in the new party leader a feeling of indebtedness to him so as to ensure his own continued control over foreign policy. This indebtedness would also reinforce Gorbachev's candidacy in the face of likely resistance within the Central Committee, although Gromyko probably exaggerated the amount of resistance involved. The fact that resistance did occur is indicated by Gorbachev's election by the Central Committee "by common consent" (*edinodushno*) and not "unanimously" (*edinoglasno*), as was the case with Andropov and Chernenko. This unusual description for a vote suggests that not all members of the Central Committee, who belong mainly to the old generation, agreed with the candidate nominated. Their critical attitude was probably due more to their fears of major reappointments and constitutional changes than to Gorbachev's age.

The Supreme Party and State Leadership Under Gorbachev

Upon his accession to power, Gorbachev possessed allies but not a special group of his own and thus no close adherents. The principal reason for this is that he had previously held leading posts only in his native district of Stavropol and in the Moscow party headquarters, where he initially dealt solely with agriculture. It was only under Andropov and Chernenko that he was entrusted with other areas of party work. Both Andropov and Chernenko afforded him an opportunity to establish personal ties guaranteeing him a majority in the Politburo. He used the experience gained under his predecessors to make important decisions and appointments at the national level with astonishing celerity after the change of leadership—all with a view to widening his power base. The process of concentration he initiated in the party and State machinery will help to consolidate his power on the national plane. Gorbachev has also resolutely continued the process (started by Andropov but slowed down by Chernenko) of purging corrupt and incompetent party and State functionaries from the various levels of administration with the aim of rejuvenating the "leading cadres."

Moreover, the election of delegates to the 27th CPSU Congress, which was held in February–March 1986, enabled him to make further reappointments and thus also to acquire a majority in major top-level bodies of the party, the Central Committee, and the Central Review Commission.

After the change of leadership, Gorbachev made use of the plenary meetings of the Central Committee held in April and June 1985 to carry out significant changes in the Kremlin leadership. First, he increased the number of his allies and drew some of them closer to himself. Second, by weakening the base of the orthodox wing, he succeeded in achieving a decisive shift of power within the Kremlin leadership. It is astonishing that he managed so quickly to oust his rival Romanov from the Politburo and the Secretariat of the Central Committee.

Gorbachev expanded and consolidated his power base with the aid of persons belonging to the two groups that Andropov had previously drawn on. Of the "Uralians," all of whom are Great Russians, he arranged for Ligachev and Ryzhkov as the two leading Central Committee secretaries to be promoted at the April plenary meeting directly to full members of the Politburo, thus bypassing candidate membership. Since Romanov's departure, Ligachev must clearly be regarded as the second secretary of the Central Committee, with prime responsibility for ideological matters. Ryzhkov had first assumed responsibility for coordinating the activities of all secretaries of the Central Committee concerned with economic issues. Of the three new Central Committee secretaries, Yelcin also belonged to Kirilenko's "group," whereas Nikonov, who is responsible for agriculture, had already had close ties with Gorbachev in the past. Finally, Sajkov, the successor to Romanov as head of the Leningrad party organization, was assigned responsibility for the armaments industry, a sector with which he is familiar.

The influence of the "Caucasians" was increased not only by Shevardnadze's promotion from candidate to full member of the Politburo at the plenary meeting in July, but also by his subsequent appointment as successor to Gromyko as foreign minister of the USSR. Close followers of Gorbachev (and members of this group) are G. P. Razumovsky and V. S. Murakhovsky. Razumovsky, the former first secretary of the Krasnodar district in the northern Caucasus, has been entrusted by Gorbachev with running the Central Committee's important department for party organization (i.e., the cadre department). Murakhovsky, the former first secretary of Gorbachev's native district of Stavropol, was lately appointed as new first deputy of the chairman of the Council of Ministers of the USSR.

Gorbachev realizes that the oligarchic structure of "collective leadership" can be limited or overcome only if the posts of the general secretary as party leader and the prime minister as head of government are closely interlinked. He has therefore deliberately dispensed with assuming the nominal office of head of state.

On the surface, Gromyko's election on July 2, 1985, as chairman of the Presidium of the Supreme Soviet of the USSR created the impression of a return to a division of offices, as was introduced after Khrushchev's fall in 1964 in order to strengthen the "collective leadership." In actual fact, owing to the existing constellation of power, this step constitutes a consolidation of Gorbachev's leadership.

Gorbachev has thus kept open the option of assuming the post of prime minister of the USSR at a later date or of assigning it to a person enjoying his confidence. In view of the advanced age of Prime Minister Tikhonov, such a change in the post of head of government did not cause any particular problems. It has simply happened earlier than expected. On September 2, 1985, Ryzhkov was appointed the new prime minister. As representative of the Uralian group he has a strong position. In connection with this change, the following dismissal of Baybakov as long-standing chairman of the GOSPLAN was not surprising. Talyzin as his successor was appointed simultaneously not only as first deputy of the prime minister but also as new candidate of the Politburo.

The election of Shevardnadze as new foreign minister—a man with little experience in foreign affairs—enables Gorbachev to exercise greater influence on the foreign policy decision-making process and hence on the shaping of Soviet foreign policy.

Of decisive importance is the question as to whether Gorbachev will succeed in carrying out a comprehensive change of generations at all levels of the establishment. Past experience has shown that middle-level cadres are the most vehement in opposing major changes to the existing system of rule and social organization. Gorbachev can achieve success only if he bases his cadre policy not just on the middle generation but also on the young one.

Stalin twice used the young generation as a lever for effecting swift revolutionary changes in the ruling machinery. The first such occasion was the time he engaged in the struggle for power after Lenin's death and enforced the "general line"; the second occurred when he carried out the great purge in the mid-1930s and reinforced his autocracy. In both instances, his action was accompanied by accelerated change in the social structure.

This method of "leapfrogging of generations" involved in both cases a loss of executive staff, a loss that the Soviet Union was no longer able to afford on such a large scale under Khrushchev. He tried to achieve at least partial rejuvenation of the leading cadres, first with the aid of "destalinization" (i.e., limited liberalization) and, second, by means of administrative reforms that were inadequately developed.

Both of these courses can still be embarked upon. However, Gorbachev can do so successfully only if he has an adequate power base and the necessary strength, but also clear plans for reform. The personal requirements are more favorable in his case than in Khrushchev's. Gorbachev is much better educated than his predecessor and would thus be accepted as an example by the young cadres. Like his predecessors he is a Russian, but he possesses greater charisma.

However, because he experienced World War II only as a child, his relationship with the military leaders will probably involve more problems than it did for Andropov and Chernenko. As a key functionary primarily responsible for agriculture, he constantly had to deal with the "iron-eaters," like Polyanski before him. For example, a veto by the military prevented the introduction of a lightweight tractor that Gorbachev had advocated in the Stavropol district on account of the specific conditions prevailing there.

As far as is known, Gorbachev does not have any close ties with the Committee for State Security (KGB) and the Ministry of the Interior (MWD). His success will depend to a crucial extent on convincing not only the bureaucratic party but also the military section of the power elite that, without a readiness on the part of the latter to subordinate its specific interests to the national interest, the Soviet Union will not be able to preserve its status as a world power. The general secretary of the CPSU is at the same time chairman of the Defense Council of the USSR. In this capacity, Gorbachev will have to ensure that he reconciles his intention of reducing the burden of armaments—a goal to which Andropov and Chernenko also subscribed—with the requirements of the military. In his speech at the plenary meeting of the Central Committee at which he was elected, he gave the armed forces the assurance that they would continue to have at their disposal everything needed "to guarantee the security of the Soviet Union and its allies."

Before the change of leadership, only the KGB was represented in the Politburo: by its chairman, Chebrikov, as a candidate of the Politburo. At the plenary meeting in April, he was promoted to a full member. He holds the rank of a general in the army. By contrast, the new defense minister, Marshal Sokolov, a 74-year-old career officer, has been granted the status only of a candidate of the Politburo.

One of Gorbachev's weaknesses is that he does not possess any direct experience of the central State machinery. One of the most difficult tasks for him will therefore be the envisaged reform of economic administration, which was demanded even by Brezhnev but has not been accomplished until now.

Domestic Transformations Since Brezhnev

Brezhnev's name stood for the second longest period in the history of the Soviet Union. By contrast, the leadership of Andropov and Chernenko turned out to be but a brief interlude. Andropov was to head the CPSU and hence the Soviet State for only fifteen months, and Chernenko for only thirteen months.

Gorbachev's accession to power marks the end of the interregnum, but not that of the transitional period. Despite the considerable consolidation of his power, he remains integrated in the "collective leadership," which, together with his problematic relationship with the armed forces and, to an extent, with the KGB as well, impairs his capacity for action in domestic and foreign policy.

The oscillations in Soviet policy during the "Brezhnev era" were largely due to changes in the constellation of power in the Kremlin and to Brezhnev's specific style of leadership. They were reinforced by the effects of sociostructural changes on developments in domestic policy. They were also determined by problems connected with the Soviet Union's rise to world power, which took place mainly under Brezhnev. On account of the increasing interdependence of domestic and foreign policy, the oscillations were reflected in growing interaction of the latter.

One of Brezhnev's achievements was, after Stalin's despotic rule and Khrushchev's vacillating style of leadership, to permit the Soviet Union to enjoy a lengthy period of domestic stability and consolidation and at the same time to bring about a certain improvement in living conditions. However, under him the bureaucratic ossification occasioned by a permanent one-party dictatorship and centralized economic planning increased considerably and led to extensive stagnation in many areas of life.

The development begun in connection with destalinization away from a totalitarian form of communist one-party State toward a more liberal authoritarian form, possibly leading later to a constitutional one-party State based on the rule of law and enjoying a measure of social pluralism, did not make much headway. The trends in this direction that emerged on the glacis of the Soviet Union were suppressed in accordance with the "Brezhnev doctrine." Although the existence of the Soviet empire was provisionally shored up in this manner, the number of unresolved problems was at the same time increased. The creation of a military basis for the Soviet Union's policy as a world power entailed high costs that posed a great strain on the Soviet economy, which was struggling with increasing difficulties in achieving growth. Ever-larger sections of Soviet society, now undergoing a far-reaching process of transformation, especially the political elite and the intelligentsia, became conscious of the existing system's lack of capacity for innovation. The feeling of being in a cul-de-sac grew.

The first change of leadership in the Kremlin—that is, when Andropov succeeded Brezhnev—took place at a juncture where a host of problems had accumulated both within the Soviet Union and in its relationship with the outside world.

Part of the upper Soviet stratum, which preferred Andropov to his rival Chernenko, hoped that Andropov, by virtue of his intelligence and experience, would succeed in bringing about a turning point in domestic and foreign policy. Andropov was fully conscious of the difficult problems facing him and tackled his task with great elan. This elan diminished rather quickly, for reasons discussed below. Although he caused a certain amount of movement in domestic affairs, he was unable to define clear goals. In foreign policy, too, he failed to bring about a reorientation owing to the further deterioration of U.S.-Soviet relations.

In the policies he pursued, Andropov laid great emphasis on domestic affairs, especially on reforms designed to help overcome the Soviet Union's economic difficulties. The measures he adopted consisted, on the one hand, of a campaign to combat corruption, cliquism, and general slovenliness. They were accompanied by demands for greater discipline, order, and productivity. On the other hand, they involved limited reforms in industry and agriculture. In conjunction with the "Food Programme" (which was established in May 1982 and which Chernenko and Gorbachev had particularly advocated), an extensive agro-industrial complex was created in the agricultural sector for the purpose of linking the harvesting of agricultural produce to subsequent processing and marketing. Introduced as part of this reorganization, "group contacts" were aimed at basing the organization of labor in collective farms to a greater extent on small groups formed by families.

At the same time, in selected branches of industry, experiments were started that involved a limited expansion of the rights of producer associations and factories as well as a reduction of central planning; they served the purpose of achieving greater productivity, whereby the end product was used as the assessment criterion. Group contracts were also introduced to a certain extent in the industrial sector. In some cases, factory directors were granted the right to lay off up to 10 percent of their work forces and to use the funds thus saved for awarding higher bonuses.

The speech by Andropov that was read out at the plenary meeting of the Central Committee on December 26, 1983 (shortly before his death)—a speech that was clearly a joint effort—indicated that the results of the economic experiments were to form "the basis for the elaboration of corresponding proposals for the entire national economy." It was pointed out that, within the forthcoming five-year plan for the period from 1986 to 1990, and in relation to the "main directions of the economic and social development of the USSR," the Politburo would draw up a long-term "complex programme for the development of consumer goods production and the services system" that would supplement the "agricultural programme." It was simultaneously announced that the time was "ripe" for developing a program to perfect the entire controlling machinery—that is, to achieve comprehensive reform of economic administration, as previously demanded by Brezhnev. This was to be "an important element" of the revision of the CPSU's program sought by Chernenko and Andropov alike.

In the speech of December 26, Andropov said: "All our efforts in the economic sphere are ultimately aimed at raising the standard of living of the people. This is the main socio-political goal of our plans"; even then, these words sounded more like Chernenko than Andropov. But there can be no doubt that with his disciplinary campaign, which treated economic administrators and workers less gently than before, Andropov managed at least temporarily to achieve a slight improvement in the Soviet Union's difficult economic situation. As a result of increased labor productivity, industrial production grew at an annual rate of 4 percent in 1983 (target: 3.2 percent), following a low of 2.8 percent in 1982. The grain harvest, which, according to Chernenko, amounted to over 190 million tonnes, was also up from previous years. However, it was not enough to dispense with imports, primarily those from the United States. All in all, official figures indicate that the Soviet economy achieved a 3.1 percent growth in GNP in 1983, compared with 2.6 percent in 1982. The actual (adjusted) figure is probably roughly 2 percent.

The reforms initiated by Andropov were continued by Chernenko, who was likewise unable to dispense entirely with the use of "administrative methods" in his effort to raise the extremely low rate of labor productivity. But Chernenko did not succeed in maintaining the economic upswing attained by Andropov. The GNP growth rate of 2.6 percent achieved in 1984 was below the 1982 level. In reality, it was probably only about 1.5 percent, thus almost reaching the low of 1979. It would have been even less had industrial production not risen slightly, from 4 to 4.2 percent. Since 1984 it has dropped again. Oil production and coal mining in that year were lower than in 1983. Only in gas production was a considerable increase achieved. Agricultural output remained at the 1983 level, thus again necessitating major grain imports from the United States.

As an adjunct to the measures designed to improve the training of leading cadres and specialists. Brezhnev had initiated efforts to enhance the vocational qualifications of workers engaged in production. These efforts were continued by Chernenko in conjunction with the educational reform of April 10, 1984.

Despite its wealth of natural resources—but because of its economic difficulties—the Soviet Union has until now failed to narrow the gap between itself and the United States (the latter has a GNP almost twice as large). The technological gap has probably widened in recent years. The Kremlin leaders fear above all that the research on the missile defense system in space propagated by President Reagan will have a technological spin-off effect that would considerably widen this gap. Gorbachev is thus particularly interested in the "complex programme for scientific and technological progress by the USSR for the period from 1986 to 2005," a project initiated under Chernenko. It is intended to be an integral part of the revised party program, which, together with the new party statutes, will have to be approved by the 27th Party Congress.

Like Andropov, Gorbachev was always more realistic than Chernenko in his assessments of the level of economic and social development attained by the Soviet Union. Yet in the end, there was not all that great a difference between him and Chernenko, as demonstrated by the latter's article ("Meeting the Requirements of Developed Socialism") in the December 1984 issue of *Kommunist* (No. 18, p. 3 et seq.). Chernenko, too, came to realize that the Soviet Union, which is only at the start of a very long phase of "developed socialism," had hitherto attained only a very low degree of maturity and, hence, that it was not appropriate to speak of "mature socialism" as he had previously done. He thus eventually concurred with Gorbachev on the view that, during this long phase, greater economic and social maturity would have to be obtained step by step.

However, Gorbachev insisted more strongly than Chernenko on getting the reforms (categorized under "Completion of Developed Socialism") implemented comprehensively and as quickly as possible. He held then, and continues to hold, the view that the desired increase in productivity can be secured only through greater intensification of the entire economy. For Gorbachev, intensification of the economy is such a central task that it must be carried out in the briefest span of time possible by using all available resources. With this in mind, he declared in his programmatic speech at the "ideological congress" on December 10, 1984, that "life is confronting us with a task of enormous political importance, namely that of raising the economy to a qualitatively new scientific, technological, organizational and economic level of making decisive progress in intensifying production by society and raising its efficiency." He went on to say that "the intensification of the economy must be a process of concern to the entire nation and acquire the same political significance as our country's industrialization did in the past." In conformity with these remarks, Gorbachev said in his speech to the Central Committee on March 11, 1985, that "we must make a decisive step forward in setting the economy on the path towards intensive development. In a brief space of time we must reach—indeed it is our duty to do so—the uppermost positions in science and technology and the highest international level of productivity through the efforts of society."

At the plenary meetings of the Central Committee on April 23 and July 2, 1985, during a discussion of questions concerning scientific and technological progress on June 12, 1985, and in speeches held at Leningrad on May 17, 1985, and at Dnyepropetrovsk on June 27, 1985, Gorbachev elucidated his "concept for expediting our country's socio-economic development on the basis of scientific and technological progress." He advocated a "new quality" of economic development permitting "rapid progress in strategically important directions." The transition to this intensification is to be achieved through a restructuring of production and a changed investment policy. Investments are, above all, intended to benefit the development of strategically important sectors of the economy. In this connection, Gorbachev singled out machine construction, electronics, electrical engineering, and biotechnology. He described these branches of industry as "catalysts of progress." Restructuring of production is to take place in these fields in particular. Gorbachev also stressed that "in the final analysis we are dealing with a restructuring of all sectors of the economy on the basis of modern scientific and technological findings." To this end, a program is to be elaborated "for the reconstruction of all factories and of all sectors."

Apart from a changed investment and structural policy, Gorbachev regards an improvement of the entire system of control and planning as the crucial condition for regaining the economic momentum lost mainly in the 1970s. For this purpose, the State Planning Committee is to be converted into a "scientific-economic body," and the State Committee for Science and Technology is to be assigned new tasks in dealing with the problem of intensifying the economy.

In the future, ministries at the national level are to focus their attention on "strategic questions," while particular controlling bodies are to be set up for the major complexes of the national economy. Concentration of ministries into larger units is to be effected mainly at the level of the republics. Central control and planning are to be retained. Even "socialist property" as the basis of the planned economy is to be "strengthened." At the same time, the competences of productive associations and factories are to be considerably expanded.

Yet the future shape of Soviet economic administration cannot be deduced from these remarks about the "completion of the economic machinery." A great deal of what Gorbachev has said is reminiscent of Khrushchev, who is now no longer regarded as a nonperson. One cannot know for certain how the contradiction between comprehensive central control and planning (with a greater part being played by the party), on the one hand, and the envisaged increased autonomy of associations and factories, on the other, is to be eliminated. Any market economy tendencies have been strongly rejected by Ligachev.

Social Trends Resulting from Structural Change

The Soviet Union's domestic difficulties, which have continued to mount since the 26th CPSU Congress in 1981, are not only of an economic nature. They proceed mainly from the fact that the existing one-party system, in which totalitarian features predominate in a centralistic and bureaucratic power system, is scarcely capable either of appreciably advancing the process of modernization or of helping to find a satisfactory solution to the problems of crucial importance to the development of Soviet society. These problems in turn derive both from the numerous contradictions discernible in the development of the Soviet Union and from the effects of far-reaching, accelerated social change.

At the 26th Party Congress, Brezhnev declared that in the 1970s there had been "further convergence of all classes and social groups of Soviet society." He also made the ideologically questionable assertion that this development justified the assumption that "the emergence of a classless social structure" would occur "mainly and essentially in the historical framework of mature socialism"—that is, during the phase of "developed socialism" that the Soviet Union considers itself to be in at present.

The process of convergence referred to by Brezhnev took place only to a limited extent and on a minor scale. By contrast, differentiation in Soviet society as a whole and in individual groups increased still further. This development was largely fostered by the continuation of the process of urbanization, by the territorial expansion of industrialization (the Asian part of the Soviet Union was affected to the greatest extent), and by a further rise of the educational level of the population.

Between 1965 and 1983, the Soviet Union's urban population rose from 120.7 million (52 percent) to 174.6 million (64.4 percent), whereas the rural population decreased from 108.9 million (47 percent) to 96.6 million (35.6 percent). Compared with Western industrial nations, the proportion of the agricultural work force is still very high (22.6 percent in 1982 in the Soviet Union compared with 2–12 percent in the West).

The developments of the last few decades reveal that the proportion of white-collar workers has increased in both urban and rural regions, whereas the proportion of blue-collar workers has risen only in rural areas. Yet efforts were made by the Soviet authorities to conceal this general trend by assigning a blue-collar status to certain categories of white-collar workers as well. The number of collective farmers has decreased still further as a result of urbanization.

Most white-collar workers today come from the "intelligentsia"; in other words, they are mainly specialists with a higher education. They increased in number from 12.1 million to 31.0 million between 1965 and 1983. The number of specialists with a university education rose from 4.9 million (40 percent) to 13.0 million (41.9 percent), and the number of specialists educated at intermediate-level technical colleges increased from 7.2 million (60 percent) to 18 million (58.1 percent).

Women accounted for 59 percent of all specialists, reaching a total of 18.3 million. Regarding specialists with university educations, the number of graduate engineers went up between 1965 and 1980 from 1.6 to 4.9 million and that of graduate agronomists rose from 0.3 to 0.6 million; graduate economists increased in number from 0.3 to 1.1 million, law graduates from 0.1 to 0.2 million, doctors from 0.5 to 0.9 million, and teachers from 1.9 to 3.8 million. In an effort to curb the flow of universities, the new educational reform places particular emphasis on providing pupils with basic vocational qualifications and, as far as possible, on letting them receive further qualifications at technical colleges.

The bureaucracy and the intelligentsia are increasingly overlapping. Not only the economic bureaucracy but also the political and administrative bureaucracies continue to obtain new staff mainly from the technical intelligentsia.

Since Khrushchev's fall, sociologically speaking, almost unrestricted rule has been wielded by the top-level bureaucracy, whose legal status was strengthened under Brezhnev. Apart from increased differentiation within the bureaucracy, which has led to growing conflicts of interest between the party and State bureaucracy and individual sections of it, several factors are preventing further consolidation of this rule. For example, the military has gained power in relation to the politico-administrative bureaucracy. Within the power elite, senior military officers now exercise greater influence in relation to the top levels of the ruling bureaucracy. Other groups and strata within Soviet society have also gained weight and confidence.

Owing to the absolute form of bureaucratic rule, the scientific and cultural intelligentsia is at a much greater disadvantage than the technical intelligentsia. It is therefore not surprising that the former group constitutes the social base not only of the dissidents of the country but also that of most other reform-seeking forces in the Soviet Union. To a lesser extent, these forces are perceptible in the technical intelligentsia, the bureaucracy, and certain sections of the blue-collar working population. In several instances, groups of workers have appealed for the formation of free trade unions.

The emergence of Soviet dissidents, who, in effect, constitute a human and civil rights movement, is directly linked to the incipient change of consciousness caused in part by the social transformation; but it also has spiritual roots, as illustrated by the growing religiousness of the movement. This phenomenon is occurring at a time when the appeal of Marxist-Leninist ideology is further declining.

In view of this development, the Kremlin leaders, who represent first and foremost the overall interests of the ruling high-level bureaucracy, are finding it increasingly difficult to integrate the divergent social forces.

Hence they are particularly disturbed by the activities of the dissidents, who reflect the intelligentsia's differing views on reform as well as the opinions of other social groups. The campaign against the dissidents has therefore been greatly stepped up since the Soviet intervention in Afghanistan and especially since Brezhnev's death. The more stringent legislation governing criminal law and the enforcement of sentences enacted under Andropov affected the dissidents in particular.

In his programmatic speech at the plenary meeting of the Central Committee on June 13, 1983, Andropov said that as a result of "far-reaching qualitative changes" in the productive forces, "a corresponding perfection of production conditions has not only become necessary, but also inevitable." With this ideological description he stressed the need for extensive reforms entailing fundamental changes in the superstructure (i.e., in the party, the State, and the social organizations) and a corresponding transformation of social consciousness. Gorbachev has expressed similar ideas.

What Andropov carefully intimated in his speech has been expressed with rare clarity in a secret study by Soviet economic and social scientists at the Novosibirsk branch of the Academy of Sciences of the USSR, for which Mrs. Tatyana Zaslavskaya, a member of the academy, was responsible. Evidently with top-level approval, this study was passed on to foreign correspondents in Moscow. The implication is that the strong criticism of the Soviet centralized planned economy expressed in the study is considered legitimate by some members of the Kremlin leadership. In place of obsolescent, centralistic forms of organization and bureaucratic methods of management with a repressive effect on the labor force, the study demands the decentralization of economic administration, the introduction of elements of a market economy, and "real incentives" for a better morale among the working population. In this connection, it places special emphasis on the effects of social differentiation among the members of the work force. It also points out the necessity of dealing with the groups of functionaries who have prevented or undermined reforms initiatied until now so as to preserve their privileges.

The study further notes that the productive forces have developed at an accelerated pace owing to the scientific and technological revolution, whereas the system of centralized economic planning established about fifty years ago—and hence the conditions of production—have remained unchanged. The key observation is that this system "never has undergone a qualitative change reflecting the fundamental transformation in the condition of productive forces." Therefore, in conformity with Andropov's remarks at the plenary meeting in June 1983, the study demands a major change so as to achieve convergence of the two economic factors that, according to Marxist theory, have had a decisive impact on social development.

Despite the continuing weakness of the forces for reform, the sociological conditions are much more favorable to a policy of reform today than they were at the time of destalinization. The representatives of "rational totalitarianism" who pilot the Soviet ship of State are increasingly confronted both with pluralist forces that are hampering the "total control from above" (a control exercised with the aid of the full-scale party apparatus) and with sections of the critical intelligentsia that are developing a social alternative. The rulers in the Kremlin could meet this challenge effectively only if, by drawing to a greater extent on the scientific and cultural intelligentsia and not only on the technical intelligentsia, they are prepared to change the makeup of the category of functionaries and not to base their rule solely on the bureaucracy.

The increasing social tensions resulting from greater differentiation in Soviet society are exacerbated by the problems connected with the Soviet Union's special nature as a State of many nationalities. The steep rise in the number of Islamic peoples in Central Asia and in the Caucasus causes the Kremlin leadership particular anxiety.

The intensified policy for Russification and centralization pursued according to the motto of a "uniform Soviet people" has led to growing unrest among non-Russian nationalities, who in some cases are demonstrating a growing self-confidence. Brezhnev was thus prompted to speak out in favor of a more cautious policy on nationalities at the 26th Party Congress. This approach was largely continued by Andropov and Chernenko, who were familiar with the nationalities problem.

Gorbachev, who comes from the Northern Caucasus (as did Andropov before him), is acquainted with this problem. In the ideological sphere, however, he emphasizes Soviet patriotism, the driving force of all-Russian nationalism. In his speech on December 10, 1984, he described Soviet patriotism as "one of the greatest spiritual achievements of our system." Such an attitude could easily be a spur to intensified Russification, which could harm instead of assist the efforts for far-reaching reforms, even though the intention is to effect these reforms within the framework of the existing system.

The Soviet Union Between Inertia and Change

Gorbachev has placed the task of accelerated intensification of the economy on a par (in terms of political importance) with the previous task of industrialization, which was decisively promoted by Stalin's "revolution from above." Thus he may be prepared to take even radical steps to handle this task. Indeed, he will hardly be able to do without such steps inasmuch as the aged leaders of the top-level ruling bureaucracy tend to shrink back from any experiments. Like large sections of the Soviet population, they seek calm and peace, and would prefer to leave the existing system as unchanged as possible, apart from a few slight corrections. The late Amalrik rightly pointed out that the bureaucratic regime in the Soviet Union is above all interested in keeping everything as it is, with the "authorities continuing to be accepted, the intelligentsia keeping mum, the system not being upset by any dangerous or unusual reforms." The regime would have been able to remain much longer in the state of internal stagnation that evolved under Brezhnev if it had not time and again been aroused from its lethargy for two reasons: First, in order to preserve its newly acquired status as a world power, the Soviet Union is obliged to compete with the dynamic industrial nations of the Western world. A discrepancy has thus emerged between its claim to world power and its economic capacity and social maturity, which are by no means sufficient to preserve and enhance its position as a world power. Second, the increased social differentiation, together with the quest of nationalities for autonomy, has led to the emergence in society of a growing number of pluralistic forces whose demands cannot be satisfied owing to the existing domestic situation.

The regime is faced with a dilemma. If it complies with the demands for far-reaching changes, there is a chance that the momentum lost can be regained. However, such changes may also unleash forces that, like the majority of dissidents, are seeking a complete reorganization of the existing system. Yet if the regime is not prepared to embark upon such a venture, there is the danger that social tensions, which have been exacerbated by the nationalities problem, will increase still further. In that event, the Soviet Union would fall even further behind in its economic and technological rivalry with the West.

The forces seeking extensive reform in the Soviet Union are still small in number. However, their quantity increased in the course of the interregnum, as can be seen from the Novosibirsk study and several other papers not stemming from dissidents. We must also bear in mind that, despite the continuing weakness of the forces for reform, the sociological conditions for a reform policy are today much more favorable than they were under Khrushchev at the time of destalinization.

One obtains the impression that the progressive sections of the intelligentsia are no longer willing to keep mum, because they consider major changes to be indispensable to the Soviet Union's further development. The same perception is gradually becoming discernible among the sections of the top-level bureaucracy consisting of "enlightened bureaucrats" and among military officers. However, the forces that are very critical of the existing State, and that meet with responses mainly from the younger members of the intermediate generation and the more aware sections of the young generation, have highly different opinions as to how the desired changes are to be carried out and what their goals are to be. In addition, there are forces that seek certain changes solely for the purpose of creating a more effective authoritarian regime of nationalist-communist making, but without the extensive liberalization that would permit a certain degree of democratization. They are all agreed that the bureaucratic ossification connected with the totalitarian form of one-party rule must be overcome so that the Soviet Union can catch up with modern developments.

In this uncertain situation, one cannot foresee the direction that Gorbachev's policy for reform will take. Andropov evidently regarded a return to Marx as a means of reinterpreting Leninism and hence acquiring greater scope for reform. He was prepared to cite certain popular democracies, such as Hungary, the GDR, and Bulgaria, as examples in individual fields. In Gorbachev's case, however, even such indications as these are lacking. He is a doer and not an ideologue. He apparently believes that attaining the goal recognized as being necessary will depend first and foremost on determination and the requisite power base. This voluntarism is more reminiscent of Stalin than of Lenin. Given this basic attitude, will he be prepared to limit the CPSU's monopoly of power and release certain areas of society from total control by the party?

In his article in the December 1984 issue of *Kommunist,* Chernenko utterly rejected self-restraint on the part of the CPSU—such rejection being the basic prerequisite for transition from a totalitarian to a more liberal, authoritarian form of one-party rule. Yet such a development, which might ultimately lead to the creation of a constitutional one-party State based on the rule of law, would not mean the end of the one-party rule that is indispensable to Leninism.

Khrushchev, who was essentially also a voluntarist, engaged in a revolutionary act with his secret speech against Stalin at the 20th Party Congress in February 1956. He was able to do so because he had the necessary backing in the Central Committee. But these preconditions do not exist for Gorbachev at present. Even if he is planning a similar revolutionary act, it hardly seems likely that he will use the 27th CPSU Congress (which, according to the party statutes, is due to start on February 25, 1986) as a forum for such an act. The numerous projects prepared during the interregnum with Gorbachev's participation will have to be confirmed by the Party Congress. They include the revision of the party program. Gorbachev will have to ensure that the provisions of the program do not excessively narrow his scope for action. Above all, the preparations and proceedings of the Party Congress afford him an opportunity to combine the expansion of his power base with a major rejuvenation of the leading party bodies to be reelected.

The 27th Party Congress will, in any event, be substantially important to the subsequent development of the Soviet Union. It will reveal whether Gorbachev intends to hold a reform congress similar to the one held thirty years ago, or whether he will embark upon a different course for the modernization of the Soviet Union.

References

Yu. V. Andropov, *Izbrannye rechi i stati. Izdannoe vtoroe* (Moscow, 1983).

R. F. Byrnes (ed.), *After Brezhnev: Sources of Soviet Conduct in the 1980's* (Bloomington, Indiana, 1983).

Zh. Medvedyev, *Andropow. Der Aufstieg zur Macht* (Hamburg, 1983).

B. Meissner, *Sowjetische Kurskorrekturen. Breshnew und seine Erben* (Zürich, 1984).

B. Meissner, *Sowjetgesellschaft am Scheideweg* (Köln, 1985).

Ch. Schmidt-Häuer, *Michail Gorbatschow. Moskau im Aufbruch* (München, 1985).

K. U. Chernenko, *Narod i partiya ediny. Izbrannye rechi i stati* (Moscow, 1984).

K. U. Chernenko, M. S. Gorbachov, *Auf das Niveau der Anforderungen des entwickelten Sozialismus* (Frankfurt a.M. 1985).

H. J. Veen (ed.), *Wohin entwickelt sich die Sowjetunion? Zur aujdsenpolitischen Relevanz innenpolitischer Entwicklungen* (Melle, 1984).

See also the articles by Boris Meissner on the changes of leadership in the Kremlin in *Problems of Communism, Osteuropa,* and *Aujdsenpolitik.*

5

Soviet Economic Trends, with Special Emphasis on Investment and Energy Policies

Marshall I. Goldman

The Soviet economy is not as robust as it was two decades ago. In those days, when economic strength was measured in terms of access to and production of raw materials, the Soviet Union proudly announced very rapid rates of economic growth year after year. There seemed to be no end to such successes, and when Nikita Khrushchev announced in 1959-1960 that the Soviet Union would overtake and surpass the U.S. economy by 1970 or at the latest 1980, the Soviet Union did indeed seem to represent the wave of the future.

Since that time, technology has been revolutionized, and the world is no longer so concerned with raw materials or even conventional machine tools. Today the emphasis is on computers, microprocessors, CAD-CAM, and biotechnology—all areas in which the Soviet Union thus far seems to be lagging behind.

Perhaps nothing epitomizes this initial success and subsequent fall from grace as much as the field of Soviet energy. Of all economic sectors, energy development is the one that lends itself best to central planning and the central allocation of the resources needed to develop that energy. Recently, however, the Soviets have discovered that after a time, even energy development requires something more than orders from the center.

A look at the life and times of the energy sector, then, should serve to provide us with a reasonably good view of the strengths and weaknesses of the Soviet economy and its traditional focus on central planning and basic industrial development. First we will look at the rise and fall of some of the energy sectors and see to what extent output has corresponded to the yearly and five-year plans; then we will examine how Soviet planners have allocated investment resources to achieve these goals; and, finally, we will examine the impact Soviet imports have had on the world energy market.

Energy Capabilities

The first thing to point out is that, even with its problems, the Soviet union is today the world's largest producer of energy. Those who fail to study Soviet energy capabilities and intentions, even when the Soviet Union seems to be having some difficulties, run some serious risks. Perhaps this fact was most vividly demonstrated in 1981-1982, when the Soviet Union's oil traders, as much as anyone, were responsible for the price cutting that brought down world prices. But deciding to study Soviet energy is not the same as actually understanding how the Soviet energy sector functions. This is due in part to official state secrecy and in part to the very different nature of the Soviet economic system and the sometimes perverse (at least by market economic standards) effects this system frequently spawns.

This is not to say that the only way energy resources can be rationally utilized is by using market economy procedures. Based on the record of this last decade and a half, the market system has frequently proven to be woefully inadequate. Fortunately for the West, the centrally planned Soviet system has proven even less useful. Nonetheless, there have been times when the Soviet energy sector emerged with a more desirable fuel balance. This result was due to Soviet economic signals, which, although they once appeared to be causing perverse effects, ended up providing more appropriate guidelines after all. In other words, it turned out that the *Western* criteria were in error, at least in the long run.

As we shall see, that is not the only paradox affecting Soviet energy. For example, by its very size, the Soviet Union finds itself with one of the richest endowments of raw materials, energy in particular, in any country in the world. Admittedly, the petroleum reserves of Saudi Arabia are larger than those so far recorded in the Soviet Union, but no other country matches the Soviet endowment in terms of energy per se. Yet that very wealth is in part responsible for some of the Soviet Union's most serious problems today. We shall examine what those problems are and how Soviet leaders are attempting to cope with them.

The Energy Balance

To appreciate current Soviet problems in the energy sector, we must examine how the Soviet energy balance has changed over the years. One sometimes forgets, however, that there are two energy balances—

one for consumption and one for production. Inasmuch as the Soviet Union has often exported as much as 25 percent of its petroleum and 10 percent of its natural gas, the two balances in the Soviet Union often lead to different results. But for our purposes, we shall rely primarily on the energy production balance.

As reflected in Table 5.1, the Soviet Union, like most other industrial countries, was very heavily dependent on coal prior to and immediately after World War II. Thus, coal accounted for approximately 60 percent of Soviet energy as recently as 1940. By then the United States' figure for coal was about 53 percent, although a decade or so earlier the United States had also relied on coal for over 60 percent of its energy.[1] Unlike most other countries of the world, particularly those in the West, the Soviet Union continued to rely heavily on coal. Thus, until almost 1970, coal production exceeded oil production, and coal consumption equalled petroleum consumption as late as 1972. In the United States that turning point occurred much earlier, during the early 1950s.

There are several explanations as to why the Soviet Union was so slow to switch to petroleum. In part, it took the Soviets time to recover from the damage done to their oilfields during World War II. But once recovery was complete, the Soviet Union exported a significant proportion of that production, just as it had done before the war. More important, therefore, is the fact that the Soviet price system, unlike its counterpart in the West, did not reflect the reduction in the price of petroleum relative to coal. In the outside world this drop in price, together with the relative ease of using petroleum and a growing concern over the environmental problems associated with the burning and mining of coal, spurred a switch in the West. As there were no similar financial or environmental incentives to switch from coal to petroleum in the Soviet Union, most energy consumers in the Soviet Union continued to rely heavily on coal.

At the time, many outside observers argued that the continued importance of coal in the Soviet Union only highlighted the irrationality of the Soviet central planning and pricing system. Wholesale prices remained fixed for long periods of time and did not respond to changing economic relationships. For example, wholesale prices in general remained constant from 1967 to 1982. There was no incentive to switch to petroleum, which in the outside world had become cheaper. Hence the Soviets lost out on the advantages of flexibility and cleanliness associated with the use of petroleum.

In retrospect, however, the Soviets may have been right (even if for the wrong reasons) when they continued to favor coal, and the rest of the world was wrong. After the 1973 oil embargo and price rise, the other countries of the world bemoaned the fact that they had turned

TABLE 5.1
Soviet Production of Major Energy Components

Year	Oil (Mil. ton)	Gas Bill (m^3)	Coal[a] (MM tonnes)
	Actual energy units		
1940	31	3.2	165.9
1960	148	45.3	509.6
1965	243	129.0	577.7
1970	353	198.0	624.1
1975	491	289.0	701.3
1980	603	435.0	716.4
1981	609	465.0	704.0
1982	613	501.0	718.1
1983	616	536.0	716.0
1984	613	587.0	712.0
	Percentages		
1940	18.7	1.8	59.1
1960	30.5	7.9	53.9
1965	35.8	15.5	42.7
1970	41.1	19.1	35.4
1975	44.7	21.8	30.0
1980	45.5	27.1	25.2
1981	44.9	28.4	24.3
1982	44.0	29.7	24.1
1983	43.3	31.1	23.6
1984	42.8	32.0	23.2

[a]Based on coal equivalent of 7000 kcalories/tonne

their backs so hastily on coal. Everyone then began to seek ways to increase the consumption of alternate energy forms and reduce their reliance on petroleum. The Soviets adopted the same policy, but they did not have so far to go. Soviet petroleum consumption never reached the high of 49 percent that it did in the United States in 1977, the peak year for the latter. In the Soviet Union, the peak of production was 45.5 percent in 1980, and the peak of consumption was 40 percent in 1975.[2]

TABLE 5.2
Soviet Energy: Actual Production and Plans

	1970A	1975P_1	1975P	1975A	1980P_1	1980P	1980A
Electricity (billion kilowatts)	740	1065	1035	1038	1380	1295	1295
Oil (million tons, including gas condensate)	353	505	489	491	640	606	603
Gas (billion cubic meters)	200	320	289	289	435	435	435
Coal (million tons)	624	695	700	701	805	745	716

A = Actual
P = Annual Plan
P_1 = Five-Year Plan target announced five years earlier

Production

It would be misleading to suggest that shifts in the energy balance of the Soviet Union were due only to changes in pricing policy or even administrative decree. Like the United States, much of the change is also due to the depletion of the reserves. Sometimes this depletion in the West was reflected in rising prices. But because energy markets in the Western world were international, depletion of petroleum supplies in the United States did not in and of itself immediately cause prices to rise or shortages to develop. Undoubtedly the knowledge that the United States was no longer self-sufficient in petroleum ultimately did contribute to an increased militancy on the part of the OPEC nations, which ultimately did raise real prices significantly in 1973. However, because the Soviet Union is a net exporter and not an importer of energy, these price increases did not have an impact on Soviet domestic pricing or shortages as was the case elsewhere. Of course, the rise in world energy prices affected Soviet interest in export markets. Yet the Soviets did manage, perhaps to a greater extent than was actually necessary, to insulate the external buildup in prices from internal Soviet economic activity.

What the Soviet authorities could not do, however, was to protect their economy from a drop in output of several of the most important energy resources. Moreover, based on a comparison of plan and actual output, there is reason to believe that the Soviets were surprised by

TABLE 5.2, cont.

1981P	1981A	1982P	1982A	1983P	1983A	1984P	1984A	$1985P_1$	1985P
1335	1325	1359	1366	1411	1416	1465	1493	1555	1540
610	609	614	613	619	616	624	613	630	628
458	465	492	501	529	536	578	587	630	623
738	704	n.a.	718	723	716	723	712	775	726

A = Actual
P = Annual Plan
P_1 = Five-Year Plan target announced five years earlier

the decline in production that did take place. Coal and petroleum production declines were particularly disappointing for them. As Table 5.2 indicates, as early as 1977 the annual plan for coal production fell 11 million tons short of actual output. The disparity grew to a 33-million-ton shortfall in 1979. Although the gap between planned projections and actual output each year is no longer as great as before, apparently little has been done to correct for what by now is a clear sign of trouble. Thus, for the tenth Five-Year Plan (1975–1980), output at the end of the plan, which was originally projected to be 805 million tons of coal, reached only 716 million tons. There is likely to be a similar shortfall between planned and actual output in the eleventh Five-Year Plan. But even more distressing, in 1979 production actually dropped from what it had been the year before and continued to decline until 1982, after which production began to decline again. The fact that the plan and actual production have seemed to bear so little relationship to one another for such long periods makes one wonder just how meaningful the central planning process has been.

A similar gap between plan and production has existed in the petroleum industry. At times various petroleum authorities have been even more optimistic than coal officials. At one point, for example, there were estimates that Soviet petroleum production would reach as high as 1,000 million tons by the year 2000. However, the Five-Year Plan and annual planning forecasts have not been too far off. For example, actual production in 1975 was 491 million tons, whereas the Five-Year Plan

TABLE 5.3
Monthly Oil Production in the USSR (in millions of tons)

	1978	1979	1980	1981	1982	1983	1984	1985
January	47.2	n.a.	50.4	51.6	51.5	52.7	52.0	50.6
February	42.9	n.a.	47.1	46.6	46.5	47.6	48.4	45.7
March*	46.0	n.a.	50.6	51.8	52.0	53.0	52.6	50.7
April	46.5	48.2	49.1	49.9	50.2	50.9	50.9	49.0
May	48.2	48.2	51.0	51.6	52.0	52.5	52.6	50.7
June*	46.8	48.0	49.0	50.0	51.0	51.0	50.5	48.0
July	48.6	49.4	51.3	51.7	52.0	52.5	52.2	50.2
August	48.8	50.1	51.5	50.0	52.2	52.6	51.9	50.4
September*	50.0	48.0	50.0	52.0	49.0	51.0	50.0	49.0
October	49.5	50.4	51.5	51.8	52.7	51.6	51.5	--
November	48.1	49.0	50.1	50.1	51.0	50.0	49.7	--
December*	50.0	51.0	52.0	52.0	53.0	51.0	51.0	--
Totals	572.0	586.0	603.0	609.0	613.1	616.0	613.0	

*Figures were estimated by calculating the residual.

had estimated 505 million tons five years earlier. Estimates for the tenth Five-Year Plan, ending in 1980, were 640 million tons as contrasted with actual production of 603 million tons. Recognizing that production was not increasing as rapidly as it had in earlier decades, petroleum forecasters soon became much more realistic. Thus, the forecast for the eleventh Five-Year Plan of 630 million tons was actually 10 million tons lower than the forecast made five years earlier for the tenth Five-Year Plan, namely, 640 million tons.

Unfortunately, there is almost no chance that the original 1985 Five-Year Plan will be met, even if it is more realistic. For that matter, even the annual plan figures set out last year at 628 million tons seems way beyond reach for 1985.

It may be part of the job description, but Soviet planners seem to be perennial optimists. Even after petroleum production began to drop in late 1983, as shown in Table 5.3, the forecast for 1984 and 1985 indicated an expected increase in production. Some argue that Mikhail Gorbachev will make a difference. His crackdown on discipline seems to be working. For 1986, production increased by 3 percent.

The relationship between planning and actual production has been somewhat different in the natural gas industry. Actual production just equalled the planned projections set out five years in advance for the tenth Five-Year Plan ending in 1980. In all likelihood the same thing will happen at the end of the eleventh Five-Year Plan plan. Equally impressive, actual production has frequently exceeded annual production forecasts (see Table 5.2). With annual production increases reaching 9 or even 10 percent, it is no wonder that Vassily Dinkov, the former minister of the Gas Ministry, was selected to replace Maltsev in the Petroleum Ministry.

Until recently, occasional annual planned forecasts of electricity generation also exceeded actual production. However, during the critically cold months of early 1985, production barely increased (especially in February); in one of Gorbachev's first moves, he pensioned off the elderly minister of energy and electricity, Pyotr Neporoznii, and replaced him with Anatoly Maiorets, a younger subordinate. Maiorets may yet be able to achieve the Five-Year and Annual Plan goals for 1985.

A Perverse Incentive System

Given the critical importance of energy production, the Soviets must do all they can to correct the problems that have arisen. The challenges in the petroleum industry are many, and for the most part conditions seem to be worse than need be. This is largely due to the perversity of the Soviet incentive system. Admittedly, many of the older petroleum fields have been depleted, but most Soviet officials acknowledge that the depleted fields have been working poorly in any case. Advanced recovery procedures have been utilized ineptly or not at all. For example, in October 1981 it was announced that E. Khalimov, the deputy minister of the petroleum industry, had been fired for importing 36 million rubles (about $50 million) of advanced recovery equipment in chemicals and then not using any.[3]

There are numerous examples of poorly or unused equipment imported for use in energy production and distribution. The Ministry of Petroleum Refining and Petrochemicals had purchased 845 million rubles worth of equipment only to leave it unused. Similar charges have been made about the Ministry of Energy and Electricity.[4]

This is not only a case of poor utilization of imported equipment. The same thing happens with Soviet-produced equipment—again, for the most part a natural consequence of the rather perverse incentive system. For example, oil drillers in the Soviet Union are paid according to how many meters they drill, not how much oil they find. Inasmuch as they can drill shallow holes faster than deep holes, Soviet drillers have been widely criticized for drilling only shallow holes.[5] The reason for the criticism is that the shallow holes tend to end up short of the reservoir. Thus, all too often the bonuses are paid despite the failure to find oil. Equally frustrating is the fact that this bonus system has been intact for many years but so far no one has revamped the system.[6]

The Soviet effort is also handicapped by the fact that Soviet technology in the energy field lags behind that of the West. For example, the Soviets continue to rely primarily on the turbo drill instead of the rotary type. Yet with the turbo drill it is difficult to drill deeper than 3,000 meters.[7] Unfortunately, most exploratory holes must go beyond that depth.[8]

On top of everything, Soviet drill pipes and bits are of such poor quality that Soviet drillers often have to stop for repairs. The geologist Arthur Meyerhoff has found, as a consequence, that an American drilling unit generally drills three times faster than a comparable Soviet drilling team.[9] Apparently, drilling problems have continued even though the Soviets completed the installation of an American-built drill bit plant.[10] Equipment inadequacies have also hampered Soviet efforts in off-shore drilling and geological exploration. Poor technology, which is a product of the Soviet industrial system, also accounts for some of the shortcomings in coal production and electricity generation.

The factory at Atommash, designed to mass-produce nuclear reactors, has had special problems—problems that, in a crude sense, can also be attributed to technology. The factory was built on a swamp and as a result the foundation keeps sinking.[11] Not surprisingly, production of the very heavy reactor units has been hampered.

Soviet technology in the gas industry has not proved to be quite the same bottleneck, in part because the Soviets are able to import most of the large-diameter pipes and compressors used in their pipeline. They were hurt by the U.S. effort to halt the sale of turbine compressors needed for the pipeline to Western Europe. Nonetheless, they were able to import most of what they needed. The surprising thing, however, is that priority efforts to build their own large-scale pipes and turbine compressors have been relatively unsuccessful. The Soviets do say that they are able to build their own 25-megawatt compressor turbines.[12] But these turbines can be used only in populated areas because of frequent breakdowns. By contrast, one of the main advantages of the General Electric prototype compressor turbine is that it is so reliable it can be left untended for long periods of time in the desolate areas through which the pipeline must pass.

But pipeline equipment aside, the Soviets seem to have abundant reserves of natural gas, and continued growth of output should prove to be no problem.

Soviet Energy Needs

The Soviets have serious energy problems to contend with. However, most of their problems have arisen because they make poor use of what they have, not because they have been poorly endowed. Undoubtedly they will someday find themselves with an inadequate supply, and, certainly, like any other country, even Saudi Arabia, the Soviet Union would just as soon have more rather than fewer supplies. But for the immediate future, the Soviets will be self-sufficient.

Part of the reason for the Soviets' own concern, however, is that for the Soviet Union self-sufficiency is not enough. The Soviet Union is very heavily dependent on energy exports to pay its hard-currency import bills. Excluding receipts from the sale of military weapons and gold, petroleum exports normally account for over 60 percent of hard-currency receipts. Natural gas accounts for not quite another 20 percent. Until recently at least, the Soviets have regularly exported as much as 25 percent of their petroleum output and about 10 percent of their natural gas production. Without these export earnings the Soviet Union would be hard put to pay for its food and technology imports. Because earnings from petroleum exports are disproportionately large, the Soviets must pay particular heed to sustaining those exports, because it will take significant quantities of natural gas to make up for the difference; moreover, there seems to be nothing else at their disposal that could be sold in large quantities in the hard-currency market.

Another reason petroleum and gas exports are important to the Soviet Union is that its East European allies have become heavily dependent on Soviet petroleum, gas, and even some electricity. On the average, the Eastern European countries import more than 90 percent of their petroleum and gas from the Soviet Union. In the early 1980s the Soviet Union cut back on petroleum exports and offset the cutback with increased exports of natural gas. The Soviets also export 1 percent of their electricity output. If and when they complete the construction of additional nuclear plants such as the one at Khmelnitskii, near the western frontier, the Soviets will export even more.

Yet it is their continued ability to sustain petroleum exports to both Western and Eastern Europe that most preoccupies Soviet energy authorities. For example, in recent years the Soviets have once again started taking reasonably large quantities of petroleum from Middle Eastern countries such as Libya, Iraq, Iran, Algeria, and, most surprisingly, Saudi Arabia. As Table 5.4 indicates, Soviet imports from these countries have risen sharply in the last few years. As the Soviet Union has almost nothing else to sell (in the case of Iran, natural gas is periodically available), the likelihood is that these imports consist primarily if not entirely of petroleum.

It is safe to assume that most of these petroleum exports are being used to pay for Soviet arms shipments. In the case of Saudi Arabia, the Saudis, who do not take Soviet arms, are probably helping to pay for shipments to Iraq and the PLO. There is also good reason to believe

TABLE 5.4
Soviet Energy Imports from OPEC Nations
(in millions of rubles)

	1981	1982	1983	1984
Algeria	---	---	1	132
Iran	433	150	350	210
Iraq	1	14	382	669
Libya	361	1,126	1,014	1,129
Saudi Arabia	---	---	157	292
Totals	795	1,290	1,904	2,432

that the petroleum imports from this area are not destined for the Soviet Union but are redirected to Eastern or Western Europe. Although the Soviets are now most likely importing and reexporting about 2.4 billion rubles (approximately $3 billion) worth of petroleum, this quantity still constitutes not much more than 20 percent of total Soviet hard-currency earnings from petroleum exports. Ironically, while the Saudis were selling to the Soviets, the Soviets in turn were driving the Saudis and other OPEC members out of the Common Market. Thus, in 1983-1984, the Soviets had displaced the Saudis and become the largest outside suppliers of crude oil and refined product to the Common Market countries.[13] However, because of the very cold weather during the 1984-1985 winter, the Soviets were forced to cut back on energy exports and thus found it necessary to declare *force majeure* in late 1984 and early 1985. The official explanation was that the exceptionally cold winter had made it impossible to pump and ship the planned quantities of petroleum. Given the cold weather, it is also likely that Soviet officials diverted to domestic uses many supplies intended for the outside. Gas exporters to West Germany in early 1985 were similarly affected.

To prevent any further drop in production, the Soviets are continuing to allocate large sums for investment in the energy sector. As indicated in Table 5.5, the Soviets have continued to increase the real amount and relative share of industrial investment devoted to the energy sector. Not surprisingly, the petroleum industry attracts 17 percent of total industrial investment. The allotment to the gas sector has increased, although, surprisingly, the percentage set aside for electricity generation has fallen sharply. Overall energy continues to receive more than one-third of total industry investment.

TABLE 5.5
Capital Investment

	1970	1975	1980	1981	1982	1983
	As a percentage of all industry (35-36 percent of total investment)					
Electricity	10.8	9.2	9.4	9.1	8.9	8.6
Coal industry	5.4	4.3	4.4	4.1	4.3	4.3
Petroleum industry	8.9	9.6	14.4	16.3	17.0	17.0
Gas industry	3.7	4.5	4.4	4.1	4.6	5.0
Totals	28.8	27.6	32.6	33.6	34.8	34.9
	In 1969 rubles (billions)					
Electricity	3.0	3.7	4.5	4.5	4.5	4.6
Coal industry	1.5	1.7	2.1	2.0	2.2	2.3
Petroleum industry	2.5	3.8	6.8	8.1	8.7	9.1
Gas industry	1.0	1.8	2.1	2.0	2.3	2.7
Totals	8.0	11.0	15.5	16.6	17.7	18.7

Sources: Nar Khoz (1983), p. 361; Nar Khoz (1977), p. 354.

The Long-Range Energy Plan and the Drive for Intensification

The aforementioned large sums reflect the importance to the Soviet Union of the energy sector. It is interesting to note the relative drop in investments set aside for electricity production. This seems particularly odd given the apparent priority attached to increasing electricity production in the 1984 long-range energy plan. Increased electricity production was listed second only to the need to increase gas production. Next in order came the call for increasing the capacity of nuclear energy output, which for the most part also means increasing electricity output. After nuclear output the document listed an increase in coal production, hydroelectric capacity, and drilling for crude oil.[14]

Continuation of the increased amount of real investment funds allocated to energy will not be easy. Soviet planners have warned that the amount available for investment has not been increasing as much as had been the case earlier. According to academician A. Aganbegyan, whereas the capital available for investment in the tenth Five-Year Plan increased 32 percent over the ninth plan, the comparable figure for the eleventh plan over the tenth was a projection of only 10 percent growth.[15] It should not be surprising, therefore, that this investment grew by only 2 percent in 1984.[16] Aganbegyan expects that the increase in capital spending in the forthcoming twelfth Five-Year Plan over the existing eleventh plan will be even less. Hampering the effort even more has been the discovery that it takes more and more rubles to generate an increase in energy output. For example, to obtain a 1-ton increase in the output of oil in 1981–1985, an almost nine-fold increased investment would be required over that needed to produce a similar increase of petroleum in 1976–1980.[17] In recent years, overall capital investment in energy has risen one and a half times faster than energy output.[18] The declining yield on the return on investment, plus the fact that the labor force has been growing at a reduced rate (and then almost entirely in Central Asia), has made the energy planner's task a very difficult one indeed.

Given these new and pressing constraints, it is not surprising that one of the main themes of the Soviets' long-range energy plan is energy conservation. Emphasis on energy conservation is spread throughout the published report. Specifically, Soviet energy planners call for a reduction of the elasticity of the energy ratio (the change in energy usage over the change in GNP) by 12–17 percent. In addition, it has been all but impossible in the last two years to find an edition of the weekly newspaper, *Ekonomicheskaia gazeta,* that does not contain at least one article about raw-material conservation and more efficient use of energy.

As with most campaigns in the Soviet Union, the theme of energy conservation is strongly supported by members of the Politburo. In fact, Gorbachev has made energy conservation a keynote of his reform effort. He calls it "intensification," but it is hard to find a speech or article of his either before or after his appointment that does not mention it.[19] Intensification in the Soviet context means retooling and more disciplined use of labor, machinery, and resources. Soviet authorities have become seriously concerned about the wastefulness of Soviet industry in its use of raw materials. A campaign has been initiated to work two full days a year on nothing but fuel and raw materials that have been freed up by more careful production.[20] The Soviets are particularly distressed by the heaviness of their machinery and output. They look at the extent to which the market economies have been able to conserve in their use of fuels and raw materials since the price increases of 1973. They seek

TABLE 5.6
Profits as a Percentage of Capital (working and fixed)

	1965	1970	1975	1980	1981	1982	1983
All industry	13.0	21.5	15.8	12.2	11.5	12.6	12.4
Electric energy	4.6	10.9	7.8	6.1	5.9	6.9	6.7
Oil extraction	5.7	27.8	16.8	8.6	6.0	27.8	23.5
Oil refineries	19.4	22.6	23.3	24.1	23.2	16.4	14.5
Gas	9.3	64.5	22.9	15.2	14.4	21.6	20.9
Coal	-17.0	7.3	1.5	-7.5	-9.4	-3.2	-7.0
Peat	0.9	6.5	2.1	-1.5	-2.7	3.1	1.7

not only increased insulation for heating but also process controls so that Soviet manufacturing procedures, such as blast-furnace operations, will be less wasteful.

Soviet economists both in and outside the Soviet Union agree that there is enormous room for improvement. The Soviet Union as well as their East European allies are among the most wasteful users of energy and raw materials. However, ordering more efficient use and actually obtaining it are two different things. Nor is there any question of malevolence on the part of Soviet factory managers. The factory managers respond to their incentive system, but this very system is unfortunately designed in such a way that the managers are encouraged to use raw materials wastefully. In fact, when they attempt to conserve raw materials, they may end up penalizing themselves.

The perversity of this system is a natural consequence of several factors. The price system in the Soviet Union plays a subordinate role in the decision-making processes of factory managers. Planned fulfillment and completion of contract agreements are the managers' prime tasks; increasing profits remains a minor concern. In any case, raw material and energy in particular have been seriously underpriced. As mentioned earlier, the wholesale prices of raw materials were held constant from 1967 to January 1, 1982. The impact of this phenomenon on raw material producers is illustrated in Table 5.6. The coal-mining industry was actually operating at a loss, and prior to the price increases the oil-extraction industry and electricity-generating plants seemed to be uncomfortably close to red ink as well.

The 1982 price increase along with an earlier doubling of retail gasoline prices apparently had some positive impact on reducing petroleum usage, although the results have thus far not been reflected in the statistics of energy usage. As helpful as price increases may be, however, they do not address the heart of the perverse incentive problems. In fact, until the Soviets turn their back and abolish the *valovaia produktsia*, or *val* (i.e., gross ruble output) system, there is little chance for meaningful improvement. Under the *val* system, managers' bonuses depend on whether they can increase the ruble value of their output. The higher the value of the output, the higher the managers' premiums. But Soviet managers concluded long ago that one easy way to increase the ruble value of their output was to utilize extensive quantities of raw materials. Value in the Soviet Union is calculated by taking the price of inputs and applying a fixed margin for profits. Obviously the more expensive the inputs, the higher the ultimate output price will be. And inasmuch as salability and appeal to the ultimate customer do not matter, the managers do all they can to increase the ultimate sales price not only by producing more but also by using excessive quantities of raw materials. This more than anything else accounts for the bulk and needless weight of Soviet products as well as the difficulty Soviet manufacturers have with miniaturization.

Soviet economists recognize that the *val* system is at the heart of their problems, and they talk about the need to outlaw the whole calculation. But despite numerous attempts, the system persists. Given the number of unsuccessful efforts to abolish *val* in both the USSR and Eastern Europe, it seems to be an almost inescapable appurtenance of the central planning system.

The pervasiveness of the *val* system therefore makes it unlikely that Gorbachev's emphasis on intensification will bear "miniature fruit." Machinery produced within the Soviet Union is likely to continue to be energy intensive, bulky, and unsuitably designed for the modern world. For that matter, even if Gorbachev decides to import energy-efficient machinery from the West to get around this problem, his difficulties will not disappear. The imported machinery may well be efficient, but Soviet managers will continue to operate it as wastefully as ever in terms of consumption of energy and other raw materials.

There is nothing obligatory in Marxism that calls for such wastefulness. Marx never mandated that a socialist or communist state must operate on a *val* basis. If anything, there is a strong possibility that the *val* system has become so pervasive because the Soviet Union was established in what used to be the Russian empire. Then and now, this vast land was noted for the richness of its natural resources. As a consequence, then, raw materials were for many years regarded as a limitless resource. There always seemed to be more somewhere else in the country. No wonder raw materials were considered to be readily expendable. But what would have happened if the Soviet Union had been founded in another country where raw materials were in short supply? For example, would a Union of Japanese or Swiss Socialist Republics have evolved such a value system? Given the shortage of raw materials in both countries, the answer is probably not. In both those countries there would have been a much higher price attached to raw materials and scarce resources because the system would otherwise have been unable to function.

In a sense the Soviet Union's vast size, one of its most important strengths, may also be one of its biggest disadvantages. As long as there seems to be more over the horizon, it will be hard to economize on raw materials and switch the emphasis to quality and miniaturization and away from quantity and gigantimania. Short of completely revamping the incentive system and, in all probability, the central planning system as well, we are hard-pressed to see at this stage of development how the Soviets will be able to give meaning to Gorbachev's code word of "intensification."

Conclusion

To the extent that Gorbachev is sincere and determined to change the way Soviet managers waste the Soviet Union's resources, he will not have an easy task. Yet as distressing as it may be, the failure to evolve another policy does not necessarily foretell an inevitable crisis for the Soviet economy. Those who are sensitive to the fact that energy raw materials are not renewable resources will continue to be distressed by the waste around them and by the knowledge of the opportunities being lost. Given the enormous size of the Soviet Union, however, it is likely that undiscovered deposits may yet be found around the next corner. Of course, such optimism cannot last forever, but for the near future the Soviet Union will continue to have more energy resources at its disposal than almost all of the world's industrial producers.

Notes

1. U.S. Bureau of the Census, *Statistical Abstract of the U.S.: 1984*, 85th ed. (Washington, D.C., 1984), p. 528.
2. Marshall I. Goldman, *The Enigma of Soviet Petroleum: Half Empty or Half Full?* (London: George Allen and Unwin, 1980), p. 52.
3. *Sotsialisticheskaia industriia* (October 4, 1981), p. 2.
4. *Izvestiia* (October 8, 1983), p. 2; *Pravda* (July 17, 1984), p. 2.
5. *Sotsialisticheskaia industriia* (July 27, 1979), p. 2; *Pravda* (July 27, 1978), p. 2.
6. *Izvestiia* (October 15, 1984), p. 2.
7. Goldman, *The Enigma of Soviet Petroleum*, p. 36.

8. Arthur A. Meyerhoff, "Sovet Petroleum: History, Technology, Geology, Reserves, Potential and Policy," in Robert G. Jensen, Theodore Shabad, and Arthur W. Wright, *Soviet Natural Resources in the World Economy* (Chicago: University of Chicago Press, 1983), p. 316.

9. Meyerhoff, "Soviet Petroleum," p. 318.

10. *Izvestiia* (June 8, 1985), p. 2.

11. *Pravda* (February 26, 1982), p. 1; *Pravda* (February 1, 1983), p. 2; *Pravda* (July 20, 1983), p. 2; *Pravda* (September 15, 1983), p. 2.

12. *Pravda* (February 19, 1984), p. 2.

13. Organization for Economic Cooperation and Development, International Energy Agency (Paris), *Quarterly Oil and Gas Statistics, 3rd Quarter 1984*, No. 4, pp. 146–147.

14. *Ekonomicheskaia gazeta*, No. 12 (March 1984), pp. 11–14.

15. *Trud* (August 28, 1984), p. 2.

16. *Pravda* (January 26, 1985), p. 1.

17. N. Baryshnikov and G. Galakhov, "Kapital'noe stroital'noe stroitel'stvo reshaiushchii uchastok sotsialisticheskogo vosproizvodstva," *Planovoe khoziaistvo* (March 1982), pp. 25–30.

18. *Ekonomicheskaia gazeta*, No. 2 (January 1985), p. 10.

19. For example, see *Pravda* (December 1, 1984), p. 2; *Pravda* (February 21, 1985), p. 1; *Pravda* (February 22, 1985), p. 1; *Pravda* (April 9, 1985), p. 1; and *Pravda* (April 12, 1985), p. 1.

20. *Pravda* (December 11, 1984), p. 3.

6

Economic Reforms in China in Light of Soviet and Eastern European Experiences

Tsuneaki Sato

As is well known, the economic system of China has already undergone many partial and experimental modifications since the Chinese political leadership proclaimed the "Four Modernizations" in 1978. The decision on "Economic Reform" adopted by the Central Committee plenary meeting of the Communist party of China (CPC) on October 20, 1984, was a milestone on the way to far-reaching economic and structural reforms. These reforms are aimed, according to the proclamations of the leadership, at establishing a new kind of socialism with Chinese characteristics (alternatively, socialism with a Chinese face). Their target, process, measures, and effects are all related to the success or possible failure of the modernization program of the world's largest socialist country. This nation is now joining the ranks of the Asian newly industrializing countries (NICs). It is quite natural, therefore, that the proclaimed economic reforms in China have received great attention in nations all over the world, including the USSR and the countries of Eastern Europe. If China's economic reforms succeed, they will undoubtedly contribute to the interdisciplinary study of economic systems theory.

However, in discussing the subject of economic reform in China, we must make at least two preliminary qualifications: First, the decision to go ahead with economic reform is a "program declaration," as is recognized by Chinese economists themselves. In this sense, China's reforms resemble an economic philosophy (according to R. Nyers, a Hungarian economist); they need further elaboration if they are to be implemented in practice. Second, the start of this reform program has been haunted by the manifestations of economic imbalances caused by an ambitious growth program and weak control over foreign trade. Nevertheless, we must try to analyze China's reforms on the assumption that no big retrogression will occur that might undermine the very basis of the reform process already started. Our analysis is further constrained by the need to focus our attention on both the intended directions of change and the reality that has already taken shape. Our discussion, in other words, remains as provisional and tentative as its subject.

General Framework of Analysis

We proceed from the understanding that

1. The process going on in China since the death of Mao is almost the same as the one that took place in the USSR and East European countries during the ten years following the death of Stalin.

2. In China, however, these changes are taking place under far more backward conditions (note the per capita GNP, for instance) and with a time-lag of nearly twenty years. Thus many of the problems that emerged in the CMEA countries in the second half of the 1960s are now appearing in China, though in a condensed and compressed way, thereby making the picture even more complicated and confused.

3. There are a number of features in common between China and the CMEA countries, including (a) de facto criticism of Mao (cf. Stalin), although this criticism was not thoroughgoing even when compared with the halfway criticism of Stalin by Khrushchev; (b) the introduction of a policy for raising the living standard of the people (renunciation of asceticism was typical of the Cultural Revolution model), even though the economic basis for it was weaker than that in the CMEA countries; (c) moves toward economic reforms; and (d) an opening up of policy toward the outside world.

4. Unlike the CMEA countries in the 1960s, economic reforms in China have dealt with specific difficulties arising from different conditions, such as (a) a low level of industrial development; (b) enormous pressure for employment—an unfavorable condition for economic reform (in the CMEA countries, relative shortage of labor was one of the factors that prompted the introduction of economic reform); (c) the shortage of competent cadres resulting from the Cultural Revolution; and (d) drastic changes in the world market following the oil-shocks, which were nevertheless compensated by the favorable fact that China could rely more on the economic aid coming from the advanced countries.

Taken as a whole, the picture is indeed confusing. The above-mentioned conditions seem to necessitate the use of a roundabout or short-cut method that transcends traditional modes of thinking about a socialist economy. An example is the introduction of the system of family production responsibility into Chinese agriculture (de facto dissolution of the people's communes), which, as I understand it, is a kind of simulation of peasant farming. This introduction might be explained not so much by the need to break from the inefficiency of collective farming (as in a people's commune) as by the pressing need for improving peasants' lives after more than twenty years of stagnation. Needless to say, in China's bold, new open-door economic policy we are seeing the new face of China. We are seeing China as a developing country eager to make up for lost time and to close the gap between itself and the Asian NICs.

Paradoxically, this situation seems to put China on a par with Hungary in the forefront of economic reforms for socialist countries. In China, the "old" problems connected with the economic reforms of the 1960s overlap with "new" problems resulting from the need to revitalize economic performance in the 1980s.

This scenario lends special relevance to a comparative analysis of economic reforms in the CMEA countries and in China. There are clear signs that the Chinese have learned quite a lot from the experiences of such East European countries as Yugoslavia and, later, Hungary. It is necessary, however, to indicate what this relevance precisely consists of. First, as stated earlier, Chinese economic reforms are most radical in agriculture and foreign economic relations; in industry, only pilot reform measures have been introduced. This bears a striking resemblance to the reforms introduced earlier in the East European countries (with the exception, of course, of certain new elements). It is not that experiences of reform in agriculture and in foreign economic relations in Eastern Europe are of relevance to China; rather, it is just the other way around. There is evidence that East European countries are showing interest in the experiences of China in these matters: Even the so-called brigade system, which is now being experimented with in Soviet *kolkhozes*, has some relevance to the Chinese experience, even though it does not touch on the general framework of the collective farm system. In some Soviet republics, especially the Georgian Soviet Socialist Republic (SSR), a kind of family production responsibility system has been introduced on an experimental basis.

Second, the economic reforms in the CMEA countries represent a series of different attempts to pull out of a centralized planning system that tried, without much success, to exercise control over all aspects of economic activity. From what we can gather from the Chinese economic literature, during the period of the Cultural Revolution (1966–1976) there was neither much planning nor detailed control over enterprises in the state sector. According to K. Nakagane, a prominent Japanese specialist on the Chinese economy, "Mao's economic model" could be characterized as a "slack centralized model" relative to the "tight centralized model" of the USSR. In my opinion, this can be explained by two factors: by the pragmatism typical of Chinese tradition, and by the relative weakness of the Central Planning Office in controlling the national economy of China. Therefore, the economic context in which current economic reforms are being introduced in China is not the same as that pertaining to the CMEA countries: Rather, it is a trial aimed at transition from a "slack centralized system" and not from a Soviet-type planning system in the narrow sense of the word. This is the case even though the symptoms of economic illness evident in China are very similar to those that have appeared in the CMEA countries, and despite the fact that Chinese economists lay the blame for the malfunctioning of the economic system on the introduction of Soviet-type planning.

Quite naturally, then, as the Chinese themselves point out, recent changes in the economic administration of state industry consist of a paradoxical mixture of attempts aimed sometimes at tighter control and sometimes at a cautious policy of granting autonomy to a number of selected industrial enterprises.

Third, it is important that we bear in mind the differences among the CMEA countries. Generally speaking, one can distinguish between two variants of economic reforms. On the one hand, as is well known, the economic reforms in Hungary over twenty years' time have radically altered the nature of the planning system. They have led to the emergence of autonomous enterprises that, at least formally, no longer receive obligatory plan targets from the Central Planning Bureau (CPB), and to the substitution of administrative measures by economic (rather indicative) instruments of control such as prices, taxes, foreign exchange rates, and credit policy. The reforms introduced in the second half of the 1980s (the second wave of economic reforms) have abolished the branch industrial ministries and replaced them with a single industrial ministry. They have also led to major changes in the administration of state enterprises coupled with cautious attempts at increasing the participation of the work force; moreover, they have resulted in steps being taken toward "pluralization" of the banking system and market prices. In the USSR and GDR, economic reforms (until now at least) have done no more than refine, with some modifications, the traditional planning system introduced since Andropov's brief tenure.

"Intermediate" variants of economic reform have also been introduced in Bulgaria under the official name of "New Economic Mechanism." The Polish variant of economic reform is more advanced than the Hungarian one in the sense that it has a built-in self-management system. However, although the blueprint is quite nice, the question remains as to whether it will function in the present atmosphere of profound political distrust and chronic economic crisis. Overall, it is quite clear that economic reforms have involved a process of increased differentiation among the CMEA countries. China is now joining this process, with an increasingly significant role to play.

The Economic System in China and Its Changes

The resolution on economic reform published on October 20, 1984, was the first attempt to provide a theoretical generalization of the reform measures introduced on an experimental basis since 1978. Two phases could be distinguished before this document was adopted. During the first phase (1978–1982), great weight was placed on the criticism of mistakes committed on the way to socialist construction since 1949: short-tempered introduction of people's communes, the "great leap forward," and the catastrophic consequences of the Cultural Revolution for production. At the same time, a process of "rethinking" and learning from abroad, from both East and West, had set in; in addition, partial reform measures were undertaken that laid great emphasis on increased incentives for the peasants, relaxation of collective coercion, and a shift of investment in favor of agriculture and light industry.

During the second phase (1983–1984), the conclusion was reached that more radical measures were needed in order to make a breakthrough on the way to the "Four Modernizations." Indeed, a decisive break had to be made from the Soviet-style centralized planned economy, which was considered to bear the major responsibility for the many faults and defects in the national economy.

The experiment now taking place in China is one of the most important and interesting reforms ever attempted in a centrally planned socialist economy. In my opinion, there are many similarities between the new Chinese reform measures and the Soviets' New Economic Policy (NEP) of the 1920s: Naturally, China today is reevaluating the Soviet economic situation of the 1920s that was buried later by Stalinism.

The resolution of the Central Committee of the CPC offered the following general conclusion: A stiff and rigid centralized planning hinders the growth of productive forces and stifles private initiative. The Communist party considered such centralized planning to be the main reason for the relative failure of economic reforms in the mid-1960s in almost all of the CMEA countries. The reform measures that stemmed out of this analysis are proceeding full-steam in the countryside and are only at the initial stage of introduction in the state industry.

In brief, these measures take a dual form. First, economic activities are being oriented on the basis of less state control and a "relative" autonomy of enterprises in the fields of production, finance, commerce, profit distribution, and the administration of personnel. In agriculture, a contract system (called the "household production responsibility system") has been developed between the collectives and the peasant households in which a right to utilization of allocated land for the maximum period of fifteen years has been stipulated. This reform is based on the separation of ownership of the means of production and its management in a socialist economic structure, as it is termed. In addition, attempts have apparently been made to introduce this "separation" in state industry in the form of a "management responsibility system."

Second, the implementation of these reform measures was accompanied by a series of far-reaching changes in the organization of the national economy. For instance, attempts have been made to create a new, less-centralized, and more flexible planning system. This system relies more on the use of economic methods than on administrative ones: State planning is intended to cover certain decisive sectors only, while the others are left to the increasing influence of market mechanisms. Price reform has also been instituted; without it, value indicators could not function in such a way as to give enterprises the incentive to increase their effectiveness. The document refers to this as "competition" between enterprises, but such competition could, in extreme cases, lead to "bankruptcy."

Thus the economic system, which is supposed to come about according to the blueprint of the reforms, could be characterized by the term *mixed economic system*. It relies on the use of different forms of planning and enterprise guidance in accordance with the importance of the economic sectors in question (i.e., differentiated approaches). And, in fact, it is yet another illustration of the "feasible" economic system of socialism that Janos Kornai referred to:

> In the official economics of socialist countries the idea was dominating for a long time that the system proceeds towards the exclusivity of the state-owned sector—the sector in "general social ownership"—and even within that towards the state-owned large firm. . . . *The reality of the socialist economy never agreed with this idea*. . . . In my view, the present Hungarian economic system may be called *"mixed economy" of a socialist type*, in the sense that it relies on the symbiosis of different kinds of ownership—and this entails a diversity of organizational and institutional forms" (J. Kornai, lecture on the economic reforms in Hungary, February 1, 1983, Tokyo).

Of course, the structure of Hungary's "mixed economy" is different from that of the Soviet NEP of the 1920s. The latter was connected with the economy of a huge army of small peasants, whereas the position of large-scale industry (commanding heights) was quite weak. Kornai's emphasis, on the other hand, was directed to the existence of and the competition or cooperation among different forms of ownership and economic activity; the state sector retained its leading role as before. Hence we are referring here to a "mixed economy" of the "socialist" type. In any case, one point is quite clear: The idea of a socialist economy approaching a "single state-owned and state-managed economy" has been abandoned once and for all. There are signs that the same way of thinking is gaining strength even in the Soviet Union (see the famous "Novosibirsk Document").

One can see more similarities between the NEP in the 1920s and the Chinese reform model than between the former and the Hungarian model. In the Chinese countryside, de facto peasant farming now predominates, thus giving rise to increased differentiation among the rural people. In addition, a bolder "concession" policy is being adopted in relation to foreign capital.

The document on reform defines the socialist planned economy as a "commodity economy based on planning and social ownership of means of production, in which the operation of the law of value should be duly taken into account." It also states that a socialist economic structure and production relations of a socialist type can be made compatible with the increased role of market mechanisms; indeed, it argues that the two elements can actually be combined. The definition of socialist planned economy as a "planned commodity economy" seems to have exceeded the conception of the combination of "plan and market" hitherto applied in many socialist countries.

We now turn to a closer examination of the systemic changes currently taking place in China's economy. Six related questions merit our attention:

1. How is ownership of the means of production actually set up?
2. What kind of mechanism is applied in order to allocate resources?
3. What system of organization governs the decision-making processes between the state and the enterprises as well as within the enterprises?
4. How are the workers motivated to work?
5. How can the policy toward the world economy be opened up?
6. What systemic changes are aimed at revitalizing the rural economy?

Only brief answers can be given due to limitations of space.

Ownership

As is generally the case in all socialist countries, three traditional types of ownership have existed in China until quite recently: state (mainly in urban industry), collective (mainly in agriculture), and individual or private (both in urban and rural areas) ownerships. Whereas the third type of ownership had almost disappeared in the urban areas in the first thirty years after the revolution, the trend has been reversed since the death of Mao and the number of collective ownerships is increasing even in the cities. The reason is that a great number of unemployed young people are returning from the countryside, where they could not be absorbed by state enterprises only—hence the need for establishing collective as well as private enterprises.

At the same time, it is now recognized officially that collective and private ownerships constitute a necessary and integral part of the socialist economic system. For instance, management of state and collective firms has recently become entrusted or leased to private persons (cf. Tibor Liska's model in Hungary). This has entailed a separation of ownership from management and a quiet but steady trend toward reforms in socialist countries; in China, too, private ownership is intended to play a supplementary role to an economy based on public ownership. In state farms the state ownership of land and big capital stock remains the same; the land is divided on an experimental basis and handed over to household management under contract obligations.

Changes can also be seen in industrial enterprises in the areas of financing and distribution of profits: On an experimental basis, enterprises are entitled to issue stocks or bonds to working collectives and to individuals who receive a dividend—a system reminiscent of the experiment introduced in Hungary in the early 1980s. In addition, mixed companies with foreign capital participation are being established in China more extensively than in other socialist countries.

Resource Allocation

Resource allocation is another aspect of the well-known problem of "plan and market." The relative weight of "plan" and "market," as well as the type of plan, varies in accordance with the kind of resource being allocated; the same is true of price-formation methods and the types of prices. In China, producer goods have traditionally been called *materials* and consumer-goods *commodities,* and their treatment was quite different both theoretically and practically. Materials were distributed by administrative methods used by supply organs (such as the Material-Technical Supply system in the USSR), and the law of value was not considered to be functioning at all in this field. Commodities, however, were administered by the Ministry of Commerce with due regard to the operation of the law of value. (Today, of course, all goods are recognized as commodities.)

Nevertheless, the names of goods hitherto in use are still employed according to the relative importance of the goods in question. *Materials* are divided into three categories: (1) centrally allocated materials such as steel and oil, for which a central balance is drawn up by the CPB, (2) materials allocated by ministries, and (3) locally allocated materials. *Commodities* are also divided into three categories: (1) those goods that are purchased and sold by the state in a unified form (such as basic foods) (2) goods of relative importance for which only normatives are given concerning procurement, distribution, and export-import, but which are not included in plan directives, and (3) all goods outside the above two categories.

Plans are divided into two types: directive and indicative. The first category includes (1) procurement and distribution of basic agricultural products; (2) products of state industries, such as important raw materials, fuels, energy, a rather small portion of machines, and a major portion of light, chemical, and construction materials of relative importance; and (3) gross investment, new productive capacities of basic products, large and medium-sized construction projects, and specialized projects.

The indicative plans include (1) production plans for basic agricultural products, (2) a portion of products from the light, chemical, construction, and machine industries of relative importance, (3) a major portion of industrial products of relative importance with complicated standards, (4) production and turnover plans for urban collective-owned industries as well as for rural (communal) industries, and (5) investment projects other than those included in the directive plans.

It is quite interesting to note that the number of obligatory plan targets for industrial enterprises decreased from twelve in 1953–1957 to four in 1957 and then increased to eight after 1975. Now the figure is thought to be on the order of four to six. In the case of machine industries, only 20 percent of total output was covered by obligatory plan targets in 1981, whereas the share was roughly 85 percent in 1979. Thus a big change can be observed here.

Prices are divided into two categories: planned and nonplanned. The planned prices are in turn divided into two subcategories: unified state prices and floating prices. Unified state prices are fixed by the state for basic foods as well as for basic raw materials, fuels, and transportation fares. Floating prices mean that prices are permitted to fluctuate within the range of 5 to 30 percent on the basis of unified state prices. Nonplanned prices are also divided into two subcategories: consultative prices, which are determined by means of negotiations between the parties concerned on the basis of, again, unified state prices, and free prices for the free markets in urban as well as rural areas.

However, the relative share of different types of prices is rather different from what one may imagine. In 1981 the share of planned prices accounted for 92.5 percent of the total retail turnover of state and cooperative commerce, whereas consultative and free prices accounted for only 3.7 percent and 3.8 percent respectively. The share of planned-price goods, excluding free prices in the total goods procured and distributed by the Ministry of Commerce, accounted for roughly 80 percent. At the end of 1982, total turnover of free markets calculated in terms of official prices accounted for 9.4 percent of the total turnover of state and cooperative commerce. The share of basic consumer goods directly planned in the total provision of consumer goods was roughly 65 percent. So, generally speaking, one could say that three-fourths of *materials* and *commodities* are distributed according to the state plans. In China planned distribution still covers the majority of products.

Yet one must bear in mind that the share of products included in the state plan is roughly 50–60 percent of the total social product only, in which direct control by the CPB covers more than 40 percent (the rest is covered by the provinces, big cities, and prefectures).

Moreover, the right to set prices is more or less centralized; distribution by free prices accounts for only a small portion of all materials, commodities, and services. In spite of this, the decision of the resolution of October 20, 1984, was to take further measures with the aim of extending the scope of indicative plans, thereby reducing that of directive plans. Beginning in 1985, as a first step, state procurement was to be abolished gradually and replaced by turnover on the market and market price formation. Hence the role of market regulation is expected to increase considerably—perhaps even more so than the reform resolution anticipates, if we take into consideration the weak control capability of the central organs.

The Decision-making Structure

Until quite recently the term *decentralization* has been understood to mean the delegation of central power to local authorities. Two such transfers of central discretionary powers to local auithorities have occurred thus far, in 1958 and in 1970; then the trend was reversed again in the direction of recentralization. On the other hand, state enterprises have always been regarded as "accessories" to the state organs and have not been treated as autonomous producers. For instance, main staffs of enterprises including directors were appointed by the ministries, while workers were allocated by the local Administration of Labor to the districts in which the enterprises in question were located.

As for the management and distribution of financial means, the principles of "unified income" and "unified expenditure" were applied (a matter of eating from the same "big rice-bowl"). From 1967 on, however, enterprises were permitted to reserve one portion of the amortization fund, but the ratio was extremely low—below 4 percent. State centralized investment accounted for almost 80 percent of total investment in 1975. Therefore, the autonomy of enterprises was reduced to almost nil: Enterprises were passive instruments by which the state plan was implemented.

Since 1979 increased autonomy of enterprises has been emphasized, and the right to distribution of profits was granted to enterprises that were entitled to retain a portion of their profits. These reserves were to be used to form three types of enterprise funds: self-investment, material incentive, and welfare—exactly the same scheme as that used in the economic reforms of the 1960s. In 1982 the profits retained with industrial enterprises accounted, on the average, for 14.8 percent of total profit—an amount four times larger than before, but still small.

There now exist several forms of profit retaining by enterprises. The most progressive of these is called "profit tax"—a system under which enterprises, after paying a fixed amount of tax to the state budget, are entitled to dispose of the remainder of their profit. Another effort aimed at enlarging enterprise autonomy involves the so-called temporary provisions for state industrial enterprises, in which detailed items to be entrusted to enterprise autonomy are listed (as of May 1984) concerning the production program, price-setting, purchase of materials, utilization of monetary means, disposition of fixed assets, organizational set-up inside the enterprises, and so on.

Regarding the decision making inside the enterprises, the direction of change has switched from "one-man management" to the principle of "director's responsibility under the guidance of factory party committee" (since 1956) and then to the separation of political guidance from economic management. After 1984 the catch-phrase "under the guidance of party committee" disappeared and "director's responsibility" gained currency. Directors are still appointed by the state, whereas deputy-directors are appointed by the state on the recommendations of the directors. Although there exists a so-called conference of representatives of employees and workers in enterprises, in reality it has been reduced to a mere skeleton. So, the real rights of workers at the workplace are smaller than they should be, and the conference remains a sort of "transmission belt."

Incentives

As is generally known, austerity, revolutionary enthusiasm, and selfless devotion were emphasized in Mao's time. The "rational low-wage system" was applied, and the real wage of workers has decreased since 1956. After 1977 the policy was changed in favor of wage increases and the introduction of a bonus system. The share of bonus in the total wages was only 2.3 percent in 1978, but it had increased to 10.9 percent by 1982. One often hears the appeal to break the so-called iron rice-bowl in order to raise labor productivity. A floating wage system has been introduced on an experimental basis, under which one part of basic wages is linked to enterprise performance (profit). Other means of increasing incentives include allowance attached to the posts held, wage adjustment according to the qualifications of workers, and loosened control over bonus payments.

One must also take into consideration the facts that (1) state control over wage funds is still rigid, and the possibility of relying on bank credits is rather limited; and (2) because of the "egalitarian" distribution of bonus funds, wage differentials between different categories of work force are small and manual workers are more favorably treated than technical staffs. One can fairly say that in the state sector at least, wage differentials are still fairly small.

Opening Up Policy Toward the World Economy

Here, several rather peculiar features can be mentioned:

1. transition from the principle of "self-reliance" to an "opening up" of the policy toward the world economy;
2. decentralization of the right to foreign trade transactions as well as of the access to convertible currencies by local authorities;
3. establishment of mixed companies with foreign capital participation as well as of "purely" foreign capital enterprises;
4. the creation of Free Zones and special economic development regions with the aim not only of developing export drive but also of absorbing advanced technologies and management systems from foreign countries. From the point of view of economic mechanism, Free Zones are supposed to rely mainly on market regulation, whereas state plans play the secondary role of occupying an intermediate position between Hong Kong (where market predominates) and inland China (where such plans are intended to play a leading role). As elements of an economic system, Free Zones are related to "state capitalism" and are considered neither capitalist

nor socialist. Thus "one state with two economic systems" is coming into being.

Changes in the Countryside

Two drastic changes that have taken place in the countryside are decollectivization of agriculture and decommunization. "Decollectivization" refers to the dissolution of people's communes and the establishment of the family production responsibility system. "Decommunization" refers to the separation of local administrative functions from the economy formerly integrated into the people's communes.

Under the family production responsibility system, while the basic means of production (e.g., land) remain under social ownership, the stable right of utilization of land is guaranteed by the state for a period of fifteen years. Households are obliged under contract to fulfill fixed-production as well as delivery tasks, and each peasant household is entitled to dispose freely of the surplus products minus a certain amount of reserves to be handed over to the brigade as collective funds. Roughly 90 percent of all households are working under this system today.

Why decollectivization? The reasons are as follows: (1) Collectivization of agriculture in 1950s was initiated from above. (2) The economy of scale of collective agriculture was rather negative in relation to the costs needed to maintain it. (3) State intervention and inefficiency resulted therefrom. And, most important, (4) pressure came from below to raise the living standard, but traditional strategies of attack did not work here at all; hence a "bypass" was needed.

Tentative Assessment

Although the picture of economic reforms in China is quite confused, one can easily see signs of the transitions under way:

1. from the absolutization of state ownership to the coexistence or symbiosis of different types of ownership as well as management forms;
2. from the predominance of planned control to the increased importance of the market;
3. from the administrative decentralization of power held by local authorities to the decentralization of economic decision making done by enterprises; and
4. from the alleged almighty role of moral to material incentives.

The ideology underlying these changes can be summed up in two words: "economic pragmatism." It found practical expression in Deng Xiaoping's famous phrase, "black or white, good cats are ______."

But three qualifications should be made here: (1) This economic pragmatism is a reaction to the "predominant role of politics" under Mao; (2) the idea of economic efficiency is recognized and emphasized; and (3) great emphasis is laid on the autonomy of economic units.

So, they are in line with the reform measures that were undertaken in the 1960s in most CMEA countries.

It should be noted here that, although the "river of Rubicon" has already been crossed and a big reversal of the present trend would be quite difficult, the economic system in China at its present stage of development could still be characterized as a "slack" centralized system in the sense that (1) the role of the market is still lower than it should be, and (2) enterprise autonomy is still kept under rigid control by the state. So, quite naturally, we see many symptoms of the "economic illness" typical of socialist economies: big stocks of unsold goods, hoarding of materials by enterprises, and long delays in construction.

One can certainly appreciate the innovativeness of the Chinese reform model in the fields of agriculture and foreign economic relations; however, crucial problems in the management of state industries—as in the case of the economic reforms taking place in the CMEA countries—are far from being solved.

It is interesting to note the rather peculiar features of the economic reforms taking place in China:

1. They are still overshadowed by the problems of a slack centralized system connected with the relatively weak capabilities of central regulation, which imparted a certain flexibility to the economic system in Mao's time but might become a fatal weakness on the way to reforming the economy.

2. The present emphasis on the importance of developing a "commodity economy" could be interpreted in terms of both the necessity of overcoming the backwardness evident in the development of a commodity economy (a unified national market, in the narrow sense of the word, is still absent) and the need to control the market by means of indirect methods of planned economy.

3. As society and economy are insufficiently differentiated, enterprises are overburdened with social tasks (such as dealing with the problem of unemployment) that hinder the solution of raising efficiency.

In my opinion, the present economic system in China is only at the initial stage of its institutionalization: The traditional "slackness" typical of China's economic system has been considerably ameliorated by the reform measures already introduced. Thus the system is free, to a considerable extent, from the rigidity characteristic of Soviet-type economies. There may even be more room for additional reforms.

At this point, we must ask: How far will these reforms go? Clearly, this is a difficult question to answer. We can say, however, that as long as the present political leadership remains in power, more realistic changes will be introduced into the economic system; moreover, a drastic reversal of these trends is rather improbable given that the changes have already been built into the system. The main line of development would perhaps be maintained, albeit with fluctuations; thus impetus would be given to the development of economic reforms in the USSR and Eastern European countries.

Finally, it should be noted that economic reforms in China have seemingly reached a point beyond which further advance will be far more difficult than before. Now that the Chinese have turned to industrial reform, they are being confronted with the most crucial problem of reforms ever attempted in socialist countries—a problem even the Hungarian reformers have not been able to solve thus far. This is the problem involved in abolishing the "paternalism" of the state in relation to industrial enterprises, thus making their "budget constraint" hard. To harden the traditional "soft" budget constraint of enterprises is as much a sociopolitical problem as an economic one. And there is no reason to believe that the solution of this crucial problem will be easier to find in China, which is otherwise burdened with an enormous pressure for employment proceeding from the population problem, than in Hungary, where a relative shortage of labor exists.

Needless to say, if China succeeds in making some headway in that direction now that it has completed its pricing reform (as proclaimed in the Decision on Economic Reform of October 20, 1985), it will have reached a new frontier. No longer repeating the sequence of reform measures in the CMEA countries (especially Hungary), China must redefine the limits of both planning and market. But the problem is terribly complex, and no proven prescriptions exist. We can be certain that China has a long way to go before it reaches that frontier and that, even if China's political leadership retains its current commitments to thorough economic reform, the progress, when it comes, will be much more gradual and much more limited than the startling changes of the past eight years might lead us to expect.

7

Economic Relations Between the Soviet Union and Eastern Europe and Their Implications for East-West Relations

Peter Knirsch

The subject being considered here—economic relations between the Soviet Union and Eastern Europe and their implications for East-West relations—is complex and quite broad, and it certainly cannot be treated exhaustively within the scope of a chapter. In order to avoid misunderstandings, I will begin by clarifying some of the possibilities for dealing with this subject, as well as the inherent limitations involved: I hope I will be able to succeed in describing the specific problems presented by economic relations within the CMEA and their influence on East-West relations. When an attempt is also made to identify the causes for these problems, it will be necessary to consider not only the special institutional, structural and development-related aspects of the external economic relations of Eastern European socialist countries but the political influences as well. This is already a very broad field to cover. To keep it within reasonable limits, I will have to refrain for the most part from examining historical developments (and this is unfortunate, as such as examination would make a significant contribution to explaining the problems being experienced today). Furthermore, to a large extent I will also abstain from using empirical and statistical data to desribe the problems being considered here; such data will be employed only to the extent that they can help clarify the current situation.

Special Features of CMEA Foreign Trade

Institutional Factors: General and Special Aspects

I will be describing a number of special features that characterize the foreign trade relations of the CMEA states.[1] Even though these special aspects play an important role in understanding the policy pursued by these countries, we should always be aware that their foreign trade relations include many features that are typical of all foreign trade and are familiar to us from our observations of foreign trade relations in the Western world market. In the CMEA countries as well, the existence of foreign trade and other forms of external economic relations indicates that there are economic relations that extend across national borders. In the CMEA countries, as in the West, the purpose of these economic relations across national borders is to increase national prosperity by taking advantage of the *international division of labor.*

In Eastern Europe, as in the Western world market, economic relations with foreign countries involve going beyond national borders for the sake of economic transactions; but this poses specific obstacles that do not exist when economic transactions take place on national territory. These obstacles often lead to higher costs—for customs duties, bureaucratic licensing procedures, or foreign transactions. In addition, they limit the influence that can be exerted by economic policy; as a rule, national economic policy cannot influence trade relations with other countries as much as it can within the country itself, since there are usually no possibilities for direct implementation in the partner country.

Considering these general conditions for all external economic relations, the economic policy component referred to above plays an especially important role in the CMEA countries: Because the economic system in these countries is based on state ownership of most of the means of production and on centralized government planning, economic policy affects a much broader area of the economy than is the case in Western market economies, where most economic activity is carried out by private entrepreneurs. In the area of external economic relations, the economic systems of the CMEA countries include special institutional arrangements that are intended to limit as much as possible the influence of external economic relations on national autonomy in the area of economic policy.

As a result of the state's monopoly on foreign trade and foreign currency as well as government planning of foreign trade, all external economic transactions are subject to control by special central government organs. It is only through these organs that links are established between domestic and foreign trade, which in theory are supposed to be totally separate from each other. This separation is particularly obvious in the area of price formation: Domestic prices are fixed autonomously by the national planning authorities, and in principle they are completely independent of world market prices for export and import goods. It is still not possible in most CMEA countries to express in an economically meaningful way the value of foreign trade transactions in domestic prices. The concrete result is that it is not possible to compare domestic costs with costs or receipts in foreign trade, such that—with a few obvious exceptions—the economic efficiency of foreign trade transactions cannot be calculated. On the whole, the indirect methods for the calculation of foreign trade efficiency that have been developed in various cases cannot provide an adequate substitute.

In the present context it is important to note that this institutional separation between domestic and foreign trade applies equally to trade among the CMEA states as well as to their trade with the rest of the world.

Thus the special characteristic of external economic relations in the CMEA countries is that, in the institutional area, all foreign trade functions are assumed by special state foreign trade organs; in addition, this activity is strictly controlled by central government organs. Thus the concept of the "state-trading countries" sometimes found in the literature definitely has a basis in reality.

During the course of economic reforms in the European CMEA countries, this foreign trade system has been modified to some extent since the mid-1960s. Such efforts have been most extensive in Hungary, where (although the state monopoly on foreign trade and foreign currency remains unchanged in principle) a larger number of enterprises have been granted foreign trade rights. Moreover, in contrast to the basic idea underlying foreign trade in the state-trading countries, an attempt is being made to establish a link between domestic and foreign prices. In other CMEA countries as well, especially in Poland, steps have been taken to relax some of the restrictions imposed by the foreign trade system described above. It is important to note that, as a result of this development, the foreign trade systems of the European CMEA states are no longer as uniform as they were ten to twenty years ago. The model for state-controlled trade described above still corresponds to a very large extent to the current organization of foreign trade in the Soviet Union. Regardless of these differences, however, in all the CMEA states today—including Hungary—foreign trade is still subject to government planning and continued rigid controls.

Structural Conditions Affecting the Foreign Trade of the CMEA Countries

The need for the various countries of the world to engage in foreign trade and their opportunities for doing so vary widely. Differences among the East European members of the CMEA are particularly evident. At first sight one cannot fail to notice the variations in the size of the seven countries concerned. On the one hand, there is the Soviet Union, by far the largest country in the world with 273 million inhabitants in 1983.[2] The Soviet Union stands in marked contrast to the six smaller CMEA countries, but even this latter group is by no means homogeneous. Poland with 37 million people and Romania with 23 million are the most populous of the six. The GDR with 17 million people and Czechoslovakia with 15 million are in the middle, while Hungary with fewer than 11 million people and Bulgaria with just under 9 million have the smallest populations.

The supply of natural resources found in each country corresponds to some extent with its size. The Soviet Union has a rich supply of natural resources at its disposal. Current geological studies show that on the whole all the mineral substances required for modern industrial manufacturing are available there in adequate amounts. In the case of specific raw materials, especially coal and natural gas, the quantities available exceed domestic requirements and thus represent an export potential. By contrast, the smaller CMEA countries have inadequate supplies of raw materials to support their industrial production and are dependent on imports of the raw materials they lack.[3] This circumstance alone—the fact that the CMEA countries have different amounts of natural resources available to them—means that the countries have varying needs with regard to maintaining foreign trade relations. For the Soviet Union this need is relatively limited, whereas all the smaller CMEA countries are strongly dependent on such economic relations.

If we had more space in which to reflect on history, we would find it revealing to examine the different attitudes toward external economic relations that have resulted from these differing needs to conduct foreign trade. Because of its more limited dependence on foreign trade, the Soviet Union in the past—especially during the 1930s and from 1949 until about 1955—has been able to temporarily place strict limits on its foreign trade with the Western industrial nations and thereby to counteract the economic and political dependence it feared would result from such foreign trade. When the smaller CMEA countries implemented a similar policy of autarchy during the 1949–1955 period, it led to major internal economic difficulties and structural distortions whose effects can still be felt today.[4]

The Economic Development and Foreign Trade of the CMEA Countries

The European members of the CMEA differ not only with regard to their size and the natural resources at their disposal, but also in their relative levels of economic development. Industrialization in these countries began at different times in history and has proceeded with varying degrees of intensity. As a result, the GDR and the CSSR today are highly developed industrial countries according to all the criteria commonly applied—their shares of national income accounted for by industrial production, the percentages of all employed working in the industrial sector, and their per capita national incomes are the highest in the CMEA.[5] At present, the Soviet Union, Poland, and Hungary are about average in their economic development by international standards (although such statistical comparisons are problematic), and Romania and Bulgaria are the least developed economically.

The differences in economic development among the CMEA states are considerable, but even the more developed of these countries lag far behind the developed Western industrial nations. This is particularly evident in the case of foreign trade: As a rule, the commodities exported by the European CMEA countries are below the technological level of the most highly developed industrial countries because of these differences in economic development, but also because of the deficiencies in their economic systems. The same applies to the quality of their export goods—in particular, to their design, packaging, delivery time, spare parts, and services offered.

The Political Dimension of the External Economic Relations of the CMEA States

All over the world external economic relations are of political significance as well. Indeed, such relations exert a mutual influence on other areas of policy—above all, foreign policy. Because of the economic system in the CMEA countries, this reciprocal influence is quite strong; all foreign trade is handled by state organs that are able to take a very direct approach in their attempts to consider the preferences of the political leadership when carrying out foreign trade transactions. This can result in the encouragement or cutting back of economic relations with individual countries or groups of countries; it can also affect the imposition of import limitations on specific goods. It is characteristic of this situation that state visits from the CMEA countries are very often associated with agreements on the deliveries of larger plants or expanded goods quotas. These political determinants of foreign trade relations became particularly noticeable in past years when, under the pressure of their indebtedness, the CMEA countries reduced their imports from the West[6] and increased their exports to these countries. Since 1982 a similar phenomenon has occurred within the CMEA, with the six smaller member countries significantly increasing their exports to the Soviet Union while their imports from there decreased or remained unchanged.

Representatives of the CMEA states frequently complain about restrictive trade practices or politically motivated embargo measures by the Western industrial nations and have demanded, among other things, that quantitative restrictions be lifted or that they be granted most-favored-nation (MFN) status. Regardless of how justified these complaints may be in specific cases, it is important to be aware that the foreign trade system of the CMEA countries permits the direct consideration of political points of view in the case of each individual foreign trade transaction. Naturally the CMEA countries also try to conduct foreign trade based on economic considerations for the purpose of achieving economic advantages, but the opportunities for institutional influence that exist have been used repeatedly for political reasons. For our purposes, it is important to note that political criteria are significant not only for the trade of the CMEA states with the West but also in intra-CMEA trade.

Economic Relations Between the Soviet Union and East Europe

General Characteristics

For all the CMEA countries the other CMEA members themselves represent the most important group of trading partners. As indicated in Table 7.1, this share of intra-CMEA trade has fluctuated significantly over the course of time. During the 1970s the share of total foreign trade conducted by Poland and Romania with the other CMEA countries decreased considerably in favor of an increased volume of trade with the Western industrial nations. At present,[7] only Romania (where trade with the other CMEA states accounted for 47.7 percent of its total foreign trade in 1983) and Hungary (with a 49.6 percent share) conduct just under half their total foreign trade with other CMEA countries, while in all the other CMEA states such trade represents a larger share. Bulgaria heads the list (as it always has) with 76.8 percent, followed by Czechoslovakia with 71.9 percent.

Of this intra-CMEA trade, the largest share is conducted by the Soviet Union, which accounted for 45 percent in 1983; the GDR follows at a distance with 12.1 percent and Hungary comes in third with 9.9 percent.[8] All nine CMEA countries accounted for 51.2 percent of total Soviet

TABLE 7.1
Regional Distribution of CMEA Foreign Trade (shares of total foreign trade in percentages)

	1970	1975	1980	1982	1983
Bulgaria					
CMEA[1]	74.4	73.8	72.8	73.0	76.8
DCC[2]	16.6	17.0	16.5	14.0	12.2
LDC[3]	5.6	7.2	8.8	11.6	9.7
Czechoslovakia					
CMEA	64.2	66.0	65.5	70.0	71.9
DCC	22.4	22.4	23.0	18.4	16.6
LDC	7.6	7.0	7.1	6.4	6.5
German Democratic Republic					
CMEA	67.3	66.2	62.7	63.1	62.5
DCC	24.4	25.9	27.4	28.1	29.4
LDC	4.0	4.4	6.7	6.4	5.8
Poland					
CMEA	63.1	49.7	53.3	54.3	68.4
DCC	27.1	41.3	34.8	31.8	21.8
LDC	6.7	6.5	9.5	10.0	7.1
Romania					
CMEA	49.3	38.0	34.0	43.7	47.7
DCC	35.8	36.7	--	--	--
LDC	8.2	18.5	--	--	--
Hungary					
CMEA	62.1	66.1	49.6	51.7	49.6
DCC	28.4	24.4	36.7	32.9	33.3
LDC	6.3	6.6	10.3	11.8	13.1
USSR					
CMEA	55.6	51.8	48.6	49.1	51.2
DCC	21.2	31.3	33.6	31.6	30.1
LDC	13.5	12.4	12.7	14.1	13.9

[1]CMEA = all CMEA countries except Vietnam. The shares for Cuba (which accounted for a 3.7 percent share of the total foreign trade of the CMEA states in 1983) and the People's Republic of Mongolia (a share of 0.4 percent) may be disregarded.
[2]Known as "developed capitalist countries" (DCCs) in CMEA statistics.
[3]Less developed countries (LDCs).

<u>Sources:</u> <u>CMEA Statistical Yearbook</u>: 1971, p. 342; 1976, p. 341; 1981, p. 335; 1983, p. 315; and 1984, p. 297.

foreign trade in 1983; the six European CMEA countries alone accounted for 44.5 percent. In 1983 the GDR was the Soviet Union's most important trading partner with a 10.5 percent share of Soviet foreign trade turnover, followed by Czechoslovakia with 8.9 percent, Bulgaria with 8.3 percent, Poland with 7.9 percent, and Hungary with 6.3 percent. It is interesting to note that Romania's involvement in Soviet foreign trade is quite limited, accounting for only 2.6 percent of Soviet foreign trade turnover, which is considerably less than the share of various Western countries or Yugoslavia.[9]

In examining this structure, we should bear in mind that, as difficult as it is to calculate, the intensity of foreign trade in the smaller CMEA states is greater than that in the Soviet Union.[10] With the exception of Romania, all the CMEA states are important trading partners for the Soviet Union, but foreign trade does not play a very significant role when considered as a percentage of Soviet national income. In the case of the smaller CMEA states, foreign trade accounts for a considerably larger share of national income, and, with the exception of Romania, the Soviet Union has been their most important trading partner since the early 1950s. In 1983 the Soviet Union accounted for the following shares of total imports and exports in each country: in Bulgaria, 55.9 percent and 51.6 percent respectively; in Czechoslovakia, 46.2 percent and 41.8 percent respectively; in the GDR 39.3 percent and 32.0 percent respectively; in Poland 37.7 percent and 31.2 respectively; in Romania 22.2 percent and 17.4 percent respectively; and in Hungary 28.6 percent and 31.6 respectively.[11] These large shares in the individual partner countries indicate (to the extent that economic dependence can be established on the basis of quanitative data) that a fairly high degree of economic dependence exists for the smaller CMEA states. The greater intensity of foreign trade, which we assume to exist, in these countries contributes to this dependence. The Soviet Union is the most important supplier and the most important market for these smaller CMEA countries.

This economic dependence is intensified even more by the commodity structure of trade between the smaller CMEA states and the Soviet Union. For all the European CMEA countries, trade with the Soviet Union has a basically complementary structure. The Soviet Union is their most important supplier of raw materials, especially fuels, and of semifinished products; it is also their most important customer for investment goods and industrial consumer goods.[12]

Positive and Negative Aspects of the Soviet Union's Trade with Eastern Europe

The economic relations of the Eastern European CMEA countries with the Soviet Union have the institutional advantage that these international relations are between countries that have essentially the same economic system, are supposed to be cooperating on the economic level in the CMEA, and have a political commitment to a common alliance. Given the similarities between economic systems with central economic planning, the CMEA countries, in principle, should be able to reach a common agreement on foreign trade relations in the long run; in addition, these relations can then be integrated into their respective national plans.[13] In a later section, where the current problems involved in such cooperation are described, we will see that the reliability of such agreements should not be overestimated and that foreign trade among CMEA countries, despite its inclusion in national planning, is not free of risk.

In the short run, the complementary commodity structure outlined above is probably to the advantage of the national economies concerned, with the respective economic potential of each country complementing that of the others in an apparently beneficial manner: The Eastern European CMEA countries receive the raw materials and semifinished products they need for their industry from the Soviet Union and find a large, almost unlimited market for their products in the Soviet Union. In this connection, the smaller CMEA states have the advantage that they can supply products to the Soviet Union that would not be competitive on the Western world market due to their quality and to other characteristics that strongly influence their marketability. In view of the balance-of-payments situation in the smaller Eastern European countries, the Soviet Union could by no means be easily replaced as a supplier and market outlet.

In the longer term, however, this advantage becomes a *disadvantage*. Because it is possible to sell products in the Soviet Union with relatively little effort, the impulse toward further technological and economic development in the smaller Eastern European countries, which in any event is already quite weak within the system of central economic planning, represents an additional obstacle to progress. As the smaller European countries do not feel sufficient pressure to reduce the gap separating them from the Western industrial nations, their inability to compete on the world market is perpetuated.

Current Problems in Soviet Economic Relations with Eastern Europe

The Soviet Union's economic relations with the Eastern European CMEA countries decisively influence the further development of economic integration in the CMEA. At present, this integration process is beset by considerable difficulties. Apparently it is not only in the West—I am thinking here about the integration problems of the European Community—that the economic integration of national states is an extremely difficult process; this is also true of the socialist countries. At an earlier point we discussed differences in the size, relative development, and supplies of natural resources available to the countries concerned; such differences mean that the *interests* of the respective countries with regard to the integration process will also vary widely. The economic and political dominance of the Soviet Union, which leads the smaller CMEA states to insist on their national sovereignty and prevents further steps toward integration from being taken due to the unanimous votes provided for in the case of more important decisions, has proven to be a particular obstacle in this connection. These basic integration problems are still unresolved. Here, however, we want to consider only those current developments which have been characteristic of the economic relations between the Soviet Union and Eastern Europe since about the mid-1970s and which are therefore important for the entire integration process in the CMEA. In this context, it is significant that a slowdown in economic growth has occurred in all the CMEA countries during the past ten years.

1. During this period the Soviet Union succeeded in persuading the smaller European CMEA countries to participate in joint investment projects, generally involving the exploitation of raw materials and sources of energy as well as their transport. In accordance with the distribution of natural resources, most of these sites are located on Soviet territory. Procurement of the required investment funds was not easy for the participating CMEA states, considering the overall scarcity of funds, and in the short run, at least, has had an unfavorable effect on their economic growth.

For a number of the smaller CMEA countries, such an attempt to secure future supplies of important raw materials and energy may nevertheless render acceptable the difficulties involved in procuring the necessary investment funds. However, with regard to their former insistence on preserving national sovereignty, this is a negative development, for their *dependence* on the respective Soviet deliveries increases as a result. The development is all the more negative given that they cannot find substitutes for cancelled Soviet deliveries by making purchases on the world market (at least not without running into difficulties), because they lack the convertible currency to make such purchases.

2. Regardless of all official declarations to the contrary, various factors have contributed over the last few years to increased doubts on the part of the smaller CMEA states in connection with their faith in the Soviet Union as an integration partner.

The first area in which the Soviet Union has let its own economic interests take precedence over solidarity toward its integration partners pertains to price formation in the CMEA. The prices agreed upon bilaterally for the goods to be exchanged between the respective trading partners, which were set for five-year periods betwen 1958 and 1975, have been set annually since 1975, using the preceding five years as a basis.[14] The result of this procedural change, which the Soviet Union wished to institute, has been an improvement of terms of trade favoring the Soviet Union in intra-CMEA trade. The reason is that by this means—although the time lag involved does have a mitigating effect, and sometimes concrete price concessions are negotiated—the dramatic price rises on the world market for oil and natural gas (as a result of the oil crises of 1972 and 1979) now affect intra-CMEA trade much more quickly. The Soviet Union has clearly been the benefactor of these new rules, for to a very large extent it supplies all the CMEA states except Romania with such energy sources.[15] Regardless of whether it would be economically rational to make these energy sources more expensive (for in the Soviet Union also, such resources are not inexhaustible, the costs of exploitation and transport are rising due to the less favorable locations of the new deposits that must now be tapped, and the market opportunities for such products on the world market represent a highly attractive alternative), this development has dramatically communicated to the smaller CMEA states that the CMEA by no means constitutes a protective alliance of countries acting in solidarity to counteract the negative influences of the "capitalist world market." The unavoidable results of this development have been far-reaching structural changes and the decline in economic growth in all the CMEA countries that were referred to earlier.

Second, it was not only the issue of price formation that shook the confidence of the smaller CMEA states in the dependability of the Soviet Union as a supplier of raw materials over the past few years. Starting in 1981, the Soviet Union reduced by 10–15 percent the oil deliveries agreed upon by contract—cutbacks that applied to the entire 1981–1985 planning period and will also apply to future planning periods. In this case, too, there may be good reasons for adopting a measure of this nature, but the smaller CMEA states are still faced with the problem that their domestic planning is based on the volume of oil originally agreed upon. It may be possible to save on oil consumption to some extent (such consumption is still relatively extensive); otherwise, the only alternative would be to obtain supplies on the world market in exchange for convertible currencies.

Third, the shift in the terms of trade referred to above has resulted in a negative balance of payments for most CMEA countries vis-à-vis the Soviet Union over the past few years. Whether the countries concerned regard this as an intensification of their economic dependence on the Soviet Union is for them to decide. In any case, our cautious assessment of the situation leads us to assume that their autonomous room for maneuver in economic and political affairs has not increased as a result.

Quite recently (i.e., since 1983), the Soviet Union has apparently been putting more pressure on the smaller Eastern European countries to improve their balance of trade with their Soviet neighbor, or to achieve a surplus in their balance of trade, by increasing their exports[16] (or at least keeping their imports at the same level) so that the Eastern European countries can reduce their indebtedness to the Soviet Union (or at least not increase it).[17] Judging by recent publications on this subject, these efforts were less successful in 1984 than during the preceding year.[18]

3. Since 1980, however, cooperation among the CMEA states has also suffered due to the events in Poland—that is, not only as a result of the need to make foreign investments or because of the uncertainties that can be observed with regard to procurement of raw materials from the Soviet Union. It is true that (at least in the short and medium terms) it has been possible to prevent almost completely the political movement in Poland from spreading to the other CMEA countries. Nevertheless, the consequences of the extremely grave economic crisis in Poland were quite noticeable with regard to their effect on cooperation within the CMEA. Bilateral trade agreements had provided for deliveries by Polish suppliers that were taken into account in the national plans of the other CMEA states. The sharp drop in Polish production between August 1980 and 1982 resulted in partial—or even cancelled—deliveries, thus leading to corresponding gaps in the domestic supplies of the other CMEA countries. The fact that Polish coal deliveries were cancelled for longer periods at the same time that Soviet oil deliveries were being reduced was extremely problematic; in addition, the other CMEA states were expected to make contributions toward stabilizing the Polish economy, in the form of either additional goods for Poland or hard-currency credits.

The consequences of the Polish crisis for CMEA cooperation are not limited to the cancellation of deliveries from Poland and the assistance the other CMEA countries had to provide. The psychological effect of this crisis appears to have been even more important. We now see that, when faced with a difficult situation, the CMEA after more than thirty years of existence was not able to realize the objective already postulated in its 1949 Founding Communiqué—namely, to provide "mutual assistance in the exchange of raw materials, foodstuffs, machinery and equipment."[19] At the same time, however, doubt has been cast upon many aspects of the possible economic benefits of international cooperation in this region: What use are trade agreements, coordination of planning, specialization, and other forms of cooperation among socialist countries if it becomes clear that there is no guarantee such agreements will be kept? During the past few years a considerable loss of trust has occurred within the CMEA, and willingness to integrate has decreased.

Future Prospects for Foreign Trade Relations in Eastern Europe

The problems that have developed in the economic relations between the Soviet Union and the Eastern European countries during the past few years leave little room for optimism with regard to future prospects. The economic deficiencies in these relations have been compounded by political problems among the respective countries. Regardless of their common ideological basis, the party and government heads of the smaller CMEA countries are concerned with achieving the greatest possible amount of national sovereignty and autonomy of action in relation to the political and economic hegemony exercised by the Soviet Union. The political conflicts that have occurred in various CMEA countries in the past—in 1953 in the GDR, in 1956 in Hungary and Poland, in 1968 in Czechoslovakia, and in 1970, 1976, and since 1980 in Poland—indicate that, despite the Soviet Union's overwhelmingly powerful position, the stability of the smaller CMEA countries in the Eastern bloc alliance is limited. On the other hand, the Soviet position vis-à-vis the Eastern European states has been strengthened due to the fact that relations among the smaller countries of Eastern Europe are frequently troubled by animosities, such that common action by all six countries appears to be practically impossible.

The consequences of this scenario in the area of economic relations have already been indicated: Under such circumstances, the states of Eastern Europe cannot be convinced to relinquish national authority (for example, to transfer authority for planning and for issuing directives to supranational organs); the individual East European states are simply not willing to reduce national room for maneuver with respect to economic policy. Distrust of the Soviet Union as an enormously powerful partner is particularly intense in this connection, and yet the smaller CMEA states need the economic power of the Soviet Union in the present situation. In the past few years, the Soviet Union has been either willing or compelled to provide a considerable amount of economic assistance to maintain internal political stability in the Eastern European states; but this could not have been an easy task in view of the obvious slowdown in economic growth that the Soviet Union itself is experiencing.

The Soviet Union has had only very limited success in employing the Council for Mutual Economic Assistance to organize economic relations in this region more efficiently: Either many of the measures provided for in its Comprehensive Program of 1971 have not yet been carried out or their implementation has been quite incomplete. In particular, we should note here that all economic transactions in the CMEA are *bilateral*; only with regard to transactions in convertible currencies is a trend toward multilateral clearing beginning to emerge among the CMEA states (although this trend is, in reality, totally alien to the prevailing economic system).

The materials from the CMEA summit referred to above provide very few concrete indications of future development trends: It was apparently not possible to reach agreement about controversial issues in this connection. However, the Soviet Union does seem to have a strong desire to reduce its economic subsidies to the smaller CMEA states,[20] although one must still question whether it will be able to fulfill this wish in the foreseeable future without incurring detrimental effects on the internal stability of the Eastern European countries and thereby on its entire system of alliances.

East-West Economic Relations Versus Intra-CMEA Economic Relations: Complementary or Competitive?

Special Characteristics of East-West Economic Relations

East-West economic relations differ from international economic relations in that they are established between countries with divergent social and economic systems; these differences are associated with political animosity, especially between the Soviet Union and the United States as superpowers. Because of this antagonism between the systems, both sides are rather apprehensive about developing such relations, and repeated attempts have been made to employ them as instruments to influence the other side in both a negative and a positive manner (an example of the "carrot and stick" approach). In the case of East-West trade, the political component is undoubtedly very significant.

Another important characteristic of such relations is that, on the whole, the West is the more affluent and economically developed area whereas the East is poorer and less developed. The implication of this, and of the different economic mechanisms concerned, is that the Western market is usually well supplied with goods of every quality and that supply outstrips demand; in the communist countries, on the other hand, there are shortages of many goods, especially high-quality technical products, so that demand for goods cannot be met by available supplies.

The Significance and Structural Aspects of East-West Trade

The political fears and hopes associated with East-West economic relations on both sides might well lead a less informed observer to believe that these relations must be of enormous significance for the national economies concerned. However, from a purely quantitative point of view, this is not the case. In the case of the OECD countries (excluding intra-German trade), only 3.1 percent of their total exports and 3.2 percent of their total imports were accounted for by the CMEA states in 1983, and in the same year the exports of the Western countries to the CMEA nations represented an average share of 0.44 percent of gross domestic product (GDP) in those countries. In the case of the United States, the 1983 share of GDP was 0.09 percent, for Japan it was 0.31 percent, for France 0.65 percent, for Italy 0.77 percent, for the Federal Republic of Germany (excluding intra-German trade) 1.17 percent, and for Austria 2.77 percent. The exception was Finland, where such trade was equal to 7.29 percent of its GDP.[21] Such trade volumes indicate that trade with the East is only of marginal significance for the OECD nations, and that it could be of greater significance only for capacity utilization in individual branches of the economy or in specific firms. In the CMEA countries, where integration into world trade is much more limited, the share of trade with the West as a percentage of total foreign trade is considerably higher; imports from the West constitute between 14 percent and 34 percent of total imports, whereas exports to the West amount to between 10 percent and 33 percent of total exports.[22]

An assessment of the political implications of the East-West economic relations outlined above is decisively dependent on the relative significance attributed to these quantitative indicators. To begin with, it is clear that the East is more dependent on trade with the West than the other way around. Inasmuch as I have discussed the problem of mutual dependence on many previous occasions,[23] my remarks here can be brief. To simplify matters, I will not discuss the dependence of Western economies on exports to the East (in Europe, where fluctuations occur over the course of time, the iron, steel, and machine-building industries are affected, whereas in the United States grain is most important) or any possible dependence on energy imports from the Soviet Union. From a macro-economic point of view, the share of foreign trade or of the national product in question is too small, and under these circumstances there can be political effects on East-West relations only in specific cases—particularly those in which the Western exporters concerned wield strong political influence in their respective countries.

Of greater political consequence for both sides is the question of how economically significant imports from the West are for the CMEA states.

A definitive answer to this question would probably be impossible to provide—and not only because the observations being made here are of a general nature. On the whole it can be stated that imports from the West continue to be the only real goal of trade relations with the West for all the CMEA countries, whereas in view of domestic shortages, exports to hard-currency countries are still regarded as an unavoidable burden for the respective national economies. In general, however, these countries have come to understand that export production, which is competitive on the world market, and a more flexible foreign trade system could significantly increase the advantages of the international division of labor for the CMEA countries. On the whole, dissatisfaction with the commodity structure of exports to the West is very intense, and the problem for the Soviet Union in particular is the fact that one product—energy—almost totally dominates exports to the West while finished industrial goods constitute only an extremely small part of such exports. On the one hand, this export structure is an unflattering indication of the weaknesses in Soviet industry; on the other hand (and this is of greater political significance for foreign trade), it means that the Soviet Union is dependent on developments in a very small segment of the world market.

It also seems possible to make the general observation that trade with the West is more important for the economies of the smaller CMEA states than it is for the Soviet Union. This situation is politically unfavorable for the development of East-West economic relations, especially since the same applies to the West, where the United States has only a relatively limited interest in trade with the East compared to the industrial countries of Western Europe. Thus the two superpowers, which confront each other as real rivals in the conflict of political systems, have only a relatively limited interest in East-West trade, whereas the smaller allies on both sides have a much stronger economic interest in maintaining or expanding East-West trade. Because of these differing interests, the use of East-West trade for political purposes over the last few years has been a subject of dispute between the United States and its Western European allies. It can be assumed that the smaller CMEA countries are also trying—with different methods, of course—to influence the Soviet Union to maintain East-West economic relations or to secure for themselves the greatest possible amount of leeway for political maneuvering in this area.

Ultimately this all adds up to one question: How important are the imports from the OECD area to the economy of the Soviet Union and the smaller CMEA states? The rapid expansion in the quantity of these imports during the first half of the 1970s suggests that the imports were most welcome. However, we still do not know whether this import activity resulted only from a general shortage of goods in the CMEA area, or whether it was the outcome of a rational economic policy strategy. What we *do* know is that Poland was at least pursuing as an objective the concept of import-induced economic growth on the basis of Western credits. Its use of imports of Western technology—primarily in the form of machinery and production facilities ("embodied technology")—as a basis placed Polish industry in a position where it could produce modern products that would be competitive on the world market, and Poland planned to repay the Western credits by exporting the new products. For a number of reasons—among others, Western technology was adopted too slowly, the long-term burdens resulting from the imports had been underestimated, and the willingness of Western markets to admit new products during a period of weak economic activity had been overestimated—this concept could not be realized, and a grave economic crisis resulted.[24]

An open question is whether a more or less consistent concept existed concerning the development of imports from the West during the 1970s; but in any case, it was never formulated as an objective anywhere else, as had been done in Poland. Moreover, there is substantial support for the assumption that an urgent need existed for the goods imported from the West, which were intended to fill the production gaps that constituted an important cause of the general slowdown of economic growth in Eastern Europe.

This impression tends to be confirmed if we look at the commodity structure of CMEA imports from the West during the past ten to fifteen years: Between 1970 and 1982 the share of agricultural products in imports from the West increased from 8 percent to 19 percent, and in 1982 semifinished industrial goods accounted for almost 45 percent of imports from the West whereas the share of capital goods declined from 38 percent to 30 percent.[25] As one observer has noted, "Imports from the West were more important for providing the economy with its day-to-day requirements of raw materials and semifinished goods than as a source of technology."[26]

This import structure seems to indicate that technology transfer—which in Western discussions is always viewed as the most dangerous contribution of trade with the East in terms of strengthening Soviet economic potential—did play a role during the rapid expansion of East-West economic relations during the 1970s, but it was *much smaller* than that played by other types of commodities. Of course, this is not to say that these other goods (for example, the grain imported by the Soviet Union) could not be highly significant for the economies of these countries; but there is a fundamental difference in such imports: Foodstuffs and semifinished industrial goods can mitigate current shortages, but they have little effect on future growth.

Thus the rapid expansion of imports from the West during the 1970s resulted in a noticeable and very welcome easing of shortages of important goods in all the CMEA countries concerned, but it made only a relatively small contribution to the necessary restructuring of the national economies involved. On the contrary, it is possible that these imports made structural change appear less urgent and therefore led to postponement of necessary measures. The stagnation of imports from the West since 1976 and their actual decline beginning in 1979 (see Table 7.2) indicate that it has been possible to do without imports from the West to some extent. But a closer examination would be necessary to determine if this reduction has significantly contributed to the general slowdown in economic growth that has occurred in all the CMEA states. In view of all the other possible influences, this apparently obvious connection should not be made heedlessly.

At the same time that imports from the West were stagnating or declining (after 1979), very intense efforts were being made by most of the CMEA countries to increase their exports to the West. Due to the widespread recession in the Western industrial nations, these efforts were not easy at first, but they have been rather successful (see Table 7.3). Since about 1983 the strained situation in East-West trade has eased considerably. On the one hand, the economic upswing in the world economy has made it easier for the Eastern European countries to export; on the other hand, the indebtedness of the Eastern European countries to the West was no longer regarded as critical in view of the extremely high indebtedness in other parts of the world—Latin America, in particular. Thus, in addition to current debt conversion actions, especially for Poland, and along with trade credits, which have never been interrupted, some (admittedly fairly modest) credits are now being granted to certain Eastern bloc countries. Indeed, East-West trade, including Western exports to Eastern Europe, seems to be recovering gradually.[27]

East-West Economic Relations Versus Intra-CMEA Trade

Following the Soviet invasion of Afghanistan in 1979 and the internal political crisis in Poland, political relations between East and West worsened considerably; in the area of foreign trade, moreover, East-West economic relations were hindered to some extent by Western embargo measures. The concern was often voiced, not only in the West but also in the smaller Eastern European countries, that the smaller CMEA states could be forced into still greater economic and political dependence on

TABLE 7.2
Eastern Europe and USSR: Import Value by Main Origins (billions of US dollars)

Imports to/from:	1970	1971	1972	1973	1974	1975
Bulgaria						
World	1.83	2.12	2.57	3.21	4.33	5.40
ECE-East	1.33	1.57	1.97	2.40	2.83	3.71
ECE-West	0.38	0.39	0.43	0.56	1.07	1.35
Other	0.13	0.16	0.17	0.24	0.43	0.34
Czechoslovakia						
World	3.70	4.01	4.67	6.07	7.51	9.09
ECE-East	2.33	2.54	3.04	3.81	4.41	5.85
ECE-West	1.01	1.12	1.22	1.69	2.34	2.52
Other	0.35	0.34	0.41	0.57	0.76	0.71
German Democratic Republic						
World	4.85	4.96	5.90	7.85	9.65	11.29
ECE-East	3.19	3.23	3.71	4.81	5.40	7.09
ECE-West	1.35	1.44	1.93	2.67	3.45	3.50
Other	0.30	0.29	0.27	0.38	0.79	0.69
Hungary						
World	2.51	2.99	3.15	3.88	5.58	7.15
ECE-East	1.56	1.88	1.98	2.33	3.00	4.48
ECE-West	0.72	0.89	0.93	1.21	2.05	2.03
Other	0.22	0.22	0.25	0.34	0.53	0.64
Poland						
World	3.61	4.04	5.33	7.76	10.49	12.55
ECE-East	2.36	2.58	3.08	3.81	4.40	5.45
ECE-West	0.98	1.18	1.89	3.49	5.41	6.31
Other	0.27	0.28	0.35	0.46	0.68	0.78
Romania						
World	1.96	2.10	2.62	3.44	5.14	5.34
ECE-East	0.94	0.97	1.17	1.37	1.64	1.97
ECE-West	0.81	0.89	1.14	1.58	2.64	2.39
Other	0.21	0.25	0.31	0.49	0.86	0.99
Eastern Europe						
World	18.45	20.22	24.25	32.21	42.69	50.82
ECE-East	11.71	12.77	14.95	18.53	21.67	28.56
ECE-West	5.25	5.91	7.53	11.20	16.97	18.10
Other	1.48	1.54	1.76	2.49	4.05	4.16
USSR						
World	11.73	12.48	16.16	20.91	24.85	36.94
ECE-East	6.63	7.26	9.34	10.89	11.35	15.67
ECE-West	3.02	3.11	4.46	6.37	8.61	14.10
Other	2.08	2.12	2.36	3.66	4.89	7.17
Eastern Europe and USSR						
World	30.18	32.70	40.40	53.13	67.53	87.76
ECE-East	18.35	20.03	24.29	29.42	33.02	44.23
ECE-West	8.27	9.02	11.99	17.56	25.58	32.20
Other	3.56	3.65	4.13	6.15	8.94	11.33

TABLE 7.2, cont.

1976	1977	1978	1979	1980	1981	1982	1983	1984[a]
5.63	6.39	7.62	8.51	9.67	10.80	11.54	12.29	12.80
4.13	4.91	5.96	6.59	7.29	7.76	8.56	9.41	9.70
1.12	1.08	1.20	1.42	1.79	2.29	2.04	1.86	1.90
0.37	0.41	0.47	0.50	0.59	0.75	0.95	1.02	1.20
9.70	11.15	12.57	14.25	15.18	14.67	15.45	16.37	17.10
6.30	7.31	8.43	9.39	9.83	9.79	10.82	11.92	12.90
2.68	2.87	3.23	3.84	4.21	3.80	3.59	3.39	3.10
0.72	0.97	0.91	1.02	1.14	1.08	1.04	1.06	1.10
13.20	14.33	14.57	16.21	19.08	20.18	20.20	21.52	22.20
9.97	9.28	9.52	9.82	11.27	12.60	12.97	13.38	13.90
4.44	4.07	4.02	5.35	6.30	6.41	5.99	6.70	6.90
0.78	0.99	1.03	1.04	1.52	1.17	1.24	1.45	1.40
5.53	6.52	7.94	8.68	9.19	9.16	8.87	8.55	8.10
2.81	3.23	3.86	4.33	4.31	4.30	4.33	4.12	3.90
2.09	2.52	3.20	3.46	3.88	3.93	3.48	3.23	3.10
0.64	0.77	0.88	0.89	1.01	0.93	1.06	1.21	1.10
13.88	14.63	15.70	17.55	19.12	15.53	10.25	10.60	10.60
6.20	7.25	8.06	8.99	10.09	9.59	5.98	6.25	6.10
6.92	6.44	6.52	6.87	6.92	4.72	3.35	3.29	3.50
0.75	0.94	1.12	1.68	2.11	1.22	0.92	1.06	1.00
6.10	7.02	8.88	10.92	13.20	10.98	8.32	7.64	7.40
2.42	2.92	3.27	3.69	4.05	3.44	3.08	3.28	2.80
2.32	2.65	3.56	4.07	4.35	3.63	2.05	1.48	1.50
1.36	1.45	2.06	3.15	4.79	3.91	3.20	2.88	3.10
54.03	60.04	67.29	76.12	85.44	81.32	74.63	76.98	78.40
29.83	34.88	39.10	42.82	46.83	47.48	45.73	48.35	49.30
19.58	19.63	21.73	25.01	27.45	24.78	20.49	19.95	20.30
4.62	5.52	6.46	8.29	11.16	9.06	8.40	8.67	8.80
38.11	40.89	50.74	57.78	68.53	73.16	77.67	80.20	78.90
16.22	18.82	24.63	26.68	29.43	29.40	33.49	37.05	37.90
14.98	14.26	17.33	21.21	25.70	28.24	28.98	27.65	25.70
6.91	7.80	8.78	9.89	13.40	15.52	15.21	15.50	15.30
92.13	100.92	118.03	133.90	153.97	154.48	152.30	157.18	157.30
46.04	53.70	63.74	69.50	76.26	76.88	79.22	85.40	87.20
34.57	33.90	39.06	46.23	53.15	53.02	49.47	47.60	46.00
11.53	13.33	15.24	18.17	24.56	24.59	23.61	24.17	24.10

Source: Secretariat of the United Nations Economic Commission for Europe, based on national foreign trade statistics. Partner country grouping: ECE-East--east European member countries of CMEA and the Soviet Union; ECE-West--ECE market economies and Japan; Other--all remaining countries.

[a]Preliminary data or secretariat estimates.

From: Economic Survey of Europe in 1984-1985, Appendix, Table C5.

TABLE 7.3
Eastern Europe and USSR: Export Value by Main Destinations (billions of US dollars)

Exports to/from:	1970	1971	1972	1973	1974	1975
Bulgaria						
World	2.00	2.18	2.63	3.24	3.84	4.69
ECE-East	1.51	1.64	2.01	2.46	2.73	3.50
ECE-West	0.32	0.34	0.39	0.48	0.55	0.55
Other	0.17	0.20	0.22	0.30	0.55	0.64
Czechoslovakia						
World	3.79	4.18	4.92	5.99	7.03	8.36
ECE-East	2.43	2.66	3.26	3.89	4.27	5.47
ECE-West	0.92	1.00	1.12	1.51	1.98	1.97
Other	0.43	0.52	0.54	0.60	0.78	0.92
German Democratic Republic						
World	4.58	5.08	6.18	7.52	8.75	10.09
ECE-East	3.13	3.50	4.39	5.20	5.60	6.84
ECE-West	1.10	1.20	1.43	1.87	2.60	2.51
Other	0.36	0.37	0.37	0.45	0.56	0.73
Hungary						
World	2.32	2.50	3.29	4.37	5.13	6.06
ECE-East	1.44	1.62	2.15	2.80	3.22	4.10
ECE-West	0.69	0.68	0.89	1.26	1.49	1.45
Other	0.33	0.34	0.35	0.40	0.77	0.98
Poland						
World	3.55	3.87	4.93	6.35	8.32	10.29
ECE-East	2.13	2.29	2.97	3.67	4.38	5.82
ECE-West	1.09	1.24	1.60	2.28	3.17	3.49
Other	0.33	0.34	0.35	0.40	0.77	0.98
Romania						
World	1.85	2.10	2.60	3.67	4.87	5.34
ECE-East	0.92	1.00	1.23	1.65	1.75	2.04
ECE-West	0.66	0.80	0.97	1.42	2.22	2.03
Other	0.27	0.30	0.40	0.60	0.90	1.27
Eastern Europe						
World	18.09	19.91	24.56	31.14	37.94	44.83
ECE-East	11.56	12.71	16.02	19.66	21.96	27.77
ECE-West	4.78	5.25	6.41	8.83	12.01	12.00
Other	1.75	1.95	2.13	2.64	3.98	5.06
USSR						
World	12.80	13.81	15.47	21.26	27.36	33.29
ECE-East	6.76	7.24	8.17	9.93	11.48	16.44
ECE-West	2.78	3.16	3.44	5.62	9.24	9.63
Other	3.26	3.41	3.86	5.71	6.64	7.22
Eastern Europe and USSR						
World	30.89	33.72	40.02	52.40	65.30	78.12
ECE-East	18.32	19.95	24.19	29.59	33.44	44.21
ECE-West	7.56	8.41	9.85	14.45	21.25	21.63
Other	5.01	5.35	5.99	8.36	10.62	12.27

TABLE 7.3, cont.

1976	1977	1978	1979	1980	1981	1982	1983	1984[a]
5.38	6.35	7.45	8.86	10.39	10.70	11.44	12.14	12.70
4.10	4.81	5.51	6.18	6.90	6.95	7.75	8.87	9.20
0.69	0.75	0.87	1.54	1.92	1.70	1.53	1.48	1.30
0.59	0.79	1.07	1.14	1.57	2.05	2.16	1.78	2.20
9.03	10.27	11.75	13.19	14.93	14.91	15.64	16.50	17.20
6.18	6.95	7.95	8.69	9.46	9.60	10.42	11.19	11.90
1.98	2.30	2.57	3.15	3.82	3.53	3.51	3.53	3.50
0.87	1.02	1.23	1.35	1.64	1.77	1.70	1.78	1.80
11.36	12.02	13.27	15.06	17.31	19.86	21.74	23.79	23.90
7.46	8.29	9.21	10.30	11.05	12.20	12.90	14.27	14.50
3.04	2.81	2.96	3.48	4.60	5.89	6.72	7.54	7.30
0.87	0.92	1.10	1.28	1.67	1.77	2.13	1.98	2.10
4.93	5.82	6.35	7.93	8.61	8.73	8.86	8.77	8.60
2.73	3.25	3.45	4.14	4.33	4.65	4.62	4.32	4.20
1.68	1.97	2.22	2.91	3.27	2.90	2.93	3.19	3.30
1.01	1.15	0.68	0.88	1.01	1.18	1.31	1.25	1.20
11.02	12.27	13.77	16.22	17.02	13.29	11.22	11.58	11.80
6.25	6.99	7.90	9.25	8.90	7.41	5.51	5.84	5.70
3.76	4.13	4.66	5.42	6.21	4.22	3.99	4.17	4.40
1.01	1.15	1.21	1.54	1.91	1.66	1.71	1.57	1.70
6.14	7.02	8.05	9.72	11.40	11.18	10.12	10.16	10.50
2.33	2.92	3.29	3.48	4.24	3.35	3.24	3.42	2.70
2.40	2.37	2.95	3.93	4.39	4.16	3.48	3.77	4.80
1.40	1.73	1.81	2.31	2.77	3.67	3.40	2.98	3.00
47.86	53.76	60.64	70.99	79.66	78.66	79.02	82.94	84.70
29.00	33.21	37.31	42.05	44.89	44.16	44.43	47.92	48.10
13.55	14.34	16.22	20.44	24.21	22.40	22.16	23.67	24.60
5.26	6.21	7.11	8.50	10.56	12.10	12.43	11.35	12.00
37.16	45.18	52.38	64.71	76.50	79.39	86.97	91.38	91.60
17.38	20.74	24.88	28.29	32.24	33.78	36.21	39.24	40.30
11.68	13.55	14.52	21.78	28.13	27.49	29.55	30.20	30.80
8.11	10.89	12.97	14.64	16.13	18.12	21.21	21.94	20.50
85.03	98.94	113.02	135.71	156.16	158.05	165.99	174.32	176.30
46.43	53.96	62.19	70.34	77.13	77.94	80.64	87.16	88.40
25.21	27.89	30.75	42.22	52.34	49.89	51.71	53.87	55.40
13.36	17.10	20.08	23.15	26.69	30.22	33.64	33.29	32.50

<u>Source:</u> Secretariat of the United Nations Economic Commission for Europe, based on national foreign trade statistics. Partner country grouping: ECE-East--east European member countries of CMEA and the Soviet Union; ECE-West--ECE market economies and Japan; Other--all remaining countries.

[a]Preliminary data or secretariat estimates.

From: <u>Economic Survey of Europe in 1984-1985</u>, Appendix, Table C4.

the Soviet Union as a result of these events and that, ultimately, the CMEA states could be cut off from the world market.

This has not yet happened, of course. As I tried to explain earlier (though my comments were admittedly quite brief), the stagnation that occurred in East-West economic relations developed more for economic than for political reasons; at any rate, Eastern indebtedness and the economic situation in the West are sufficient in and of themselves to explain such stagnation. At the same time, no spontaneous growth has occurred in intra-CMEA trade; the larger shares it now represents are largely the result of stagnating trade with the West and of price increases. The experience of the past years seems to indicate that, at present and in the foreseeable future, intra-CMEA economic relations are not and will not be in a position to replace East-West trade. The CMEA states are dependent to a fairly large extent on specific products from the West, and this includes not only technology-intensive products but various raw materials and semifinished goods as well. Regarding many areas of Eastern European economies, the sometimes much higher quality of Western goods and their short-term availability make them a significant complement to domestic production and procurement possibilities, and it is precisely in such cases that intra-CMEA trade can provide no adequate substitutes. In this connection, the economic significance of the goods imported from the West is probably greater than is indicated by their quantitative share, for supplementary deliveries from the West often consist of only a few individual components for equipment that has otherwise been manufactured domestically or in the CMEA area—but without the import of these Western components or follow-up deliveries, the entire plant cannot be built or maintained in working order.

It thus seems justifiable to regard East-West economic relations as complementing intra-CMEA relations in a significant way. East-West economic relations will probably retain their significance in the foreseeable future precisely because of the difficulties being encountered in connection with efforts to improve cooperation among the CMEA nations. The interest of the smaller CMEA countries in maintaining East-West economic relations may be influenced by the consideration that such trade with the West somewhat reduces their dependence on the Soviet Union. The Soviet Union will have to accept this fact, since it can by no means offer substitutes for Western goods and, in fact, even participates more intensively in East-West trade than do the other CMEA states.

To this extent it is possible to take seriously the (not overly profound) declaration of inention made at the 1984 CMEA summit conference, where it is stated: "In the future the CMEA member countries will also be willing to develop mutually advantageous economic and trade as well as scientific-technical relations with the developed capitalist countries, with all the nations of the world."[28]

Acknowledgments

This chapter has been translated by Mary Hess, Berlin.

Notes

1. Of the ten countries that were members of the CMEA as of 1985, only the European members—the Soviet Union, Poland, the German Democratic Republic, Czechoslovakia, Hungary, Romania, and Bulgaria—will be considered here, in keeping with the subject of this chapter. The six smaller nations just mentioned will usually be treated as a group and referred to as the "CMEA countries" or the "smaller European CMEA states." At times I will also refer to the seven European CMEA countries as the "East." The non-European CMEA members—Mongolia, Cuba, and Vietnam—will not be considered in this study. Under economic relations we will basically consider only foreign trade relations. It will not be possible for me to deal with international financial relations or special forms of economic cooperation.

2. These figures were taken from Sovet Ekonomičeskoj Vzaimopomošci, [hereafter referred to as SEV], Secretariat, ed., *Statističeskij ežegodnik stran-členov SEV 1984* (Moscow, 1984), p. 7.

3. Thus, to name only a few important resources, Poland has deposits of hard coal and copper, the GDR has brown coal and potash, Hungary has bauxite, and Romania has some oil.

4. I have discussed these questions in greater detail in my article. See Peter Knirsch, "Ost-West-Wirtschaftsbeziehungen zwischen Kooperation und Konfrontation" [East-West Economic Relations Between Cooperation and Confrontation], *Europäische Rundschau*, No. 4 (Vienna, 1984), pp. 84–87.

5. SEV, *Stat. ežegodnik 1984*, pp. 39, 363–366. These tables are inconsistent in many respects; statistical criteria in the various CMEA countries are obviously not uniform for this type of data.

6. In the present discussion we consider the "West" to be the Western industrial nations that work together in the OECD; for the most part these are the Western European members of the European Community as well as the United States, Canada, and Japan.

7. At the time this chapter was written, basically only the foreign trade figures for 1983 were available along with some preliminary and incomplete figures for 1984.

8. SEV, *Stat. ežegodnik 1984*, p. 298.

9. For example, the Federal Republic of Germany, as the most important Western trading partner, accounted for 5.5 percent of Soviet foreign trade, Finland for 4.1 percent, Italy for 3.5 percent, France for 3.2 percent, and Japan for 2.3 percent. The figure reported for Yugoslavia is 3.9 percent. All these statistics are based on *Narodnoe chozjajstvo SSSR v 1983 g.* (Moscow, 1984), p. 592.

10. There are no dependable calculations of foreign trade intensity for the CMEA states because it is not possible to convert foreign currency values into domestic prices.

11. These figures were supplied by the following publications: Bulgaria: *Statističeski godišnik na Narodne Republika Bulgarija* (Sofia, 1983), pp. 367ff.; GDR: *Vnešnjaja torgovlja SSSR v 1983 g.* (Moscow, 1984), pp. 9–10, and SEV, *Statističeskij ežegodnik 1984*, p. 296; Czechoslovakia: *Statistická vočenka ČSSR* (Prague, 1984), pp. 462ff.; Poland: *Vnašnjaja borgovlja SSSR v 1983 g.*, p. 10, *Narodnoe chozjajstvo socialističeskich stran v 1983* (Moscow, 1984), p. 193ff., and *Tribuna Ludu* (Warsaw, March 2, 1984); Romania: *Anuarul Statistiz al Republicii Socialiste Romania 1984* (Bucharest, 1984), pp. 254, 256; and Hungary: *Statistisches Taschenbuch Ungarns 1983* (Budapest, 1984), p. 188.

12. This structure becomes particularly clear in the case of such CMEA countries as the GDR, or Czechoslovakia, where industrial development is more advanced. Thus, in 1981 the basic materials and production goods industries accounted for 66.6 percent of the GDR's imports from the Soviet Union, while capital goods accounted for only 13.8 percent and consumer goods for 1.8 percent. On the other hand, 57.1 percent of the GDR's exports to the Soviet Union consisted of capital goods, and 9.8 percent were consumer goods. See Deutsches Institut für Wirtschaftsforschung (DIW), publisher, *Handbuch DDR-Wirtschaft* [Handbook of the GDR Economy], 4th ed. (Reinbek bei Hamburg, 1984), p. 402.

13. This is also the case with Hungary's foreign trade with the Soviet Union. Despite all the changes in the planning system, the contracted deliveries of Hungarian enterprises to other CMEA countries continued to be under the system of detailed planning with mandatory compliance.

14. See the very clear description of this subject in *Lexikon RGW* [The CMEA Encyclopedia] (Leipzig, 1981), pp. 186–188.

15. Thus the GDR still meets about 85 percent of its import needs for oil through oil deliveries from the Soviet Union. See DIW, *Handbuch DDR-Wirtschaft*, p. 305.

16. The final document of the CMEA summit conference, entitled "Declaration of the Main Directions for the Further Development and Intensification of the Economic and Scientific-Technical Cooperation of the CMEA Member Countries," mentions that future Soviet deliveries of energy and raw materials will be dependent on expanding deliveries of "products needed by the Soviet Union." The German text can be found in *Wirtschaftsberatung des RGW auf höchster Ebene vom 12.-14. Juni 1984 in Moskau* [Economic Consultations of the CMEA at the Highest Level from 12–14 June 1984 in Moscow] (East Berlin, 1984), p. 23.

17. The exact amount of indebtedness to the Soviet Union incurred by the Eastern European countries, most of which arose after 1975 (due to the oil price rise together with the new price formula for intra-CMEA trade), is not known; nor are the credit terms known. Jan Vanous, in "Eastern European Economic Slowdown," *Problems of Communism*, No. 7/8 (Washington, D.C., 1982), p. 7, cites the seemingly fantastic figure of 100 billion U.S. dollars as the amount of Soviet assistance given to the Eastern European countries between 1972 and

1981 in the form of price concessions and credits. The DIW's *Handbuch DDR-Wirtschaft,* p. 307, refers to a cumulative GDR trade deficit vis-à-vis the Soviet Union amounting to 14.4 billion VM (valuta marks, 1 VM = 0.214 rbl) for the 1975–1982 period.

18. See the more detailed analysis in Economic Commission for Europe (publisher), *Economic Survey of Europe in 1984–1985,* pre-publication text (Geneva, 1985), pp. 5.45–5.64.

19. *Pravda* (January 25, 1949).

20. See the passage cited in Note 16.

21. The figures from OECD statistics are quoted according to Jan Stankovsky, "Ost-West Handel 1984/85: OECD Importe aus dem Osten belebt" [East-West Trade 1984/85: OECD Imports from the East Increased] (Vienna: 1985), pp. 39, 46. See also the Vienna Institute for Comparative Economic Studies, *Forschungsberichte,* No. 104.

22. SEV, *Stat. ežegodnik 1984,* p. 297; see also Table 7.1 of this volume.

23. See Peter Knirsch, "Interdependence in East-West Economic Relations," in *From Marshall Plan to Global Interdependence: New Challenges for the Industrialized Nations* (Paris: OECD, 1978), pp. 135–167; Peter Knirsch, "The Significance of Economic Interdependence Arising from East-West Relations," in *Partners in East-West Economic Relations: The Determinants of Choice,* edited by Zbigniew M. Fallenbuchl and Carl H. McMillan (New York, 1980), pp. 51–75; Peter Knirsch, "Economic and Political Interdependence Between East and West Reconsidered," *East-West Economic Interaction: Possibilities, Problems, Politics, and Prospects,* edited by Bo Huldt and Atis Lejins (Stockholm, 1981); The Swedish Institute of International Affairs, *Conference Papers 1,* 1981, pp. 55–78; Peter Knirsch, "Grenzen der Ost-West Interdependenzen: Politische Aspekte der Wirtschaftsbeziehungen" [Limits to East-West Interdependence: Political Aspects of Economic Relations], *Aujdsenwirtschaft. Schweizerische Zeitschrift für internationale Beziehungen,* No. 1, Vol. 37 (Diessenhofen, 1982), pp. 31–44.

24. See the detailed discussion in Zbigniew M. Fallenbuchl, *East-West Technology Transfer: Study of Poland 1971–1980* (Paris: OECD, 1983).

25. OECD statistics were cited according to Friedrich Levcik, "Die Wirtschaftsbeziehungen swischen Ost und West in den siebziger und achtziger Jahren" [The Economic Relations Between East and West in the 1970s and 1980s] (Vienna: 1983), pp. 11ff. See also the Vienna Institute for Comparative Economic Studies, *Forschungsberichte,* No. 92.

26. "Ost-West-Handel unter schwierigen Bedingungen" [East-West Trade Under Difficult Conditions], published by Deutsches Institut für Wirtschaftsforschung, *Wochenbericht,* No. 46 (West Berlin, 1982), p. 567.

27. A detailed discussion of the current situation is presented in Economic Commission for Europe, *Economic Survey of Europe in 1984–1985,* pp. 5.65–5.93.

28. *Wirtschaftsberatung des RGW,* p. 27.

8

Continuity in the Pattern of Russo-Soviet External Behavior

Kenichi Ito

In this chapter I have tried to deal with the Soviet Union's foreign policy in its broadest sense, from the longest possible historical perspective, and with the deepest possible insight into the root of the problem. In doing so, however, I might have overemphasized the aspect of continuity. But, in my view, it is this aspect that has been so much neglected in the past.

Let me clarify a few points regarding my standpoint. To start with, I have to reiterate one thing that is elementary but at the same time confusing to some people, who claim that it is meaningless to talk about the patterns of external behavior of any nation, because, in their view, what is regarded as characteristic of the external behavior of one nation is always found in that of another nation. It is true that any specific pattern of the external behavior of a nation should not be regarded as peculiar to that nation only and, accordingly, can be imitated by any other nation. Yet the pattern must be wrong if we conclude that we can therefore paint the external behavior of all nations in one color.

History tells us how differently the Greeks and Persians thought and behaved in the Persian War and how the Romans and Carthaginians differed in the Punic Wars. Let me quote what Harold Nicolson said in this regard:

> There are marked differences in the theory and practice of the several Great Powers. These differences are caused by variations in national character, traditions, and requirements. One can thus distinguish types, or species, of diplomacy and it is important that these distinctions should be recognized. All diplomatists (the professionals scarcely less than the amateurs) are inclined to assume that their own conception of the art of

negotiation is shared more or less by those foreigners with whom they are negotiating. This fallacy leads to misunderstanding.[1]

Second, some people, even after admitting the necessity of distinguishing different patterns or types of external behavior of a nation, remain skeptical over the availability of "scientific" methodology to "prove" that certain patterns or types are attributable to a certain nation. I intentionally put the words "scientific" and "prove" in quotation marks. As is well known, the Marxist-Leninist ideologists are fond of using the word "scientific" to describe their own dogmas as something legitimate while labeling all other incompatible propositions as "unscientific."

Though not in the Marxist-Leninist terminology, if the word is used in the same sense as that in the scientific study of natural phenomena, then I must say it is too naive to think the same "scientific" methodology possible for "proving" any proposition in the study of most social phenomena, particularly the political variety. Frankly speaking, we must admit that we cannot "prove" things in the study of social phenomena as we do in that of natural phenomena. As a matter of fact, we had better be humble enough to be aware that what we can achieve in the study of social phenomena, which are subject to far more complex factors than natural phenomena, is at best to convince the majority of other people of the validity of a proposition and never in any circumstances to prove it in a way that will forbid the counterargument of any person. It is in this context that we find the role of such quantitative information as statistical data helpful but only as auxiliary bases of judgment, whereas, on the other hand, we find crucially important the role of such qualitative information as the insight and knowledge of a person who personally experienced the phenomena in practice. In this presentation, my efforts will be concentrated more on generalization of conceptions than on analysis of the elements of a particular object. Such generalization will be intended to serve as the basis for an overall judgment we may need to make regarding the fundamental nature of the Soviets' external behavior.

In the process I would like to pay particular attention to the fact that we unwittingly tend to see the external behavior of the Soviet Union independent from, and even irrelevant to, that of Tsarist Russia. But to do so is to grossly neglect reality. Just as the external behavior of modern Japan is inseparable from that of old Japan before the Meiji Restoration of 1868, so is the external behavior of modern Russia, which is the Soviet Union, from that of old Russia (Tsarist Russia) before the Russian Revolution of 1917. Of course, factors of disruption were imposed by the force of the Restoration in the case of Japan and by that of the Revolution in the case of Russia. But, if so, it will be all the more important to distinguish between continuing and disrupting factors in the external behavior of either nation. Without such fundamental knowledge, our perspective of the future behavior of the country concerned would be basically circumscribed.

Before entering into the main topic of continuity in the pattern of Russo-Soviet external behavior, I must ascertain what should be identified as the pattern of Russo-Soviet external behavior. I admit that this is a huge question—a question that clearly cannot be satisfactorily answered in a mere twenty pages or so. So I must admit my own recklessness at the beginning.

Anyhow, I must start, and the first thing I have to do is define what external behavior means. Usually it means diplomatic negotiating tactics. We often ask whether a certain country is trustable or not. The answer could be an expression of the diplomatic tactics of the country in question. However, in the transition from peace to war, the characteristics of military strategy that the country might employ come to occupy a dominant position in the judgment of the country's external behavior. If we want a longer-term historical perspective of the country's external behavior, we need to know something more about the country, such as the fundamental traits inherent in its external behavior. Some people call it the grand strategy of the country. But a grand strategy in this case is not necessarily limited to being a product of conscious planning of the leadership of the country; rather, it can be extended to include a response of the country to the challenge of environments in the form of unconscious impulses and/or inertia.

At the Level of Grand Strategy

In 1939 Nicolson described the German type of external behavior as a "warrior" type and the British type as a "mercantile." According to him, both types have displayed remarkable continuity.[2] Regarding German external behavior, he wrote as follows:

> Underneath all the solid and magnificent virtues of the German race there lies a layer of nervous uncertainty. This uncertainty (which has been defined by Friedrich Sieburg as "spiritual homelessness") is due to a lack of any sharp geographical, racial or historical definition or outline. . . . "We are," writes Sieburg, "shifting sand, yet in every grain there inheres the longing to combine with the rest into solid, durable stone." It is this desire to find some real focus, some centre of gravity, which has impelled the Germans to regard the conception of "unity," as expressed by the State, as something mystical and almost religious. It has also led them to find in physical unity, and therefore in physical power, that sense of

> solidarity which they lack as individuals. The whole of modern German political theory from Fichte, via Hegel and Stewart Chamberlain, to Hitler is coloured by this emphasis upon some mystic union.[3]
>
> German policy has been deeply affected by this philosophy. It is inspired by the ideal that German Kultur is some virile but inspired force which in the interests of humanity should impose itself upon the world. This ideal is essentially mystic. "Germany," writes Sieburg, "is a destiny, not a way of life." To that destiny the German individual citizen is prepared to sacrifice his mind, his independence, if necessary his life. . . . In every German there is an element of suicidal mania.[4]
>
> The practical interpretation of this ideal assumes several forms. In so far as foreign policy and diplomacy are concerned it expresses itself in two ways. On the one hand there is the belief that force, or the threat of force, are the main instruments of negotiation. And on the other hand there is the theory that the "*raison d'état,*" or needs of the State, take precedence over all individual religions or philosophies. German policy, therefore, is essentially "*Machtpolitik*" or "Power policy." Her diplomacy, as I have indicated before, reflects this warrior or military conception. It seems to them more important to inspire fear than to beget confidence; and when, as invariably happens, the frightened nations combine to protect themselves, the Germans complain of "*Einkreisung*" or "encirclement," wholly ignoring the fact that it is their own methods and menaces which have produced this reaction.[5]

Of course, we must take into consideration the transformation the Germans have undergone since the above-quoted statement was made by Nicolson in 1939. If Nicolson had analyzed Japan's external behavior in 1939, he would have been surprised in 1985 to see the transformation the Japanese have achieved in about half a century. But still I wonder if Nicolson would be ready to admit that new Germany and new Japan were created in complete severance from their pasts, which were deeply rooted in immutable geopolitical and sociocultural conditions. Here again it becomes important to distinguish between the factors of continuity and those of disruption.

With regard to the "mercantile" conception of British external behavior, Nicolson said as follows:

> Essentially, British diplomacy is but the expression, in terms of international contacts, of those principles of policy which, owing to history, geographical position, imperial responsibilities, liberal institutions and national character, have, in the course of centuries, been found best suited to British requirements. What are those principles? . . . Sir Eyre Crowe took as his axiom the incontestable premise that British policy was determined by geography. On the one hand you had a small island situated on the exposed flank of Europe. On the other hand you had a vast Empire

> stretching across the world. The law of self-preservation necessitated the maintenance of the food-supplies of the island and the safety of its communications with its Empire overseas. This dual necessity implied preponderance of sea-power against any possible enemy. . . . It is the corollary of this proposition which applies to my present argument. Sir Eyre Crowe argued that this maritime supremacy would, if pressed, arouse feelings of resentment and jealousy throughout the world. It must therefore be exercised with the utmost benevolence and with the minimum of provocation. It must be "closely identified with the primary and vital interests of a majority of other nations." What were these primary interests? The first was independence; the second was trade. British policy must therefore maintain the open door and must at the same time display "a direct and positive interest in the independence of small nations." The doctrine of the "Balance of Power" thus assumed for Great Britain a peculiar form. It meant that she must be "opposed to the political dictatorship of the strongest single State or group of States at any given time." This opposition, Sir Eyre Crowe stated, was for Great Britain "a law of nature."[6]

Already in 1939 Nicolson was saying, "Such, for more than one hundred years, have been the directives of British foreign policy. It is possible, now that Great Britain may appear to have lost her invulnerability, that these principles may be modified. It is probable that the former policy of alternating isolation with intervention may have to be supplanted by some more planned system of collective security and that to this extent the old doctrine of the Balance of Power will be abandoned."[7] Thus, in the case of the British as well, we notice the necessity of making a distinction between what continues to be valid and what does not as given conditions change in historical perspective.

I will now turn my attention to the Russians and try to determine the characteristics of their external behavior at the level of grand strategy. At this level, I have to pay attention to the same geopolitical factor as that pointed out by Nicolson with regard to the Germans—namely, what he described as "a layer of nervous uncertainty or spiritual homelessness due to a lack of any sharp geographical, racial, or historical definition or outline." In the case of the Russians, the impact of geopolitical conditions has been even stronger. As George Vernadsky has noted,

> All civilizations are to some extent the product of geographical factors, but history provides no clearer example of the profound influence of geography upon a culture than in historical development of the Russian people. Russia is divided into two distinct zones—the forests in the north and the steppes spreading southward below them. . . . Today there is little to differentiate these bands, which through the centuries have been welded into a single broad agricultural area, but in ancient times the forests and the steppes were sharply divided.[8]

The importance of the roles of the forests and steppes in the formulation of the ways of thinking and living of the Russian people has long been pointed out by many scholars of Russian history. It is said that the Russians, when they were still a weaker and smaller nation, acquired a cautious and prudent trait in the forests, where they found shelter from invading nomads. When they came out of the forests into the steppes after finally overthrowing the rule of the Mongols in Russia in 1480, they quickly became obsessed with the idea of securing their safety by means of buffer zones around the sphere of life of the Russian people.

It is interesting to note that they often use the word "space" (*prostranstvo*) to mean "territory." For instance, the Russian word for "territorial sky" is "*vozdushnoe prostranstovo*" (air space). This comes from the way the Russians perceive "territory." Living in the steppes, which provided no such natural barriers on the frontier as the Alps, the Pyrenees, the English Channel, and the Rhine (which in turn had made the French feel secure in their own territory), the Russians could feel the presence of "space" but not that of "territory." In other words, for the Russians the border lines of their territory were no more than the lines describing their sphere of life, which was demarcated and protected by their military.

Thus, for the security of the Russian state under the rule of the grand duke of Moscovy, which occupied about 300,000 square kilometers (about the size of contemporary Poland), conquest and annexation of the land adjacent to its territory had to be undertaken. An uninterrupted pursuit of conquest and annexation over the next 500 years made the Russian people occupants of a territory covering 22,800,000 square kilometers, or one-sixth of the total land area on the earth. Some people might say that Russia was not alone in its expansionist tendencies—that Britain and France and other imperial powers were similar. I admit that this is true. But it would be a strange argument to claim that Russia was not expansionist because Britain was also expansionist. Moreover, Britain, France, and all other former imperial powers seem to have ceased to be expansionist at some point of historical development, but whether Russia also ceased remains an open question.

Russia's conquest and annexation were unique not only in terms of the consistency of its expansional efforts but also in terms of its selectiveness of the target for expansion. In pointing out those two characteristics at the same time, I position my approach in the middle of the two extreme approaches in the study of Russo-Soviet external behavior. If I had indicated the first alone and had failed to mention the second, my approach would have been similar to that of the "essentialists," who claim that the only guideline of Soviet foreign policy is its expansionism and that the Soviet Union is distinct in this regard from all other nations in the world. If I had done the opposite, my approach would have coincided with that of the "contextualists," who claim that there is nothing inherently distinct in Soviet foreign policy and that the Soviet Union behaves just like any Western nation. I think the true approach can be found between these two extremes. In this regard, Richard Pipes has observed that "history has taught Russian rulers to accommodate themselves to a superior power with cunning when they were weak and to act in an unmistakably imperial manner when they were strong."[9]

It must be said that these rulers were basically irrelevant to the "mercantile" conception of the British, who placed great importance on the exercise of power "with the utmost benevolence and with the minimum of provocation." They may be said, in a sense, to be closer to the "warrior" conception of German behavior, because they share with the Germans not only a "spiritual homelessness" but also a cultural and ideological messianism, a belief in "power policy," and even a sense of "encirclement."

However, in one sense, the Russians are fundamentally different from the Germans. The Russians have no "element of suicidal mania." They can change their attitude whenever they find their opponent stronger. They have made it a rule to respect their opponents' strength and have always been willing to find terms of coexistence with such superior powers. In other words, the Russians have always known how to wait until the wind changes.

Under the present nuclear circumstances, we must also note in this connection that the Soviet Union is a nation that will be more easily deterred if the West is strong enough. As was demonstrated by the Soviet invasion of Afghanistan, however, the Soviets are easily tempted, in the absence of deterrence, to resort to the use of force as a means of settling international disputes. As compared with the German "warrior" and the British "mercantile" conceptions of external behavior, the Russian external behavior is of the "hunter" type, given its basically prudent but essentially aggressive character.

At the Level of Military Strategy

Now that we have examined the pattern of Russian external behavior at the level of grand strategy, we can turn our attention to military strategy. It can safely be said that at this level the Russians have historically demonstrated two distinct characteristics: first, an unusually salient disparity between their defensive strength and their offensive fragility, and second, an inherent tendency to try to compensate their qualitative weakness by quantitative superiority. An excellent illumination of these characteristics of the Russo-Soviet military strategy is provided by Edward Luttwak. After citing the record of "the centuries of successful expansion" of the Russian empire at the expense of either small tribes and weak emirates or old Asiatic empires in decay, he concludes that "we thus find not one case of successful war deliberately launched against a first-class power."[10]

In my view, two factors may be cited to explain the Russians' strength in defeating invasion as demonstrated when they fought against the invading armies of Napoleon in 1812 and those of Hitler in 1941–1945. The first is geopolitical and the second is sociocultural. The first is further divided into two elements. Luttwak cites the first of these in his explanation of the reason why the Germans who succeeded in invading so deeply into the heart of the Russian land in 1941 had to be turned back by the counteroffensive of the Russians:

> It is the enemy that attacks first, and very successfully in this case. But then the enemy army finds itself thinned out along the front, since Russia's width increases from West to East as the Baltic and the Black Seas curve outwards. The enemy's lines of supply are more and more stretched, and it is harder and harder for his stock of vehicles to resupply the receding front. Local resisters and stranded soldiers can thus combine safely to form many little armies that begin to wage guerrilla war on the long and thin lines of supply. Thus the enemy's offensive momentum is exhausted."[11]

Of course, I may add to this first element of Russia's increasing geographic width from West to East the second element of the climatic effect of the Russian *moroz* (cold), which in winter reaches extremes unimaginable to invaders from outside.

As for the sociocultural factor, the role that the Russian *mudhik* (peasant) can play has always been great. Having inherited the militant tradition from the Cossacks, peasants-in-arms could wage a spontaneous guerrilla warfare even in the absence of coordinated orders from above.

The Russians' weakness in offensive operations as demonstrated in their wars against the Japanese in 1904–1905 and against the Finnish in 1939–1940 can be explained in terms of the backwardness of the society itself. The poor quality of junior officers in the expeditionary army reflected the lack of a middle class in the society. Yet in mounting offensive operations, the advance of the armies coordinated by advance planning must be adjusted to the change of circumstances, move by move; and upon arrival at the front, fighting decisions need be made swiftly, often without orders from above. It was in this regard that the Russians were at a great disadvantage. An army of any country is the product of its society. Thus the backwardness of the Russian society has been reflected in the qualitative weakness of the Russian army. Not only managerial but also technical inferiority have been inherent in that army.

The task of military doctrine has always been to solve the problem of how to circumvent these qualitative weaknesses. Of course, since the days of Peter the Great, the Russian appetite for modernization of its society and for importation of Western advanced technology has always been great. But in failing to modernize its society and lagging behind the Western countries in technology, the Soviet Union has always adhered to a doctrine of compensating for the managerial weakness of the junior officers by exploiting the tenacity and excellent fieldcraft of the peasant-soldiers, and of compensating for the technical inferiority of their weaponry by exploiting the numerical superiority of their army.

Mikhail Tukhachevskii, commenting on the temporary "Field Service Regulations" of 1936, advocated the need "to exert influence on the enemy not only directly at the front line, but to break through his position and attack him simultaneously in the whole depth of his order of battle";[12] he also stressed the importance of tanks, aviation, and parachute troops in the future war. Tukhachevskii's desire to modernize the Red Army reflected the strong motivation behind his doctrinal advocacy, but no less important was the traditional Russian military conception persisting in the mind of every Russian soldier since the days of Aleksandr Suvorov—namely, the notion of compensating for technical inferiority by numerical superiority.

In this regard it is interesting to note how a contemporary Soviet military writer boasts of the genius of Suvorov. Oleg Mikhailov writes as follows:

> In contrary to the then existing strategic principles, he [Suvorov] placed the main purpose of war not on taking cities and fortresses but on annihilating the enemy's living forces. In distinction from West European cordon strategy, which disposes its troops in open order, Suvorov demanded a concentration of forces in the decisive direction to destruct the enemy in parts. F. Engels, characterizing the leading nature of Suvorov's military act, wrote in the middle of the 19th century that Suvorov's strategy was close to the contemporary strategic system.[13]

In spite of Tukhachevskii's purge in 1937, his concept of the "operation in depth" as an application in modern times of the traditional Russian doctrine of exploiting numerical superiority in the battlefield seems to have survived and is now included in the Warsaw Pact Organization's strategic concept of Operational Maneuvering Group (OMG). Another example is the composition of the Soviet strategic nuclear arsenal, whose heavy reliance on such quantitative factors as the number of launchers, the megatonnage of destructive power, and the throw-weight of ICBMs may lead us to think that the traditional Russian doctrine is still alive in contemporary Soviet military thinking.

At the Level of Diplomatic Tactics

At the level of the diplomatic negotiating tactics, the Russians are known as tough negotiators. First, let us see what a few of our most experienced former ambassadors to Moscow have said on this topic.

Former U.S. Ambassador Foy D. Kohler: "More than once in recent years we have engaged in lengthy, laborious, acrimonious, and seemingly hopeless negotiations with the Soviet government on particular issues, have talked for months and years without any sign of progress, and then have suddenly found the Soviet Union ready to come to terms within a matter of hours."[14]

Former U.K. Ambassador William Hayter: "The Soviet diplomat's lack of inhibitions about truth and consistency, so useful for propaganda, means that he seldom inspires confidence."[15]

Former U.S. Ambassador Charles Bohlen: "Men of Moscow are never troubled about consistency and close their books at the end of every day."[16]

Those diplomats (whether Western or non-Western) who have never personally experienced negotiations with the Russians may instantly understand what these former ambassadors were trying to say. As one such diplomat who spent three years in Moscow, I share with those former ambassadors the opinion that the indifference the Soviets show toward the need to maintain even a minimum appearance of logical consistency in what they say and do seems to be a salient factor in their negotiating style.

In this regard I am, of course, aware of Nicolson's comments about the German style of negotiation, to the effect that "it seems to them more important to inspire fear than to beget confidence." I may also point out that Great Britain, too, is known for its hypocrisy in the international community, as is often indicated in connection with the phrase "perfidious Albion." In fact, as a symbol of the British preference for deception and machination, we can quote another good phrase, one invented by Winston Churchill during World War II: "bodyguard of lies." Japan was no exception. It was thought to be an infidel when it expanded its military fronts in China every time its government declared its policy of nonexpansion during its war with China in the late 1930s.

Am I talking now about a characteristic almost omnipresent in the international community? For that matter, am I talking about something peculiar to the Russian negotiating style? I must answer "no" to both questions. As is well known, Charles Bohlen, in his book *Witness to History 1929–1969*, defined Stalin's character not as "immoral" but as "amoral."[17] In my view, however, that was true not only of Stalin. When German or British or Japanese diplomats deceived or lied, they were, with the exception of Hitler and his inner associates, acutely conscious of their guilt in doing so. But when Russian diplomats did the same, they apparently did so because such behavior stemmed from their way of life at home. They were simply not cognizant of the fact that what they were doing could be morally prohibited in other cultures. To know where this cognizance comes from, in my view, one must know the cultural climate of the Soviet Union, the basis of which is the "rule of force." But I also want to make clear the fact, that, in saying this, I am not making a value judgment. In fact, I must admit that for most Soviet people it is not necessarily an uncomfortable thing to live in this cultural climate. Generally speaking, the diplomacy of a country is a product of its domestic politics. Its tactics and machinations evolve from its experiences in the internal power struggle. The final say in the decision-making process of foreign policy is the responsibility of the final survivor of the domestic power struggle. Moreover, the process itself is nothing more than a part of the mechanism of domestic politics. If we look at the Russian tradition of diplomatic tactics from this point of view, we may observe that the factor most greatly affecting the diplomatic tradition was the lack of the notion of "rule of law." Neither the throne of the tsars nor the title of the CPSU general secretaries offered its holder security of tenure. The rule in force has always been the "rule of force" in both Imperial and Soviet Russia. The political culture of Russia is thus explained by the lack of respect in the society for the notion of contract.

Ivan V. Kireevskii, one of the most influential slavophiles in the nineteenth century, proudly made a distinction between Russia and Western Europe. In his view, Russia was superior to Western Europe because it had not inherited Roman law and could therefore exempt itself from the individualism and rationalism that had so contaminated Western Europe. Thus, when *lichnosti* (personality) was denied in the society, either *samoderdjavie* (autocracy), as in the case of Nikolai M. Karamzin, or *mir* (community), as in the case of Aleksandr I. Gertsen, had to become the central value of the society. It is interesting to note that these two concepts still constitute the basis for the "rule of force" in contemporary Soviet society.

Russia was placed outside both the dominion of the Roman empire and that of international relations under the Peace of Westphalia (1648). As Richard Pipes has noted,

> The background of Russia's diplomacy was primarily Oriental, the reason being that the Russian state grew up on the fringe of Asia. Its attitudes toward both domestic policy and international relations were first developed vis-à-vis its sovereign, the Golden Horde, then its successor states, and until the early eighteenth century with diverse Eastern countries like the Ottoman empire, Iran, China, and various nomadic civilizations. The principles of this kind of diplomacy are very different from those of the West. There is, for example, no concept of the fundamental right of every state to exist.[18]

In my understanding, this means "no concept of contractual obligation among equals to abide by treaties." The international relations of the Peace of Westphalia were later expanded to include other states outside Western Europe. But the countries that wanted to be accepted as members in this society of nations had to prove themselves qualified as such. It was in this context that Japan had to demonstrate the Westernization of its domestic legal system as a requirement for such qualifications in the 1880s and 1890s. But in the case of Russia, the Revolution of 1917 proved to be another barrier that resulted in the seclusion of Russia from the rest of the world.

The Russians' preference in diplomatic negotiations for "force" over "sincerity," for "winning" over "compromise," and for "faits accomplis" over "give and take" is well known. It may well reflect the mentality prevailing in their domestic politics—hence the striking parallels between Tsarist and Soviet Russia. The following illustration of the style of the Tsarist Russian diplomacy provided more than 100 years ago by Lord Palmerston (1853) reminds us vividly of the current state of Soviet diplomacy:

> The policy and practice of the Russian government has always been to push forward its encroachments as fast and as far as the apathy or want of firmness of other governments would allow it to go, but always to stop and retire when it was met with decided resistance, and then to wait for the next favorable opportunity to make another spring on its intended victim. In furtherance of this policy, the Russian Government has always had two strings in its bow—moderate language and disinterested professions at Petersburg and at London; active aggression by its agents on the scene of operations. If the aggression succeeds locally, the Petersburg Government adopts them as a "fait accompli" which it did intend, but cannot, in honor, recede from. If the local agents fail, they are disavowed

> and recalled, and the language previously held is appealed to as a proof that the agents have overstepped their instructions. This was exemplified in the Treaty of Unkiar-Skelessi, and in the exploits of Simonovich and Vikovich in Persia. Orlov succeeded in extorting the Treaty of Unkiar-Skelessi from the Turks, and it was represented as a sudden thought, suggested by the circumstances of the time and place, and not the result of any previous instructions; but having been done, it could not be undone. On the other hand, Simonovich and Vikovich failed in getting possession of Herat, in consequence of our vigorous measures of resistance; and as they failed, and *when* they failed, they were disavowed and recalled, and the language previously held at Petersburg was appealed to as proof of the sincerity of the disavowal, although no human being with two ideas in his head could for a moment doubt that they had acted under specific instructions.[19]

Factors of Continuity and Disruption

Factors of continuity and disruption are intricately interlocked. They are mutually affected and interdependent. Yet for the purpose of our discussion it may become necessary and justified to draw a line between the two categories of factors. The factors of continuity in Russian history are, first, geopolitical or natural factors and, second, historical or human factors. As a geopolitical or natural factor I have already mentioned "the importance of the roles of the forests and steppes in the formulation of the ways of thinking and living of the Russian people," which paved the way both for the Russian version of belief in "power policy" and for the uniquely Russian trait of prudence in dealing with superior powers.

Regarding historical or human factors, I would like to stress the importance of the influences exerted by the Byzantine and Mongolian empires on the birth of the Russian empire. As previously noted, Kireevskii was proud of the fact that Russia had not been conquered by and incorporated into the Roman empire. Thanks to this historical fact, according to him, Russia remained free from individualism and rationalism. But in my view, it was precisely because individualism and rationalism (which gave rise to Western democratic values) were absent that Russia inherited the unity of the church and state from the Byzantine empire and the absolute subjugation of the individual to the collective from the Mongolian empire. In the former case, the state was given the right to meddle in an individual's acts.

I truly believe that to understand the Russian society, one must realize that not only the masses but the leaders and the intelligentsia as well, during almost all stages of its history, have remained and still remain utterly indifferent to fundamental human rights or the notion of citizens' freedom. After all, the Russian intelligentsia, both before and after the Revolution, could not and did not want to understand the value of human rights and democracy. There may be no sentence more difficult for the Russians to comprehend than the following, which I excerpted from the Declaration of Independence of the United States: "We hold these truths to be self-evident, that all men are created equal, that they are endowed by their Creator with certain inalienable Rights, that among these are Life, Liberty and the pursuit of Happiness."

Let me now turn to the factors of disruption. I would like to point out three in particular. The first concerns the impact of Marxism on the Russian way of life. An overestimation of this factor would be misleading; if anything, we should not underestimate the impact of the Russian way of life on Marxism. As is known, a legitimate offshoot of the revolutionary stream of native Russian thought was that of *Narodniki* and their successors, the Socialist Revolutionaries. As Gertsen has noted, they estimated the value of *mir* highly and aimed directly at the construction of Russian-style socialism by bypassing the process of capitalism in Russia. It should be stressed that in this enterprise the urban workers were not expected to play an important role, and that the peasants and intelligentsia were declared to be leading bearers of the flag of the revolution.

On the other hand, there were those Russians who wanted to import an orthodox Marxist thought. They were called *Mensheviks*. Georgi V. Plekhanov, the father of Russian Marxism, was so loyal to Marx that he made clear that they would wait until Russian capitalism matured and the urban proletariat emerged. But such was nonsensical to Lenin and the *Bolsheviks*, who claimed to be orthodox disciples of Marx in Russia although they did not hesitate to apply whatever modifications to the Marxist orthodoxy they believed were required for seizing power. The Machiavellian concept of placing the highest value on seizing power itself and of disregarding all other questions as secondary was a nurtured product of the Russian soil. In this spirit they learned a lot from the revolutionary thought and practice of the *Narodniki* and Socialist Revolutionaries, who were the most legitimate children of the revolutionary tradition of Russia.

The russianization of Marxism took place when the *Bolsheviks* adopted the revolutionary heroism of the *Narodniki* and gave a disproportionately high importance to the role of the intelligentsia in the Russian Revolution. At this time the initiative of the Revolution moved from the hands of the proletariat to those of the professional revolutionaries. In spite of the fact that Marx wanted to realize the "dictatorship of the proletariat," his self-appointed disciples in Russia pursued and realized the "dictatorship of the vanguard party." The difference was decisive. At certain stages of history this dictatorship escalated into the "dictatorship of an individual." Under the "dictatorship of the proletariat," the people are at least theoretically allowed to appear as sovereigns when the class finally disappears in the socialist society. But under the "dictatorship of the vanguard party" such is not allowed, as was demonstrated in Article VI of Brezhnev's Constitution of 1977. The article makes it clear that the CPSU is the leading force in Soviet society and that it determines the principles of internal and external policy. The party, which is one bureaucratic machine independent of the will of the people, is thus allowed to govern the people; thus it is equivalent to the proletariat of contemporary Soviet society.

It is not my intention to make value judgments about the Soviet system. My purpose is simply to describe the cultural climate in the Soviet Union—a climate that, in essence, has not changed since the Revolution. In this connection, let me add that such a climate is not unique to the Soviet Union. Even in the contemporary world this climate is prevalent outside the so-called industrialized democracies. Iran under the leadership of Khomeini is one example. But the Soviet Union is a superpower whose words and acts are of vital concern to every other nation in its daily life, whereas Iran is not necessarily so.

A second factor of disruption concerns the impact of technology, particularly that of nuclear weapons and the related effect of "nuclear stalemate." Undoubtedly, such developments have deeply affected the traditional pattern of Russo-Soviet external behavior. For the Soviet Union, war has ceased to be a universal means of settling international disputes, even when it is militarily superior to its opponent. Such is particularly the case in relation to the risk of war with the United States and its allies. Yet the Soviet Union may still resort to the use of force to settle international disputes when and where it feels it is not deterred by the threat of retaliatory nuclear strikes. (As noted, this was demonstrated when the Soviet army invaded Afghanistan in 1979.)

In connection with the progress of military technology, we should also note that the meaning of buffer zones, in the classic military sense, has undergone a great change. Now that Pershing-II missiles deployed in West Germany can hit Moscow within ten minutes, an invasion of the Soviet Union could never be a repetition of the marches that Napoleon and Hitler pursued in the past. Under such circumstances, the important question to be asked is this: What kind of reevaluation will the Soviet Union make regarding the role and meaning of buffer zones in the contemporary world?

The third factor of disruption concerns the unprecedented international status to which the Russian nation has finally elevated itself. For the first time in its history, the Soviet Union finds itself to be one of the two superpowers in the world. We might naturally expect the Soviets to behave with greater responsibility toward humanity than before. But nobody knows whether they will develop a sense of flexibility and generosity toward other members of the international society, or whether they will persist in their old "hunter" type of external behavior, obsessed with deep suspicions and a fear of inferiority. Whatever the answer to this question, the future fate of humanity hangs in the balance. Particularly important will be the attitude and response of the Soviet Union to the arms control negotiations with the United States in Geneva.

In conclusion, let me quote a concluding remark from *After Brezhnev: Sources of Soviet Conduct in the 1980s:*

> If the United States and its allies should succeed in improving the quality of life in their societies and establishing consistency and coordination in their foreign policies, they may be able to nudge the Soviet Union into policies that make the system more tolerable for its citizens and less threatening to the world. But if the world outside the Soviet empire descends further into economic and political disarray, the incentives for the Soviet leaders to reform their internal system and to moderate their ambitions abroad will correspondingly decline.[20]

Notes

1. Harold Nicolson, *Diplomacy,* 3rd edition (London: Oxford University Press, 1963), pp. 127–128.
2. Ibid., p. 144.
3. Ibid., pp. 144–145.
4. Ibid., p. 146.
5. Ibid., pp. 146–147.
6. Ibid., pp. 132–134.
7. Ibid., pp. 137–138.
8. George Vernadsky, *A History of Russia* (New Haven, Conn.: Yale University Press, 1961), p. 8.
9. Richard Pipes, "Diplomacy and Culture: Negotiation Styles," in Richard F. Staar, ed., *Arms Control—Myth Versus Reality* (Stanford, Calif: Hoover Institution Press, 1984), p. 155.
10. Edward N. Luttwak, *Grand Strategy of the Soviet Union* (London: Weidenfeld and Nicolson, 1983), p. 13.
11. Ibid., p. 18.
12. M. N. Tukhachevskii, "O Novom Polevom Ustave RKKA," in *Izbrannye Proizvedeniya,* Vol. 2 (Moskow: Voenizdat, 1964), pp. 255–256.
13. Oleg Mikhailov, *Suvorov: Istoricheskii Roman* (Moscow: Sovetskaya Rossiya, 1984), p. 339.
14. Foy D. Kohler, "Negotiation as an Effective Instrument of American Foreign Policy," *U.S. Department of State Bulletin,* Vol. 38 (June 2, 1958), p. 910.

15. Sir Wiliam Hayter, *The Diplomacy of the Great Powers* (London: Hamish Hamilton, 1960), pp. 30–31.

16. Quoted in Joseph C. Harsch, "Moscow Loves the French—Again," *Christian Science Monitor* (November 2, 1978).

17. Charles E. Bohlen, *Witness to History 1929–1969* (New York: W. W. Norton, 1973), p. 339.

18. Pipes, "Diplomacy and Culture," p. 155.

19. Evelyn Ashley, *The Life of Henry John Temple Viscount Palmerston, 1846–1865* (London: Richard Bentley & Son, 1876), p. 25.

20. Robert F. Byrnes, ed., *After Brezhnev: Sources of Soviet Conduct in the 1980s* (Bloomington: Indiana University Press, 1983), p. 440; translated by Kenichi Ito.

9

The Military Factor in Soviet Foreign Policy

Tsuyoshi Hasegawa

In the late 1970s there emerged in the West a hot debate as to whether the Western nations should continue the policy of détente with the Soviet Union. The central issue in this debate was the role of the military in Soviet foreign policy. Specifically, the debate focused on the problem of how to interpret two actions pursued by the Soviet Union in the 1970s: first, the Soviets' enormous military buildup and, second, their rapid expansion in the Third World. To some observers the growth of the Soviet military represented a relentless pursuit to achieve military superiority over the United States. To others it seemed merely an attempt to catch up. To the critics of détente, arms control was nothing but an excuse behind which the Soviet Union could expand its military power while halting U.S. military expansion. To the supporters of détente, arms control provided a real chance not only to reduce the danger of catastrophic nuclear war but also to achieve mutual reduction in nuclear arsenals.

The Soviets' aggressive foreign policy in the Third World—especially as manifested in the expansion of Soviet influence in Angola, Ethiopia, and South Yemen—seemed to create an "arc of crisis" that posed a serious threat to Western security. When this expansion was combined with an enormous military buildup in the Far East and the establishment of a foothold in Cam Ranh Bay, many began talking about a Soviet global strategy for expansion. Finally, the Soviet invasion of Afghanistan seemed to represent a new Soviet determination to commit military force outside its sphere of influence. The supporters of détente, on the other hand, contended that such actions did not represent the Soviet expansionistic policy but, rather, that each case was dictated by specific local and international situations. In the case of Afghanistan, it was primarily a defensive action motivated by Soviet security concerns.

Thus, the debate about détente centered on the nature of Soviet foreign policy and the role of military power. In this debate two diametrically opposed views emerged. The first view, which might be called the "essentialist" approach, held that Soviet foreign policy springs from the innate nature of the Soviet Union. Expansion is not an accidental, temporary phenomenon but, rather, is rooted in the very nature of the Soviet state. It would be a mistake to treat the Soviet Union as an ordinary nation-state and to expect it to behave as such, because its policy is fundamentally different from that of Western nations. Proponents of this first view argue in essence that Soviets will be Soviets, and that the most important task for Soviet specialists and policy makers is to learn what makes the Soviet Union different from the West.

The second view might be called the "contextualist" approach. Its proponents assert that there is nothing inherently distinct in Soviet foreign policy, and that the Soviet Union, despite all its ideological pronouncements, behaves exactly like an ordinary nation-state in its conduct of foreign policy. According to this view, the Soviet state's ultimate objective is not the expansion of communism to every corner of the globe but, rather, the protection of security and the enhancement of its national interests. Soviet international behavior is not predetermined by a master plan for world conquest but, instead, is dictated by complex domestic and international situations in much the same way as with any Western nation's behavior. The emphasis of this interpretation is that Soviet foreign policy is by no means monolithic, that the important thing is to pay more attention to the subtle differences of opinions among Soviet foreign policy makers.

In this chapter I shall attempt to reexamine some of the basic assumptions held by the "essentialists" and the "contextualists," as expressed in (1) historical factors, (2) ideological factors, (3) military power, and (4) military doctrine. I will also offer a few tentative conclusions intended to provide a basis for further discussion.

Historical Factors

According to the "essentialists," there are two elements that make the nature of Soviet foreign policy expansionistic. They are history and ideology.

Richard Pipes has forcefully argued that expansionism is rooted in the nature of the Russian state that preceded the Soviet Union.[1] Dismissing the widely held view that Russia's insecurity was fostered by numerous invasions suffered from outsiders, Pipes argues that Russian history is a history of aggressions, as illustrated by the Muscovite annexations of Kazan and Astrakhan in the sixteenth century, the conquest of Siberia in the seventeenth century, the continuous offensives against the Ottoman empire and the partitions of Poland in the eighteenth century, and the conquest of Turkmen and seizures of Chinese territories in the nineteenth century.

Common sense tells us that a nation's sense of security is shaped by its history; but historical determinism, if too rigidly applied to reality, becomes arbitrary and useless. There are three things wrong with Pipes's conclusions. First, Pipes never questions whether such examples were uniquely Russian, given the standards that existed at the time. The annexations of Kazan and Astrakhan might not be considered an extraordinary example of aggression when measured against the standard prevailing in the age of successive crusades by other European nations against the infidels. The conquest of Siberia was no more brutal than the U.S. westward movement. The Ottoman empire was attacked not only by Russia but also by other European nations, and the partition of Poland was not Russia's doing alone—Prussia and Austria were also culprits. Not only Russia but other imperialistic nations plundered China. In other words, expansionism was at one time or another a common characteristic of all European nations.

Second, Pipes's selection is arbitrary. By picking examples that fit one's hypothesis alone and by ignoring others, one can prove almost anything. If Pipes's examples were historical facts, there are also numerous examples of Russia having fallen victim to foreign invasions. The point is not whether aggressions or foreign invasions were more responsible for the predominant character of Russian behavior but, rather, that they both complemented each other in forming Russia's unique sense of security. Russia's borders, not protected by natural barriers, were exposed to attacks from adversaries. The open steppes in the south and the flat land in the west provided a highway through which enemies invaded Russia. To ensure security Russia had to use the same highway to attack neighboring states.

Russia's expansion can largely be explained by the absence of strong neighboring states. As Edward Luttwak has noted, there was not one instance (with the possible exception of Peter the Great's war against Sweden) in which Russia won a victory in a war deliberately launched against a first-class enemy.[2] In this sense, Russia's expansion was not of the same nature as that of the Nazis.

Third, Pipes ignores the fact that his examples pertained to Russia's contiguous regions. In this sense, Russia's expansion was inferior to that of the major European nations that had established vast colonies overseas. Luttwak attributes Russia's lack of overseas expansion to the vastness of its territory, its landlocked geographical position, and the poor quality of Russian junior officers.[3] These factors, which were not so detrimental to the waging of a defensive war on its own territory, proved prohibitive in offense beyond its borders. History, therefore, not only offers examples of aggression but also illustrates the limitations of expansionism.

This is not to say, of course, that expansionism was nonexistent in Russian history. Expansions did take place, as Pipes asserts, but they were not necessarily the results of those innate forces from within that were uniquely Russian in character. Three factors are important to explain the motives behind Russian expansions: security, nationalism, and imperialism.

Russia's perception of threat, reinforced by geography and a history of foreign invasions, contributed to its desire to weaken potential threats, to turn its neighbors into docile client states, and even to absorb them into its empire. Security concerns were also closely connected with nationalism. The desire to achieve national independence and irredentism also served as a strong motivation for expansion. Finally, in the age of imperialism, when a nation's prestige was measured by the degree to which it expanded its influence beyond its borders, Russia also began to seek expansion for geopolitical reasons. All three factors transcend the watershed in 1917 and continue to play an important role in Soviet foreign policy. The point is that these factors are not necessarily exclusive attributes of the Russian-Soviet state; they are also applicable to the foreign policies of other nations.

Whether for offensive or defensive reasons—and in my opinion both were complementary—Russia traditionally allocated disproportionately large resources to the military, as Pipes points out. In fact, Tsarist Russia could have been characterized primarily as a bureaucratic-military state. Yet, I suspect that Russian militarism was not so much an instrument of insatiable appetite for expansion as evidence of backwardness in social development and military technology. To create military power that could compete with major powers in Europe, Russia had to pour all its resources into the military, thus further retarding social development. The inherent weakness caused by this vicious circle was revealed in the Crimean War and World War I. The defeat in the Crimean War forced Alexander II to launch the Great Reforms, but the unsuccessful prosecution of World War I led to the collapse of the tsarist regime itself.

It is precisely this connection between wars and changes in the state structure that I consider important in relation to the historical legacy that was carried into the Soviet period.

The Mongol invasion of the thirteenth century destroyed Kievan Rus. But the Muscovite state that grew in the appanage period was an absolute state based on the new military class known as *dvoriane*. The Livonian War of the sixteenth century was partially responsible for the collapse of the Muscovite state and for the Time of Troubles. But the foreign invasions during the Time of Troubles inspired the national spirit and contributed to the creation of a renewed Muscovite state in the seventeenth century. Peter the Great's reforms were basically ad hoc measures necessitated by the exigencies of the Great Northern War. The Napoleonic War of 1812 severely tested the strength of the autocratic state and gave rise to expectations of internal reform when the autocratic regime failed to respond to them. The frustration of these expectations then led to the Decembrist Revolt—the first spark of the revolutionary movement. Defeat in the Crimean War led to the Great Reforms of Alexander II, and the 1905 Revolution took place after Russia suffered a humiliating defeat in the Russo-Japanese War. The Russian involvement in World War I exposed the internal contradictions of the autocracy, which was overthrown in the February Revolution of 1917. And, finally, the inability of the Provisional Government to extricate itself from the war contributed to the Bolshevik seizure of power in October 1917.

These examples amply demonstrate that throughout Russian history, wars were not merely a matter of security of the nation; they were also a matter of security of the regime.[4] It is precisely this combination of national security and security of the regime that the Soviet state inherited from its past. From its very inception the Bolshevik regime lacked legitimacy, and it feared that foreign invasions would touch off popular rebellion against the regime. Military power was an essential instrument for survival against foreign enemies as well as against real or perceived internal enemies. When the communist regime abandoned the dream of world revolution and accepted the necessity of socialism in one country, the military factor became a prerequisite for the survival of a socialism beset by hostile imperialist nations outside and potential class enemies within. The Bolshevik Revolution, therefore, did not part with the traditional bureaucratic-military regime but, in fact, perpetuated it.

The Nazi invasion of 1941 exposed the Soviet regime once again to a danger that could have been fatal to the existence of the regime itself. But Stalin's regime bounced back and succeeded in turning the Fatherland War into a chance for the communist regime to gain a hitherto elusive legitimacy. The war also provided the Soviet regime with another opportunity to establish a buffer zone in Eastern Europe. But the acquisition of Eastern Europe also meant that the Soviet Union could not free itself from the combination of national security and security of the regime, even if communist legitimacy was established within the Soviet Union.

It cannot be denied that Russian history offers many clues to the military role of Soviet foreign policy. But Pipes's conclusion about the innate nature of Russian expansionism is not convincing. Rather, Russian expansion was motivated by nationalism, national security, and imperialism—factors operating to an equal degree in the nations of the West.

History also demonstrates the limitations of Russian expansionism. If history is helpful in suggesting the continuity between the old regime and the Soviet regime, the following three factors pertain: (1) Russia's aggressions are often connected with its sense of insecurity; (2) Russia was traditionally a military-bureaucratic state, as necessitated by the backwardness of social development and military technology; and (3) national security was often associated with the security of the regime.

Ideological Factors

The second factor often cited by the "essentialists" as a source of the innate Soviet urge for expansion is ideology. The Soviet state, based on Marxism-Leninism, is not an ordinary nation-state but a state with a mission to achieve world revolution. Moscow is said to have a grand global strategy to fulfill this mission, and Marxism-Leninism is considered the driving force behind the expansion of communism.[5]

Marxism contributed to the political theory of war. Contrary to the Western liberal tradition, which stressed consensus as the basis of political community, Marxism saw in the conflict between classes the basis of social relations. Behind the façade of seeming social harmony there is violence in the form of exploitation exerted by the exploiters over the exploited. Social progress is made only when the exploited turn violent against the exploiters to overthrow them. A metaphor of war was used to describe this struggle. At the same time, a real war between nations was regarded not as a serious breakdown of international relations but as an extension of class struggle. In other words, Marxism saw in peace an element of war, and in war nothing extraordinary. This approach, one must admit, added a valuable insight to our understanding of society and international relations.

The danger in the Marxist approach comes when it ceases to be a useful antidote to the prevailing bourgeois political philosophies and is turned into the sole official ideology. As Pipes has noted, Lenin turned Clausewitz on his head and advocated war as the extension of politics by violent means.[6] Indeed, Lenin was probably the first politician to militarize domestic politics. In examining Lenin's writings during the revolutionary days of 1917, one is struck with his imagery of war. The Civil War was not merely imposed by outside forces hostile to the Bolshevik regime; it was a logical consequence of Lenin's strategy, which Lenin clearly foresaw and encouraged.[7]

The metaphor of war was transformed into real war in the Soviet Union. The distinction between war between nations and war waged in society was obliterated, and the methods used only in wars between states were indiscriminately applied within society. The civil war mentality fostered the communist habit of settling differences by military means. Even at the end of the civil war, the mentality of *kto-kogo* did not disappear; rather, it was reinforced by the isolation of the communist regime in a sea of imperialist nations. Domestically as well, the communist regime was surrounded by essentially hostile class enemies such as Nepmen and the kulaks. It is no accident, to borrow a common Soviet phrase, that at precisely the time economic liberalization was taking place during the NEP period, the internal freedom of the Communist party was stifled. It was characteristic of Lenin to make a primarily military reference. In criticizing the opposition faction within the Communist party, Lenin blurted out that it was better to "discuss with rifles."[8] Furthermore, in his major report on NEP at the 10th Party Congress in 1921, Lenin stated:

> Then discipline must be more conscious and is a hundred times more necessary, because when a whole army retreats, it is not clear to it, it does not see where it will stop, it sees only retreat; then sometimes a few panic voices are enough to start everyone running. Then the danger is immense. When such a retreat is being carried out with a real army, machine-guns are brought out and, when the orderly retreat becomes disorderly, the command is given: "Fire." And quite right. . . . At such a moment it is indispensable to punish strictly, secretly, unsparingly the slightest breach of discipline.[9]

I suspect that the mentality of militarization advocated by Lenin was enthusiastically endorsed by the young communist elite who had won the civil war. Against this prevailing current, the attempt by Bukharin and his supporters to reconstruct a theory of the socialist state on the basis of social peace and reconciliation had no chance of gaining acceptance.[10]

The application of military methods in domestic politics was further accelerated by Stalin's revolution from above. The collectivization was an "offensive against the kulaks." The military factor in the industrialization was unmistakable. In his famous speech in 1931 justifying the accelerated tempo of industrialization, Stalin stated: "We are fifty or a hundred years behind the advanced countries. We must make good this distance in ten years. Either we do so, or we shall go under."[11] Julian Cooper's study makes it clear that the first priority of the industrialization drive during the period between 1929 and 1941 was the military, thus diverting necessary resources away from even heavy industry.[12] The slogan during the industrialization drive was "There is no fortress that the Bolsheviks cannot take." As Seweryn Bialer has stated, military images were firmly entrenched even in the language:

> In Stalinist Russia one did not solve a problem, one "attacked" it; one "retreated," "regrouped," organized a "campaign"; one was "at war" and organized one's own "camp" against the "enemy"; one acted on various "fronts"—ideological, industrial, agricultural—and one had a "strategy" and "tactic" for each "sector."[13]

The militarization of society relentlessly pursued by Lenin and Stalin not only prepared the country for a possible war; it was also used to fan a class warfare in a society in which enemies did not even exist. And its logical conclusion was the Great Purge and the madness of the Gulag Archipelago.

Ironically, however, Marxist-Leninist ideology has not been applied in Soviet foreign policy as clearly and relentlessly as it has been in the society itself. According to Pipes, Marxism, "the child of the age of Social Darwinism . . . views history as the record of uninterrupted class warfare and . . . advocated the continuation of class war as a means of abolishing, once and for all, classes and the exploitation of man by man."[14] Furthermore, he argues, "Marxism-Leninism is an international doctrine. As it perceives them, the phases in the evolution of mankind are global in scope and cannot be contained . . . within the limits of the nation-state."[15] All this is true in theory. But it is difficult to subscribe to Pipes's view that in reality Soviet foreign policy has been primarily guided by such a global strategy based on Marxism-Leninism.

Four factors contributed to the diminishing role of ideology and to the eventual end of its role as an operating principle in Soviet foreign policy. First, the Soviet Union had to survive in a world of nation-states, and ideological purity had to be sacrificed for the sake of survival of the state. The choice was made early in the game, when the young Bolshevik regime had to choose between peace or war at Brest Litovsk in 1918. Ever since the Soviet regime chose peace for survival of the state at the expense of revolutionary war, it subjugated ideology to the dictates of national interests. Henceforth ideology ceased to be the guide of policy; instead, it became a tool for justification of policy.

Second, after World War II there emerged a different path to socialism. The Sino-Soviet split had a profound influence on the devaluation of Marxist-Leninist ideology. The Soviet Union could no longer claim to be the sole fatherland of socialism to which all communists in other countries had previously sworn blind obedience. The Soviet Union was portrayed by the Chinese as an industrialized European White power with its own imperialist designs. The mystique that once surrounded the Moscow-led communist movement was once and for all destroyed.

Third, the Soviet model of industrialization, which had once captured the imagination of intellectuals in the underdeveloped nations clamoring for modernization, no longer serves as an attractive alternative to capitalism. Moreover, the revelations of Stalin's terror, and the repressive measures taken even after Stalin, "where the regime was more devoted to the policeman than to the worker,"[16] disillusioned the potential revolutionary leaders of the Third World.

Fourth, as I will discuss in more detail below, the existence of nuclear weapons fundamentally altered the Marxist approach to war.

The end of ideology as the operating principle of Soviet foreign policy raises two questions. First, can we assert, as the "contextualists" might, that the Soviet Union now basically acts like an ordinary nation-state, and that the Soviets view the world exactly as we do? Second, what is the consequence of the end of ideology in terms of Soviet military power?

The end of ideology as the operating principle in foreign policy does not automatically suggest that ideology has become totally meaningless. Ideology still provides the Soviet citizens in general and the foreign policy elite in particular with a frame of reference from which to view the world. As Bialer states, ideology serves a "conscious cognitive function, [as] the analytical framework that the Soviet leadership applies to its evaluation of world events and trends, and as the unconscious *motivating* function that defines a priori images, biases, and beliefs that the leadership brings to its perception of international reality and that are almost never spelled out and enunciated in analytical terms."[17]

Even if ideology is understood in this context, Marxism-Leninism provides the Soviet leaders and foreign policy elite with a powerful framework. First, the Marxist dialectic would contribute to their habit of seeing the world in terms of a conflict between the forces of socialism and the forces of reactionary imperialism. The outcome of this struggle will be determined by an objective reality called "correlation of forces." Thus, the Soviet leaders are apt to approach international relations as a zero-sum game.

Second, the use of force itself is neither good nor bad; if force is used to enhance the interests of the socialist camp, it is good; if it serves the interests of imperialists, it is bad. But when force is used, it is not regarded apologetically as a necessary evil; rather, it is advocated positively, unequivocally, and without one iota of moral hesitation. Furthermore, it is considered criminal *not* to exercise force when it is necessary, because the other side is always prepared to use it just as readily. The mentality of *kto-kogo* dies hard. It is well to recognize that the Soviet leaders have no respect for the kind of pacifism that Japan has subscribed to after World War II. Without questioning whether the West or the Soviet Union has exercised more violence in pursuing foreign policy, one must admit that the Soviet notion of force is more brutal than that of its Western opponents. We should not delude ourselves into believing that the Soviets think and view the world in exactly the same way we do.

In this connection, it is important to ponder the significance of the Soviet recognition that a thermonuclear war might annihilate humanity—and socialism as well. The emergence of this theory, which is essentially at variance with the main tenets of Marxism-Leninism, should not be dismissed merely as a propaganda ploy to deceive the West; indeed, it should be taken seriously as a sign of new realism. Even Marxism-Leninism in the Soviet Union is not necessarily a colorless repetition of the dead canons; it can change according to new situations. But in the final analysis it would not change the basic approach to world politics, which is still considered to be the arena of the decisive conflict between the two camps, and in which the use of force continues (or so it is believed) to play a major part. The existence of nuclear weapons introduced a new variable in the Soviets' calculations of the correlation of forces, but it has not fundamentally changed their basic approach to international relations.

The second question concerns the consequences of ideology as the operating principle of foreign policy in the Soviet Union. The fact that the Soviet Union can no longer expect to use ideology or economic achievement as the instrument of foreign policy means that the military has become almost the sole reliable means on which the Soviet leaders can count. It is therefore necessary to examine next the meaning of Soviet military power.

Soviet Military Power

Both "essentialists" and "contextualists" accept the basic fact that because of the enormous military buildup that occurred under the Brezhnev regime, the Soviet Union has finally caught up with the United States in military power. Since specifics are well presented in the literature, I will sketch here only the most important features of the Soviets' military achievements.

First, the Soviet Union has reached strategic parity with the United States. Some indicators suggest that the Soviet Union is actually ahead of the United States in term of strategic nuclear weapons. Soviet technological backwardness has been largely overcome; in particular, the Soviet fourth-generation missiles have reached or significantly narrowed the gap of accuracy relative to the U.S. Minuteman missiles. With the deployment of the new SLBMs, the Soviets are quickly developing invulnerable strategic reserve forces. When the land-based missiles alone are compared, the Soviet missiles with their large yields and increased accuracy could theoretically take all the U.S. land-based missiles in a first strike.

Second, an enormous military buildup has occurred in all regions, in all services, and in all weapons systems. With the development of theater nuclear forces, notably the SS-20s and the Backfires, the theater balance in Europe has actually tipped in favor of the Soviet Union. A similar buildup has occurred in Asia. Altogether, fifty-two divisions are deployed along the Chinese border, and the Far Eastern Fleet has become the largest fleet in the Soviet Navy, which is now acquiring a foothold in the strategic position of Cam Ranh Bay. The Soviet Navy, which was no more than a coastal defense force in the 1950s, can now operate anywhere in the world, and with its modern submarines, surface ships, and naval aviation, it can threaten the Western sea-lanes of communication. Likewise, the Soviet Air Force has significantly narrowed the gap in air power, which was once dominated by the West, whereas the Western advantage in air-to-ground capabilities has diminished due to the development of Soviet air-defense capabilities.[18] The Soviet ground forces, which were more numerous even in the 1950s, are now equipped with modern armored carriers, tanks, antitank weapons, tactical nuclear weapons, and chemical weapons. Even with helicopters—an area in which the United States once had overwhelming superiority—the Soviets are now narrowing the gap.

Third, the Soviet Union has made enormous progress in its power-projection capability. It has acquired the capability of projecting its forces anywhere in the world.

The most significant consequence of the Soviet military buildup is that the Soviet Union, for the first time, now has global power status. Under Stalin, and even under Khrushchev, the Soviet Union was a regional power whose influence was primarily restricted to the European continent. The Soviets' global power status can be expressed in two ways. First, given their destructive nuclear power, the Soviet Union and the United States alone hold the fate of mankind. The SALT I Treaty represented a truly significant moment for the national prestige of the Soviet Union, which had finally reached equal status with the other superpower of the world—a fact that was also recognized by the United States.

Second, the Soviet Union acquired global power status in the sense of power projection. If one compares the Soviet expansion of influence in Ghana, Egypt, and the Congo in Khrushchev's time with the Soviet expansion in Angola, Ethiopia, and Afghanistan, the difference becomes immediately clear. Whereas the former relied basically on economic aids, the current expansion has been accomplished primarily through military power and demonstrates above all the enormous leap in the Soviets' airlift capability. The Soviet leaders' proud pronouncement that there is no problem in the world that could be resolved without the participation of the Soviet Union is therefore not an idle boast. The Soviet Union now demands a place in the sun—a place that had been denied until now.

The attainment of global power status is thus purely a function of military power, without which the Soviet Union would lose all its influence and prestige. In the future the Soviet Union is not likely to relinquish the only card it holds.

The nuclear stalemate that resulted from the Soviet Union's achievement of strategic parity with the United States has also paradoxically opened up opportunities for small nations to maneuver and manipulate the superpowers in order to gain advantage in local conflicts. Herein lies the Soviets' opportunity to undermine Western influence and to expand its own. It is no longer ideology for social transformation but military hardware and advisers that the Soviets can export to these customers. And there is no reason to doubt that the Soviets will jump at the chance to take advantage of such opportunities in the future.

Soviet military power, however, reveals not only a threat to Western security but weaknesses in the Soviet system as well. First, the Soviet Union cannot expect to achieve unilateral military buildup of such magnitude without provoking a reaction from its adversary. The Soviets' grievous error in judgment in believing that the U.S. withdrawal from world commitment in the 1970s represented an irreversible change in the correlation of forces inevitably provoked the United States to seek an activist foreign policy and a vigorous attempt at military buildup. It also contributed to the renewed attempt at military buildup by the Western European nations and Japan. Now that the Soviets have been challenged by the United States' attempts to achieve superiority through SDI, even the military parity they spent so many years to achieve is in danger of erosion. In other words, we cannot be certain that the enormous buildup by the Soviet Union has brought a commensurate increase in the security of the Soviet Union.

Second, the Soviet Union has found it difficult to integrate the gains it acquired by military means in the Third World into their own imperial sphere of influence. In many cases, the nations of the Third World face tremendous problems in carrying out modernization. The Soviet Union is quite helpless in aiding them beyond military means and construction of the instrument of repression. It was quite an embarrassment for the

Soviet Union, for instance, when it could not extend any help to the starving population of Ethiopia, its own client state, while aid poured forth from the Western nations.

Third, the enormous military buildup has exacted sacrifices in the domestic economy. The ever-increasing stagnation of the Soviet economy is sooner or later bound to affect military capability as well.

This is not to suggest, as some commentators do,[19] that Soviet military power based on inferior military technology must in itself be inferior, and that what has been presented as a Soviet military threat does not in reality exist. The Soviet defense industry, which is basically separate from the civilian economy, has so far succeeded in producing military hardware comparable in quality to its Western counterparts. But the more sophisticated and expensive modern weapons become, the more difficulty the weak Soviet economy has in competing with the West.[20]

Luttwak sees this as the greatest danger of all. The Soviet Union, now that it is ahead in military and hopelessly backward in economy, may find it necessary to strike before it is too late. He argues:

> But aside from the usual dynamics of imperial power, there must also be a degree of urgency in the Soviet case. It is not just a question of using uncommitted divisions . . . to expand the empire further, but rather of employing a transient military advantage before it is too late, to gain a permanent enhancement in the security of the empire. . . . But inevitably Soviet planners must now foresee that the superiorities thus gained will evaporate during the 1990s. All the sacrifices and all the discipline will have been for naught—unless the power thus accumulated is wisely employed to achieve a permanent improvement in the security position of the Soviet Union.[21]

Luttwak's prescribed solution is primarily military in nature. Only the Western military buildup could deter the Soviet Union. But in my opinion, the unilateral military action in the West, without any accompanying effort to reach agreements on arms control, will bring the world dangerously close to the possibility of catastrophic nuclear war. In order to explain why this is so, I must now turn to a discussion of Soviet military doctrine.

Soviet Military Doctrine

It was argued in the late 1970s that Soviet military strategy was basically at variance with the concept of mutual assured destruction, which lay at the foundation of the U.S. military strategy. Instead, that strategy was considered to be based on the philosophy of warfighting.

The Soviets were said to believe that they could "fight and win a nuclear war," to quote the title of Pipes's article. Further, the "essentialists" contended that the Soviet military posture aimed at first-strike capability and acquisition of military superiority against the United States. They recommended, therefore, that in order to counter such a strategy of nuclear warfare, the United States should abandon the traditional approach to military posture based on mutual assured destruction, cease attempts to reach arms control agreements, and launch unilateral military buildup to seek the acquisition of warfighting capability.[22]

It is true that the military doctrine enunciated in the Khrushchev period, which continued until the middle of 1970s, held that (1) if an imperialist power attacked the Soviets, it would deal them a crushing blow; (2) as Soviet military power is essential to deter imperialist aggression, military superiority is the only guarantee of peace; and (3) in the event of a nuclear war, the Soviet Union would emerge victorious (although it would suffer unprecedented damage) and capitalism would perish.[23]

However, it would be a mistake to think that such a view represented the permanent, unchanging features of Soviet strategic thinking. In fact, the military doctrine that prevailed from 1960 to the middle of the 1970s departed significantly from the military doctrine in the postwar Stalin period. As a study by Stephen Meyer clearly demonstrates, the Soviet strategy evolved, with remarkable flexibility, according to the changing threat perceptions and the availability of technology.

Therefore, it is not surprising to find that Soviet military doctrine was actually making an important transition in the late 1970s.[24] In the background of this change, there was the reality that the Soviet Union had reached strategic parity with the United States. Only when parity was reached did the Soviet leaders become concerned with the outcome of seeking superiority. As David Holloway has stated, "The choice the Soviet leaders faced was not one between parity and superiority (for superiority is clearly desirable), but between parity and a dangerous competition for superiority, the outcome of which was by no means certain."[25]

In January 1977, during his speech at Tula, Brezhnev stated: "The defensive potential of the Soviet Union ought to be sufficient so that nobody will risk disturbing our peaceful life. Not a course aimed at superiority in armaments." The joint communiqué issued after Brezhnev's visit to West Germany in May 1978 indicated that "the two sides consider it important that no one should seek military superiority. They proceed from the assumption that approximate equality and parity are sufficient to ensure defense."[26] Furthermore, in his report to the 26th Party Congress, Brezhnev declared: "Military strategic parity that exists between the Soviet Union and the United States and that exists between the NATO nations and the Warsaw Pact nations is an objective guarantee for world peace. We never intended in the past and do not intend now to seek military superiority against our adversary." In the same speech, he referred to "dangerous madness . . . to count on victory in nuclear war."[27]

These statements by Brezhnev make it clear that at least the political leadership has made a serious revision in the previously held military doctrine by accepting mutual deterrence "in the sense of mutual vulnerability to devastating retaliatory strikes."[28] However, there seemed to be a degree of resistance and hesitation on the part of the military leadership to accept the revision of the military doctrine. Marshal Ogarkov, chief of the general staff, stated in 1976 in the *Soviet Military Encyclopedia* that "Soviet military doctrine . . . gives a program of actions for ensuring military-technical superiority over the armed forces of probable enemies." In 1979, he referred to the Soviet Union's "objective possibilities for achieving victory" in a nuclear war.[29] In a pamphlet published in 1981, Ogarkov went on to say that "an important aspect of the military-technical component of Soviet military doctrine in the nuclear age is to defeat the enemy under any conditions."[30]

This seeming contradiction baffled Western observers. Some completely rejected the significance of the change, dismissing it as yet another attempt by the political leadership to deceive the West. There was a division of opinion even among those who took this change seriously. Dan and Rebecca Strode, for instance, concluded that serious differences of opinion existed within the Soviet leadership.[31] Holloway, on the other hand, argued that Soviet military doctrine should be interpreted as a synthesis of the political and military aspects of the military doctrine. The task of the political leadership would be to prevent war from occurring, while the task of the military would be to prepare for the possibility of war when deterrence failed. But, in Holloway's opinion, the political aspect of the military doctrine always assumes more importance, and, to that extent, the change in the military doctrine must be taken seriously.[32]

Whatever differences existed between the political leadership and the military now seem to have been resolved in favor of the former. Ogarkov himself revised his previous position in the interview given in *Krasnaia zvezda* on May 9, 1984:

> The number and diversity of nuclear missiles that exist at present in the United States and the Soviet Union would make it difficult for one side to destroy the system of the other side in a preemptive first strike. It has become inevitable that a decisive retaliatory attack with even the limited

> number of nuclear weapons that remain in the hands of the defender could inflict unacceptable damage to the aggressor.[33]

It is conceivable, as Cynthia Roberts suggests, that the Soviet leadership may not feel wholly comfortable with strategic stability based on mutual vulnerability, and that despite the change in doctrine, it has had a minimal impact on Soviet weapons development, which continues to be oriented toward counterforce missions.[34] Nonetheless, the revision in the doctrine suggests that the Soviet military doctrine is not stationary, unchanging, and monolithic but, rather, that it can change according to challenges posed by military situations and technological development.

This brings us to my explanation of why the Western unilateral attempt at military buildup to counter the Soviet threat may result in a dangerous situation. In this context we must review the Soviet reaction to the Reagan administration's military program. As generally accepted, the Soviets are threatened by Reagan's SDI program. In fact, it was most likely their fear of SDI that brought them back to the negotiating table of arms control, after they walked out of both the INF and the START negotiations. Obviously, they are concerned about the economic cost of the arms race resulting from SDI, particularly given that the newly established Gorbachev regime apparently wishes to concentrate its energy in long-overdue economic reforms. Moreover, the Soviets are well aware that they could not possibly catch up with the United States in the competition of SDI, which would make use of computers and high technology in which the Soviet Union lags far behind the West. But it seems to me that we ought to pay more attention to what the Soviets are saying in opposing SDI. The Soviets view SDI as an attempt by the United States to achieve military superiority. Their argument is that while they are developing first-strike counterforce weapons such as MX missiles, Trident II SLBMs, and B-1 bombers, the United States is trying to develop a shield of strategic defense. The Soviet leaders, both political and military, declare that the Soviets will have to respond to prevent the U.S. acquisition of military superiority at any cost. There is no reason to doubt their intention.

Specifically, the Soviets will be forced to increase the number of nuclear warheads at an accelerated pace, develop new strategic missiles as well as cruise missiles, deploy a network of ABMs, and accelerate the development of ASAT technology. But this would mean the complete collapse of the arms control regime, which has continued to operate up to now since 1972 and which, despite all weaknesses too well known to be cited here, has at least provided both countries with a certain degree of strategic stability and predictability. In the absence of arms control agreements, the Soviet Union would be forced to write a new military doctrine to replace the old one based on the reality of parity and mutual vulnerability. I see no reason to believe that the new direction would be a pleasant change for the West. If Luttwak is correct in predicting that the Soviet Union might be forced to strike before it is too late (although he himself discounts the possibility of nuclear attack), then the attempt by the West to launch a unilateral military buildup, in which the Soviets see an attempt to seek military superiority, seems a sure prescription for the Soviets to launch a preemptive strike before SDI completes construction of its invulnerable shields and before the Soviet Union loses its military competitive edge. The Soviet Union may not be crazy enough to launch such a preemptive attack, the outcome of which, according to the current Soviet military doctrine, would be mutual annihilation.

Even if the Soviet Union was not provoked to launch a go-for-broke attack, the resulting arms race would still create a precarious situation. But in all likelihood, the world will continue as it is now, filled with intense social and international tensions; and in ensuing conflicts the United States and the Soviet Union will persist in jockeying to preserve and expand their interests and influence. Any conflict, even one that does not pose a serious threat to the national security of each nation, but in which one side will find it necessary to use force, may irrevocably lead to a catastrophic confrontation—particularly if military doctrine is rewritten in such a way that it lowers the nuclear threshold and reemphasizes preemption, and if there is no will on either side to reach an agreement of crisis management. If such a world jeopardizes the Soviets' sense of security, it certainly would not increase our own security, either. The history of MIRV technology should serve as a reminder to us that an attempt to seek a strategic edge against the Soviet Union may in the end sharply reduce our own security.

I do not pretend to have a solution as to how to approach the Soviet Union, and how to meet the challenge posed by the Soviet military threat. What I am suggesting here, however, might serve as a basis for further discussion.

First, we should begin by rejecting two illusions. The first illusion is to imagine that the Soviet Union is a kind of expansionistic maniac bent on world domination, with force as its primary means to achieve that goal and whose nature is so fundamentally different in terms of state and foreign policy goals that normal relations other than confrontation are impossible. As Holloway cautions, if one is seized by this illusion, two consequences will follow: "First, one does not have to listen to what the Soviet Union says, because one knows essentially what it is trying to do; second, one does not have to heed the effect of one's actions on the Soviet Union, because Soviet policy remains essentially the same."[35] Actually, Soviet foreign policy, even in such fundamental issues as its military doctrine, has demonstrated a capacity for change. In addition, an inflexible confrontational policy based on this illusion would not increase our security but, rather, would diminish it.

The second illusion is the notion that the Soviet Union has become an ordinary nation-state like any other nation and that good behavior will result from our goodwill and unilateral concessions. The Soviet Union's distinctive historical background and ideological framework will continue to cause the Soviet leaders to approach the world differently from their Western counterparts. They will continue to exploit every opportunity that presents itself to undermine the interests of the Western powers and Japan. There will undoubtedly be occasions in which Western determination, with force if necessary, will be the only way to resist Soviet actions. In arms control negotiations, the Soviets will continue to be tough negotiators, exploiting every opportunity to preserve and enhance their own military power while arresting and retarding the development of Western military power.

The fundamental nature of the relationship between the Soviet Union and the United States and between the Soviet Union and the Western alliance will continue to be one of conflict. But in the nuclear age, both sides have the common interest to prevent an outbreak of nuclear war. Our challenge is to find ways—without illusions—to manage our conflicts and thus ensure our mutual survival.

Notes

1. Richard Pipes, "Militarism and the Soviet State," in Pipes, *U.S.-Soviet Relations in the Era of Détente* (Boulder, Colo.: Westview Press, 1981), pp. 196–200.

2. Edward N. Luttwak, *The Grand Strategy of the Soviet Union* (New York: St. Martin's Press, 1983), p. 13.

3. Ibid., pp. 16–17.

4. I borrowed the phrase *security of the regime* from Takayuki Ito, "Tenkanki no To-O Anzen Hosho Shisutemu" [The East European Security System in the Period of Transition], *Kokusaimondai*, No. 303 (June 1985), pp. 32–34.

5. Pipes, "Soviet Global Strategy," in *U.S.-Soviet Relations*, pp. 171–193.

6. Ibid., p. 175.

7. See Yonosuke Nagai, *Gendai no senryaku* [Contemporary Strategy] (Tokyo: Bungeishunjusa, 1985), pp. 289–294.

8. E. H. Carr, *The Bolshevik Revolution*, Vol. 1 (London: Macmillan, 1960), p. 199.

9. Ibid., p. 211.

10. Regarding Bukharin's attempts to reconstruct a new theory, see Stephen F. Cohen, *Bukharin and the Bolshevik Revolution: A Political Biography, 1888–1934* (New York: Random House, 1973).

11. Alec Nove, *An Economic History of the USSR* (London: Allen Lane, 1969), p. 188.

12. Julian Cooper, "Defense Production and the Soviet Economy, 1929–1941," CRESS Discussion Paper, No. 3 (1976).

13. Seweryn Bialer, *Stalin's Successors: Leadership, Stability, and Change in the Soviet Union* (Cambridge: Cambridge University Press, 1980), p. 22.

14. Pipes, "Soviet Global Strategy," p. 172.

15. Ibid., pp. 172–173.

16. Luttwak, *The Grand Strategy of the Soviet Union,* p. 63.

17. Seweryn Bialer, "Soviet Foreign Policy: Sources, Perceptions, Trends," in Seweryn Bialer, ed., *The Domestic Context of Soviet Foreign Policy* (Boulder, Colo.: Westview Press, 1981), p. 424.

18. Luttwak, *The Grand Strategy of the Soviet Union,* pp. 45–47.

19. See, for instance, Andrew Cockburn, *The Threat: Inside the Soviet Military Machine* (New York: Random House, 1983); Eiichi Shindo, "'Bocho shugi' ron no nakano soren gaiko—ideorogi, gunjiryoku, senryaku [Soviet Diplomacy in the Theory of "Expansionism"—Ideology, Military Power, and Strategy], *Sekai* (April 1985).

20. See Tsuyoshi Hasegawa, "Soren ni okeru heiki-chotatsukatei no seijigaku [Politics in the Weapons Procurement Process in the Soviet Union], in *Kokusai seiji* (January 1986).

21. Luttwak, *The Grand Strategy of the Soviet Union,* p. 82.

22. See Richard Pipes, "Why the Soviet Union Thinks It Can Fight and Win a Nuclear War," *Commentary* (July 1977); also in Pipes, *U.S.-Soviet Relations,* pp. 135–170. See also Benjamin Lambeth, "How to Think About Soviet Military Doctrine," Rand Corporation Paper, P-5939 (February 1978).

23. Harriet Fast Scott and William F. Scott, *The Armed Forces of the USSR* (Boulder, Colo.: Westview Press, rev. ed., 1984), Ch. 2; Stephen M. Meyer, "Soviet Theatre Nuclear Forces: Part I: Development of Doctrine and Objectives," *Adelphi Papers,* No. 187, pp. 3–34.

24. Raymond L. Garthoff, "Mutual Deterrence and Strategic Arms and Limitation in Soviet Policy," *International Security,* Vol. 3, No. 1 (Summer 1978).

25. David Holloway, "Military Power and Political Purpose in Soviet Policy," *Daedalus* (Fall 1980), p. 22.

26. Both statements were quoted in Holloway, "Military Power," p. 30.

27. *Pravda* (February 24, 1981).

28. Holloway, "Military Power," p. 22.

29. *Sovestskaia Voennaia Entsiklopediia,* Vol. 2 (Moscow: Voenizdat, 1976), p. 253; ibid., Vol. 7 (1979), p. 564.

30. N. D. Ogarkov, *Vsegda v gotovnost' k zaschite otechestva* (Moscow: Voenizdat, 1982), p. 58.

31. Dan L. Strode and Rebecca V. Strode, "Diplomacy and Defense in Soviet National Security Policy," *International Security,* Vol. 8, No. 2 (Fall 1983).

32. Holloway, "Military Power," pp. 19, 23–24, 28; David Holloway, *The Soviet Union and the Arms Race* (New Haven and London: Yale University Press, 1983), pp. 29–31, 48–55.

33. *Krasnaia zvezda* (May 9, 1984).

34. Cynthia Roberts, "Soviet Military Policy in Transition," *Contemporary History* (October 1984), pp. 332–333.

35. Holloway, "Military Policy," p. 28.

10

The U.S.-Soviet Rivalry in East Asia

Donald S. Zagoria

Although Europe remains the critical region of superpower rivalry and the Middle East the most dangerous, it can be plausibly argued, as John Erickson does, that "the Soviet leadership sees the strategic center of gravity moving slowly but inexorably in the direction of East Asia, the source of a potentially critical challenge to Soviet power and prestige."[1]

Indeed, in the late 1980s and 1990s, Moscow faces the prospect of a fundamental shift in the Asian balance of power through growing Sino-American military cooperation; significant Japanese rearmament; the probability of a successfully modernizing China, which will remain a permanent adversary; and a more assertive United States at the head of an informal security coalition including China, Japan, South Korea, the ASEAN countries, and ANZUS.

In no other region of the world is there such a gap between Soviet military power and Soviet political influence. Moreover, the longer-range trends are against the Russians. By the year 2000, Japan is likely to be the second greatest industrial power in the world, China may have a GNP of close to $1 trillion, and the emerging Pacific community of free market economies may be closer to reality.

The Russians clearly recognize these adverse trends. As recent Soviet commentaries have pointed out, Japan already has the fourth largest fleet in terms of tonnage and is eighth in overall military spending. It could quickly become a nuclear power.[2] Moreover, "any special relationship with the United States may prove to be illusory. . . . Tokyo is following its own program."[3] At the same time, the United States and Japan also have "far-reaching plans for South Korea," which is to become "the third member of a Far Eastern NATO."[4]

Even more alarming for the Soviet Union is the growing prospect of a Sino-Japanese entente, a phenomenon that, as Erickson points out, is "fraught with serious strategic consequences" and brings "added defense problems in northeast Asia as well as along the inner Asian frontier lines."[5] According to *Red Star,* which commented on the recent visit to China by the deputy chief of the Japan Defense Agency, China seems to have an "active approach" to the expansion of military ties between the two countries as well as a "positive approach" to the U.S.-Japanese security treaty. Nor is China complaining about the growing U.S. military presence in Asia or the buildup of Japanese military potential.[6]

At the same time, as the Soviets have also noted, Chinese military relations with the United States are intensifying. U.S. Defense Secretary Weinberger, former Chief of Staff Vessey, and all the U.S. service chiefs have visited China in the past two or three years; the Chinese minister of defense has visited Washington; and U.S. naval ships have made a port call to Qingdao in what was the first U.S. naval visit to a Chinese port since 1949.

What makes these trends in Sino-American and Sino-Japanese relations even more alarming for the Russians is the fact that Sino-Soviet relations, although they have improved in the economic and cultural arenas, remain deadlocked on the basic security issues—Afghanistan, Cambodia, and the Soviet forces along the Chinese border. One of Moscow's shrewdest political observers, Alexander Bovin, recently conceded that "internally [the Chinese] are not yet ready to develop better relations with the USSR on so broad a basis. The causes of this may be varied, but the fact itself is indisputable."[7] Bovin went on to complain that Beijing "supports the American policy of militarizing Japan" and also favors the deployment of new U.S. weapons in Western Europe. He concluded that Sino-Soviet relations were "full of contradictions."

But if the Soviets understand the nature of their Pacific dilemma, there are as yet few signs that they understand their own role in helping to bring it about. They continue to increase their own formidable military power in the region; they show no signs of substantially thinning out their forces on the Chinese border or of returning the disputed northern territories to Japan; they remain determined to impose a communist government in Afghanistan; and they continue to support Vietnam's occupation of Cambodia.

Under these circumstances, it would be naive to expect that there can be any substantial accommodation between the Soviet Union and the United States in Asia. On the contrary, the United States is presently engaged in building up its own military power in the region. The U.S. Seventh Fleet is being equipped with Tomahawk cruise missiles, some of them nuclear-capable; the Carl Vinson, a nuclear-powered attack carrier, and the New Jersey, a battleship retrofitted with cruise missiles, have been added to the U.S. Pacific Fleet; two additional squadrons of F-16s are being based on Japanese territory; and a second battleship group, led by the *U.S.S. Missouri,* will greatly increase U.S. surface strength.

The Soviets will have to contend with the Japanese fleet as well. The Japanese navy, although it needs to be modernized, is the fourth largest and "one of the best maintained and trained fleets in the world."[8] Some 80 percent of that fleet is operational at all times. In view of the much lower estimated operation rate of the Soviet Pacific Fleet, the addition of the Japanese fleet to the U.S. Seventh Fleet is not at all insignificant.

But if the Soviets have their problems in the Pacific, the Western position is far from secure. The continuing growth of Soviet military power, the growing economic "cold war" between the United States and Japan, the insurgency in the Philippines, the unpredictability of North Korea and the potential instability in South Korea, the uncertainty about China's policies after Deng Xiaoping—all of these challenges and many others will have to be surmounted.

In this chapter, I will first offer some general observations on the serious internal and external problems facing the Soviets in the coming years. If I am right about the gravity of these problems, they are bound to condition Soviet foreign policy in the years ahead, both in Asia and elsewhere. I will then examine the superpower rivalry in Asia in some detail, with particular emphasis on the "weak links" in the Western position in Asia. Finally, I will conclude with some observations on how to cope with Soviet power in Asia, including some thoughts on possibilities for reducing regional tensions.

The Global Setting

The late 1980s and 1990s are not likely to be a promising decade for the Soviet Union in its drive to become an effective challenger to the United States in the global arena. First, the trends in the strategic competition are becoming increasingly unfavorable for Moscow. A series of U.S. strategic modernization programs—the MX, the "Midgetman," the new, more accurate Trident submarine-launched ballistic missiles, the revived B-1 bomber, the advanced-technology (Stealth) bomber, and Pershing II, as well as ground-, sea-, and air-launched cruise missiles, will soon enhance the U.S. nuclear arsenal. These systems will increasingly endanger the large, land-based Soviet ICBM force, which is the very cornerstone of Soviet strategic nuclear power. Moreover, "superior U.S. technology in such areas as sensors, computers, computer programming, signal processing and exotic kill mechanisms being harnessed in connection with President Reagan's Strategic Defense Initiative is bound to increase Soviet anxiety about the possible shape of the strategic balance in the years ahead."[9]

Second, the Soviet Union faces severe economic and social stagnation at home. Some Soviet intellectuals have been warning that, if present trends are not soon reversed, the "Polish disease"—disaffection within the working class—could spread to the Soviet Union.[10] The new Soviet leader, Mikhail Gorbachev, has implied that the Soviet Union, unless it improves its technology and economic productivity, may not be able to maintain its present strategic position in competition with the West. In a brutally frank report delivered on December 10, 1984, three months before he became general secretary of the Soviet Communist party, Gorbachev attributed the "slowdown of growth in the late 1970s and early 1980s" to the "stagnant retention" of "outmoded production relations." He warned that the ills of the system were of "truly tremendous scale" and that it would be a "titanic task" in terms of innovation and complexity to deal with them. At stake, he concluded, was nothing less than the need to make sure that the Soviet Union could "enter the new millennium worthily, as a great and flourishing power." And, in an unusually candid admission, he conceded that because of Soviet economic failures, the West was winning not only the economic and technological race but the ideological competition as well.[11]

On June 11, 1985, Gorbachev continued his dire warning. He said that "urgent measures" were required to improve the economy because he could not cut social programs or reduce defense expenditures in the face of the "imperialist threat." He may yet be forced to do one or the other.

Declining trends in the strategic competition and severe economic difficulties at home are not Gorbachev's only problems. The Soviet Union is still bogged down in Afghanistan, and it faces a possible insurrection in Poland. Elsewhere in Eastern Europe, its economically hard-pressed satellites want greater independence and increased trade with the West. Some of them want to experiment with Chinese and Hungarian-type economic reforms. A harshly worded *Pravda* article reacted to all of this by warning the Soviets of the dangers of "revisionism" and even of "Russophobia."[12]

In the Far East, the Soviet Union is increasingly "odd man out." In Europe, despite clumsy Soviet efforts to split NATO and to prevent the deployment of the Pershing IIs and cruise missiles, the Western alliance is still firmly intact and the missile deployment has proceeded on schedule. In the Gulf area, Iran's revolutionary regime has greatly increased its trade with Pakistan and Turkey, two U.S. allies, and continues to broadcast revolutionary Islamic propaganda to Moscow's predominantly Muslim southern republics. The other major power in the Gulf, Iraq, has been establishing closer economic relations with the West.

More broadly in the Third World, Moscow faces armed insurgents in almost all of its desperately poor client states; there is almost universal condemnation of the Soviets for their policies in Afghanistan and Cambodia; and many less-developed countries have increasingly come to recognize the limits of Soviet economic assistance and are looking more and more to the West for aid, credits, technology, and know-how.

In the meantime, the U.S. economy continues to recover, and President Reagan has launched the most sustained U.S. military buildup in postwar history.

None of this means that Gorbachev is going to opt out of the international competition with the United States. The Soviets continue to add to their already huge military arsenal, and Gorbachev will almost certainly try to exploit differences within the Western alliance and to improve relations with China. The Soviet media continue to stress Western Europe's adherence to the spirit of détente and the opportunities this presents for Soviet diplomacy. But the problems Gorbachev faces are formidable and deep-rooted; they cannot be solved quickly. It could take a decade or more just to begin a turnaround in the ailing Soviet economy, particularly as Gorbachev seems to have ruled out Chinese or Hungarian-type market reforms as too risky. Consolidation of the fragile Soviet empire in an era of economic austerity will be an equally long-term and uncertain process. All of this means that Gorbachev will need a long period of calm in relations with the United States while he concentrates on internal and imperial problems.

The need for "breathing space" is precisely what new Soviet Foreign Minister Edward Shevardnadze hinted at in a speech to the Helsinki Conference in July 1985. In an unusual linkage between Moscow's internal and foreign policy, Shevardnadze said that "the foreign policy of any state is inseparably linked to its internal affairs" and that, in order to implement its vast internal plans to improve the economy, "the Soviet Union needs a durable peace. . . ."

But for the purposes of this chapter, the more important point is that the Soviet Union is now entering a period when, for its own reasons, it requires a period of calm in relations with the West. In such a mood, it does not want to stir up tension with the United States in Asia or in any other region. This is not a guarantee of peace and stability in Asia. But it is an encouraging element in the overall picture and one that could be exploited by an alert adversary to help reduce tensions.

The Soviet Stake in Asia

Although Europe remains the region of key concern to the Soviet Union, it has vital security interests at stake in East Asia. Geography, geopolitics, and economics all ensure the enormity of this stake.

Geographically speaking, the Soviet Union, though generally regarded as a European power, is actually the second largest Asian power (next to China). One-third of its vast territory lies east of Irkutsk in East Asian Siberia. Moreover, large stretches of Soviet Siberia border on China and Mongolia; the Soviet Pacific coastline is close to Japan, Korea, and China; and, as a result of the Russian conquest of much of Central Asia in the nineteenth century, 50 million people, or some 20 percent of the Soviet population, are Asians.[13]

Geopolitics is another critical factor in shaping Soviet policy in East Asia. The Soviet Union's presence in the region and its status as a world power are inseparable from Moscow's global strategic competition with the United States. Yet the United States, by dint of its naval and air power, its bases, its alliance system, and its economic and cultural influence, remains the strongest power in the Pacific.

The Soviets are determined to weaken that U.S. alliance system, to contain China while improving relations with it, and to project their own power and influence in this important region. Moscow's acquisition of new bases in Vietnam in the late 1970s represented an important strategic gain; it was perhaps the most significant strategic change in the Pacific during the past decade. These new naval and air bases will enable the Russians to project their power more readily into the Gulf area and the Indian Ocean.

A third factor shaping Soviet policy in the Asia-Pacific region is economic in nature. In the remaining decades of the twentieth century, and far into the twenty-first, Moscow will seek to develop Siberia, a region that contains a large proportion of potential Soviet wealth in the form of energy and precious metals. The development of these Siberian resources will become increasingly important toward the latter part of the 1980s, when the Soviet Union may be facing an energy crunch.

Finally, Soviet policy in Asia is shaped by certain fears and insecurities—some of them rooted in reality, others in paranoia; some inherited from the past, others rooted in recent developments.

1. There is the fear of having to fight on two fronts in the event of a general war. The Soviets still vividly remember World War II. If Japan had joined Germany and attacked Russia in 1941 instead of turning south against China and Southeast Asia and then against the United States at Pearl Harbor, the Soviet Union would almost certainly have

been defeated. As late as the battle of Stalingrad, the Russians kept large forces on the Siberian front to guard against such a danger.

2. There is the fear that one day a strong, huge, irredentist China may claim back the territories grabbed from a weak Manchu empire by Tsarist Russia in the middle of the nineteenth century. The Russians surely cannot forget what Mao Zedong told the Japanese Socialists in 1964 when he was sympathizing with their demands for a return of the Kuriles—that China had not yet presented *its* bill to the Soviets for *its* lost territories.

3. There is a sensitivity about the vast borderlands with China. Is a powerful China likely to be reconciled to the Soviet domination of Mongolia? The Kazakhstan/Sinkiang frontier will also remain sensitive because of minority races on both sides of the border.

4. There is the fear of a powerful Japan, already the third largest industrial power in the world and a country with which the Soviets have had an unpleasant history and an intractable territorial dispute.

5. There is concern about the geopolitical vulnerability of Siberia, a region that is sparsely populated and a long distance from European Russia, with long, overland lines of communication that are vulnerable to interdiction.

6. And, finally, there is uncertainty about the loyalty of some 40 million Muslims in Soviet Central Asia at a time when an Islamic awakening is occurring on Russia's southern border.

An Asian Overview

By and large, Soviet policy in East Asia has been a spectacular failure. The reasons for this failure are varied. Some have to do with the success of U.S. policies; others with the heavy-handedness of Soviet diplomacy; and still others with the extraordinary economic dynamism of the region itself. But a brief overview of the region will demonstrate that the basic trends (with some notable exceptions to be discussed later) are extremely encouraging for the West and quite unfavorable for the Soviet Union.

1. The Asia-Pacific region is one of extraordinary economic dynamism. The Pacific economies have displayed the greatest resilience and the highest rates of growth in the world. The economic output of the Pacific region as a whole now equals more than two-thirds of total U.S. GNP. U.S. trade with East Asia, which only a decade ago was $42 billion, rose to $170 billion in 1984 and accounts for almost 30 percent of total world trade. U.S. direct investment in the Pacific is now conservatively estimated at more than $30 billion.

2. Not unrelated to its economic dynamism, the Asia-Pacific region with the notable exception of Cambodia, is basically at peace. Peace

and prosperity are interrelated. Without peace, the region would not have enjoyed such economic prosperity. Without economic prosperity, the region would almost certainly have been more unstable.

3. Despite serious trade frictions, the U.S.-Japan strategic alliance remains strong. Under Prime Minister Nakasone, Japan has moved from being a passive ally to being an active one. There are joint planning, joint basing, and joint training exercises. Japan has agreed to participate in research on the Strategic Defense Initiative. It is expanding aid to key countries throughout the world, some of which (e.g., Turkey, Egypt, and Pakistan) are threatened with instability—not just traditional Japanese trading partners. Japan is taking responsibility for the defense of its sea-lanes. And public opinion in Japan is becoming increasingly favorable to the U.S. alliance. Even the Japanese Socialist party, the largest opposition party, is trying to break away from its earlier position of "unarmed neutrality."

4. Since 1978 China has been embarking on a historically significant reform and modernization program comparable to Japan's Meiji Restoration in the nineteenth century. If it continues to be as successful over the next fifteen years as it has been in the last seven, China, by the early twenty-first century, will have a GNP approximatley equal to that of the Soviet Union today. Moreover, China's experiment with market reforms is bound to have an enormous impact on the Third World, on Eastern Europe, and on the Soviet Union. It has already had an impact on North Korea, which has recently instituted a new tax program designed to attract foreign investment. So long as China is absorbed with domestic modernization, it will have a continuing stake in Asia's peace and stability, and in expanding its economic and other cooperative ties with the West—even as it simultaneously seeks to reduce tensions with the Soviet Union. In foreign policy, China now shares with the West an interest in containing Soviet power, in a strong U.S.-Japan alliance, in improving relations with South Korea while restraining North Korea, in forcing Vietnam out of Cambodia while improving relations with ASEAN, in removing the Soviet Union from Afghanistan while shoring up Pakistan. Over the long run, although China will certainly not be anyone's "card," it will remain—for reasons of geography, history, and national interest—a massive barrier to the spread of Soviet power in the Pacific and a deterrent to Soviet adventurism elsewhere.

5. Yet another piece of good news is the developing dialogue between North and South Korea. The North is even suggesting a summit meeting. All of this portends a significant change in North Korean policy that is attributable partly to economic difficulties at home, partly to China's encouragement, and partly to the vitality of South Korea, which now has a GNP more than four or five times that of North Korea.

6. In Southeast Asia, since the fall of Saigon ten years ago, the dominos have not so much fallen as banded together in a unified ASEAN, one of the world's most successful regional organizations.

7. More broadly speaking, communism as an ideology and a moral force—as a model for development—has, with the single exception of the Philippines, lost much of its appeal. China's open questioning of Marxism, the enormous successes of free market systems, and the economic weaknesses of communist countries from the Soviet Union to Vietnam and North Korea, have put communism on the historical defensive.

8. Also, despite its substantial military buildup in the Pacific, the Soviet Union has failed to convert its military power into political advantage and, in fact, is unlikely to do so in the future. Indeed, it is pursuing counterproductive policies in the Asia-Pacific region and will find it difficult to retreat from these policies. I have in mind the Soviet invasion of Afghanistan and the indications that the Soviets will remain; the Soviet-supported Vietnamese invasion of Cambodia; the Soviet military buildup on the northern islands, which are being disputed with Japan; the enormous Soviet buildup on the Chinese border, including its forces in Outer Mongolia; and the crude handling of Asian sensibilities. All of this has contributed to a new strategic consensus in the Asia-Pacific region that has been developing since 1978.

9. In the Pacific, as elsewhere, a substantial resurgence of U.S. military power has occurred in recent years.[14]

10. Then, too, in the Far East, as in no other region of the world, the East-East conflict is playing a major role in helping to maintain a favorable balance of power. In Asia today, with the sole exception of the Korean peninsula, which still remains divided along East-West lines, the most serious and bitter confrontations are those between contiguous communist states: Russia against China, China against Vietnam, and Vietnam against the communist insurgents supported by China in Cambodia. All of the Asian communist states are finding that their most active and dangerous adversaries are not faraway Western powers but neighboring communist states with which they share disputed and heavily armed borders and a historical record of conflict going back several centuries—a record undiminished by a supposedly common ideology. These East-East conflicts are likely to last. They are deeply rooted in history and geography. The divisions among the communist states contribute to a new balance of power in East Asia that is more favorable to the West than anyone could have imagined ten or fifteen years ago.

11. Finally, and not least important, there is growing in the West a recognition of the strategic interdependence of Europe, Asia, and the

United States. The Soviet deployment of medium-range ballistic missiles—the SS-20s—has highlighted this interdependence. Japan and China have manifested a clear interest in preventing any redeployment of the SS-20s from Europe to Asia. The West has an equally clear stake in ensuring that any Soviet-Chinese détente does not lead to a transfer of Soviet forces from the Siberian border to Europe.

In sum, for the West, the situation in the Asia-Pacific region is extremely encouraging. The region is prosperous and generally peaceful, relatively stable and basically pro-Western. The overall balance of power in the region favors the West. But for the Soviet Union, the region must look quite disturbing.

Moscow's Future Prospects

This generally favorable situation for the West in Asia could change. But if adverse changes were to take place, they would more likely come about not as a result of Soviet actions but through bad management of the Western alliance, political or economic instability in key countries, and so on. Before examining some of these possibilities, we must briefly review the relations of the Soviet Union with the various countries in the region. Such a review will expose Moscow's weak political position.

Despite recent improvements in Sino-Soviet relations, the Soviets remain well aware that China is a long-range adversary. The clash between Russia and China is an old-fashioned contest between two huge land empires with potentially unstable buffer zones lying across their long common frontiers. As a Eurasian empire, the USSR has a special concern about China because it has not been able to fully assimilate its own Central Asian peoples. The long-range "China threat" is made even more serious in Soviet eyes by the U.S. strategy of trying to tie down Soviet power in Asia in order to weaken Soviet capabilities elsewhere.[15]

Moreover, there are conflicting geopolitical interests between the Soviet Union and China in Mongolia, Indochina, and southern Asia; there is an unresolved border conflict; there are deep-seated mutual suspicions and fears on both sides; and, eventually, China will modernize its armed forces, particularly its nuclear forces. It will then pose a real threat to Soviet security.

To be sure, a tactical détente is now in effect, and it will probably continue. It will remain in the interests of both countries so long as both need to concentrate on internal economic problems. But this détente will almost certainly be limited. Over the long run, the Soviet Union knows that a more powerful China will be a more dangerous China.

In assessing the future prospects for Sino-Soviet relations, we will find it useful to divide the obstacles to normalization into two sets of problems. First, there are the intractable geopolitical issues. Second, there are the bilateral issues, which are somewhat more susceptible to compromise because they do not involve third parties.

China's geopolitical demands on the Soviet Union are well known. The Chinese insist that the Soviets must pressure the Vietnamese to pull their troops out of Cambodia, that they themselves must pull out of Afghanistan, and that they must remove their forces from Outer Mongolia. It is quite unlikely that there will be substantial progress on any of these particular demands in the foreseeable future. The Soviets do not have the leverage necessary to force Vietnam out of Cambodia, and they are unlikely to exercise great pressure. The Soviet acquisition of naval and air bases in Vietnam has greatly increased Soviet power projection throughout the Western Pacific, and Moscow is not likely to risk the loss of those bases for what is yet a will of the wisp in Beijing. A unilateral Soviet withdrawal from Afghanistan would, under the present circumstances, lead to the collapse of Moscow's client government in Kabul and to its replacement by an anticommunist and anti-Soviet government. A negotiated withdrawal still seems very unlikely despite the recent flurry of talks at the United Nations and elsewhere. And, although the Soviets have made some reductions in the forces in Outer Mongolia, they will not withdraw from that region, as it constitutes a buffer country of great strategic importance and one to which the Chinese have laid claim in the past.

In contrast to the issues involving "third countries," the bilateral issues between Moscow and Beijing are theoretically more susceptible to compromise. The most critical of these issues—and the one that has proven difficult to resolve in more than a decade of negotiations—is the border dispute and the related presence of large numbers of Soviet troops in forward positions along the border. Throughout the past decade or more, the Chinese have insisted that the Soviets withdraw their troops from "disputed areas" of the border as a precondition to resolving the border conflict. They have also insisted that the Soviets formally acknowledge that the treaties signed between Tsarist Russia and the weak Manchu dynasty in the nineteenth century were "unequal treaties." The Soviets, on the other hand, have refused to concede that there are any "disputed areas," and they insist that the Chinese recognize the legality of the nineteenth-century treaties.

Given the political will in both countries, it is not difficult to imagine a number of compromises that could resolve the issue. The Soviets could unilaterally pull back some of their troops from the border as a gesture of goodwill. The Chinese could drop their unrealistic demands on the

Russians to recognize that the nineteenth-century treaties were "unequal"—demands that seemed largely intended for psychological warfare purposes in any case. Such concessions could be followed by a thinning out of forces on both sides of the border and the signing of a variety of "confidence-building measures." These measures could set the stage for a breakthrough on the border conflict, and, ultimately, the Soviets and the Chinese could sign some type of nonaggression pact or "friendship treaty" similar to what the Soviets have been offering Beijing in recent years.

But the obstacles to progress on these issues are substantial. First, the troop deployments along the border are such that the Soviets, who are forward deployed, would have to do most of the withdrawing. It must be assumed that conservative leaders in the Politburo, who are strongly supported by the military, will oppose such a move. The trans-Siberian railroad runs very close to the Chinese border, and it will be argued that Soviet troops need to be forward deployed in order to protect that vulnerable railroad. It will also be argued that unilateral Soviet pullbacks from the border will be interpreted by the Chinese as a sign of weakness. Even more important, it will be impossible for the Soviets to dismantle the huge military infrastructure they have built on the border—depots, airfields, underground silos, barracks, and so on. And it will be impossible for Moscow to pull back from some of the disputed areas—particularly the one located on the very environs of Khabarovak. Then, too, the strategic importance of Siberia is bound to grow in the years ahead as the Soviet Union seeks to develop its vast natural resources and to build up its labor force. This will be an argument not for reducing but for strengthening Soviet forces in Siberia.

In addition, there will be strong arguments for modernizing and strengthening the Soviet forces opposite China as a result of the planned increases in the U.S. Navy, the closer security cooperation between the United States and Japan, the increases in Japan's defense spending, and the still-present threat of a U.S.-Chinese-Japanese "united front" against the Soviet Union.

Thus, in a country where "worst-case" scenarios are common, where a belief in large, if not excessive, amounts of military power is deeply rooted in the national history and national psychology, where a new leader is heavily dependent on the marshals for consolidating his power base, it seems unlikely that significant Soviet concessions to China will be made on the question of Soviet forces in Siberia.

On the Chinese side, there are equally important constraints on flexibility. Why should the Chinese drop their insistence on a significant Soviet pullback from the border? Tensions along the border have already been reduced. What more could the Chinese realistically hope to gain?

And even if progress could be made toward "confidence-building measures" and a "nonaggression pact," would this really be in China's interest at this time? Success in such negotiations would run the risk of profoundly disturbing China's newly acquired "friends" in the United States, Europe, and Japan, many of whom would point to any Sino-Soviet "deal" on the border as an indication that China could not be trusted as a long-term opponent of Soviet expansionism. As a result, China's access to Western technology could be jeopardized at a time when the Reagan administration has lifted some restrictions on such technology transfers to Beijing.

To sum up, a modest improvement in Sino-Soviet relations limited to increases in trade and exchanges and to reductions in tensions is not going to alter certain key facts in the strategic triangle.

1. The Soviet Union and the People's Republic of China will remain potential enemies, and China will have less to fear and more to gain from a United States that is hostile to the Soviet Union than from the Soviet Union itself.
2. The Soviet Union will continue to maintain one-quarter of its army and one-quarter of its nuclear forces opposite China.
3. China will seek to maneuver within the strategic triangle in order to improve its position in it. But the Chinese will not be able to afford "equidistance" between the superpowers. On the crucial matters affecting the overall strategic balance, China will "tilt" toward the United States.

Japan, too, is almost certain to be a long-range Soviet adversary. Despite recent Soviet efforts to woo Japan, relations between the two countries are at one of their lowest points in the entire postwar period.

A number of reasons can account for this. First, there is an enormous suspicion of the Soviet Union in Japan, a suspicion nourished by the nineteenth-century rivalry over Korea and Manchuria, the Russo-Japanese War of 1904, fighting on the Manchurian-Mongolian border in the 1930s, and the entry of the Soviet Union into Manchuria and Korea during the last days of World War II, when the Russians captured tens of thousands of Japanese soldiers and confined many of them to prison camps. Quite recently, one of Japan's best sellers was a book entitled *Why Do We Hate Russians?*

Second, Japanese trade with the Soviet Union has declined substantially in recent years and is unlikely to increase much in the future. Japanese businessmen and the Japanese government are losing interest in Siberian development as a result of the energy glut and easier access to other sources of oil in China, Canada, Indonesia, and elsewhere. Japanese trade with China has been expanding much more rapidly than trade with the Soviet Union, and this pattern is likely to continue.

Third, the territorial dispute between the two countries will be extraordinarily difficult either to resolve or to put aside. No elected Japanese prime minister could make concessions on the issue. Even the Japanese Communist party (JCP) wants the four Kurile Islands back; indeed, the JCP claims Sakhalin as well. This is a good barometer of Japanese public opinion on the issue.

But the Soviets are equally intransigent. Despite repeated Western speculation, no Soviet government is likely to make any concessions on the islands. There are a variety of reasons for Soviet intransigence. The Soviets have a territorial "domino complex"—a fear that returning the territory acquired from Japan after World War II would stimulate the claims of other nations whose territory the Soviet Union also acquired at the same time. But the most important consideration from the Soviet point of view has to do with the strategic importance of the northern islands.

The disputed islands and the northern island of Japan, Hokkaido, command one of the key straits leading from the Sea of Japan to the Pacific. A hostile power in command of these straits could block the sea-lanes of communication between Vladivostok, Moscow's main naval base in the Pacific, and Petrapavlovsk, an important submarine base for the Soviet Pacific Fleet. During recent years, and especially since the late 1970s, the Soviets have been developing a Sea of Okhotsk–Sea of Japan–Maritime Province complex that could be used as an "ocean bastion" in which the Soviets could submerge their strategic submarines without having to worry about their being tracked by the U.S. Seventh Fleet. The disputed northern islands have become an important link in this complex.

A dramatic breakthrough for the Soviets on the Korean peninsula seems equally implausible. The visit by Kim Il-Sung to Moscow in May 1984, his first in seventeen years, produced a new warming trend in Soviet–North Korean relations. Diplomatic contact has increased; and the Soviets have begun to sell MIG-23s to Pyongyang, a break with their past policy of withholding modern aircraft from North Korea. In return, the Russians have been given overflight rights over North Korean territory, and port calls have been made by Soviet warships to North Korean ports. Still, suspicions between the two countries run deep.

The Soviets can hardly view Kim as a satisfactory vehicle for expanding their own influence on the Korean peninsula. To begin with, North Korea under Kim during the past three decades has generally been much closer to China than to the Soviet Union. Second, Kim has, at least until quite recently, opposed Soviet policy in Afghanistan and Cambodia.

He continues to provide a residence in Pyongyang for Prince Norodom Sihanouk, the nominal leader of the anti-Vietnamese resistance in Cambodia and a man routinely described by the Soviet media as a "hireling of the imperialists." Third, Kim has in the past publicly accused the Soviet Union of "dominationism" and of efforts to exploit the North Korean economy. Fourth, during the past several decades, Kim has developed into something of a state religion in his philosophy of *chu'che* (self-reliance), and although he has not been able to live up to this philosophy to the extent that he has preached it, it does symbolize his determination not to become dependent on the Soviets. Moreover, despite what have probably been considerable Soviet pressures for North Korea to provide the Soviet Union with military facilities and to join COMECON, the Soviet-sponsored Council for Mutual Economic Assistance, Kim has thus far resisted such pressure. Finally, Kim is a "hot potato" who has frequently involved the Soviets in unwanted confrontations with the United States.

Kim is equally suspicious of Moscow. His distrust of the Soviets stems from a number of deeply rooted considerations. First, he does not need to be reminded how close the Soviets came to incorporating North Korea into the Soviet Union during the period from 1945 to 1950. Kim knows only too well how the Soviets use their military and economic advisers, their troops, and their KGB agents to infiltrate the governments they intend to dominate.

Moreover, Kim has witnessed the fates of a number of the Soviet Union's neighbors from Eastern Europe to Outer Mongolia to Afghanistan. And he knows about the "Brezhnev Doctrine" by which the Soviets have arrogated to themselves the right to intervene in the internal affairs of any "socialist state" that defies Moscow. For such reasons alone, he would tend to keep his distance from the Soviet Union.

Second, Kim saw for himself during the Korean War that the Soviet Union would not risk war with the United States in order to salvage North Korea. Even at a time when U.S. troops were marching toward North Korea's Tumen River border with the Soviet Union, the Soviets gave no indication that they were prepared to intervene in the war. It was only the Chinese intervention that saved Kim Il-Sung's regime from being toppled by the Americans.

South Korea is tied to the United States, and it is likely to remain so as long as Korea is divided and surrounded by two giant communist states. Taiwan continues to be economically dependent on the United States and is extremely unlikely to make any moves toward warming relations with Moscow.

In Southeast Asia, the ASEAN countries—the Philippines, Indonesia, Singapore, Thailand, Malaysia, and Brunei—are all quasi-authoritarian, capitalist, anticommunist states, and so the Soviets start with a great handicap there. Any kind of communism is regarded by those governments with suspicion—for internal security reasons if for no other. Furthermore, the Vietnamese invasion of Cambodia has greatly alarmed all of the noncommunist states of Southeast Asia—particularly ASEAN's "hardline" states, Thailand and Singapore. Thailand, because it has now lost its Cambodian buffer to its traditional Vietnamese enemy, is determined to get the Vietnamese out of Cambodia. Because Thailand shares this interest with Beijing, it has moved perceptibly closer to the Chinese. This "pro-Chinese" position on the part of Thailand worries some of the other ASEAN members, but as Thailand is the "front-line" state, and as ASEAN prizes unity above all else, the Thais in effect hold a veto over ASEAN strategy on the Cambodian problem. And the Thais will almost certainly continue to oppose the Vietnamese occupation by subsidizing and supporting the resistance inside Cambodia.

Moreover, the Soviet invasion of Afghanistan greatly stiffened ASEAN; at recent meetings of the UN and other international groupings, a successful ASEAN strategy has been to link the Soviet invasion of Afghanistan with the Vietnamese invasion of Cambodia. As a result, the ASEAN countries have developed a community of interests with many of the Islamic countries, which in turn has led to a considerable weakening of Soviet influence in the "nonaligned" movement.

For the Soviets, the one big bright spot in the Pacific is their alliance with Vietnam and Vietnam's two client states, Laos and Cambodia. But we cannot assume that this Soviet-Vietnamese alliance is easy on either partner. There are many signs of strain. The Vietnamese are proud nationalists; they fought a thirty-year war against the French and the Americans, and they are not likely to surrender their independence to the Soviets.

Challenges for the West

Although the basic outlook for the West in the Pacific is extremely positive, a number of serious problems and challenges remain. Some of these problems are related to Soviet policies, but others—perhaps the most important ones—are not. I want to discuss some of the more serious potential challenges to Western interests in the Pacific.

1. Although the United States maintains naval and air superiority over the Soviet Union in the Pacific, the margin of this superiority has been decreasing. In the fifteen years or so prior to 1980, the tonnage of the Soviet Pacific Fleet more than doubled while that of the U.S. Seventh Fleet was reduced by one-third. The Soviet submarine force is the largest in the world, and the Soviets are currently producing or

testing seven different classes of submarines. The trend in major surface warship programs has been toward larger, more technologically sophisticated ships. Substantial numbers of Backfire bombers now represent a considerable threat to the U.S. Seventh Fleet. At the same time, the Soviets, by deploying more than 100 SS-20 intermediate-range nuclear missiles in Siberia, pose a serious threat to the entire U.S. base structure in the region. In addition, the Soviets continue to maintain more than 50 troop divisions opposite China. The danger of this impressive Soviet military power in the Pacific is not so much that it is likely to be used in overt military activity. Opportunities for the use of Soviet forces in Asia will probably remain limited. Rather, growing Soviet military power could encourage the Soviets to use coercive diplomacy against their adversaries; it could also encourage a drift toward political neutralism in Asia.

2. There remains the possibility of a backlash against China's "open-door" policy that could lead to a substantial reorientation of Chinese domestic and foreign policy. The Chinese, though successful thus far in implementing their ambitious reforms, are running into major problems of inequality, inflation, corruption, and so on. Recent student riots in China triggered a major shakeup in the leadership, including the ouster of a key reformer, former Party Leader Hu Yao Bang. A future post-Deng leadership may seek to curtail ties with the West and to revert to a more traditional, Soviet-style centralized economic system. If this were to be accompanied by continuing U.S.-Chinese frictions over Taiwan and a more rapid improvement in Sino-Soviet relations, it could have an adverse effect on the overall balance of power in Asia.

3. North Korea is pursuing a double-track policy that is still fraught with uncertainty. On the one hand, it has entered into a dialogue with South Korea for the first time in a decade. On the other hand, it has purchased advanced fighter planes from the Soviet Union, deployed U.S.-made helicopters that were smuggled into the country, and increased its menacing forward deployment near the demilitarized zone.

4. South Korea enjoys a precarious stability. It remains to be seen whether power will be transferred peacefully in 1988 or whether there will be a new and familiar cycle of liberalization leading to unrest and crackdown.

5. Vietnam shows no sign of removing its 180,000 troops from Cambodia or of negotiating a political solution there that would be acceptable to China or ASEAN.

6. Antinuclear sentiment is rising in the South Pacific. A Labor government in New Zealand is committed to banning from its ports all nuclear-powered and nuclear-armed ships, thus imposing serious strains on ANZUS, one of our oldest alliances.

Finally, there are three "weak links" in the present pro-Western balance of power in the region that seem to me the most serious of all. They have to do with the U.S.-Japanese trade rivalry, the continuing instability in the Philippines, and the growing Soviet pressure on Pakistan. It is to these problems that I now wish to turn in somewhat more detail.

Perhaps the greatest single threat to the United States' position in the Asia-Pacific region is not the Soviet Union but the emerging economic cold war between the United States and Japan. A growing number of U.S., Japanese, and Asian leaders share a nightmare—that of the United States and Japan sinking into a bitter trade war, with the United States setting up walls to keep Japanese goods out while the Japanese, embittered, gradually push out of the U.S. orbit.[16]

In recent years U.S. trade deficits have reached unprecedented proportions, and projections indicate that further dramatic deteriorations are likely. These huge deficits have produced several ominous consequences: increased protectionist sentiment in the United States; the demands of powerful constituencies in the United States for greater "reciprocity" in U.S.-Japanese economic relations; and growing Japanese resentments over U.S. pressure to open and liberalize the Japanese economy.

Most alarming is the fact that many influential figures on both sides of the Pacific are escalating their rhetoric and putting most of the blame on the other side. Many Japanese are beginning to view the United States as a helpless giant, unable to compete economically and unable to pursue a clear course politically.

Many Americans, on the other hand, are focusing on the need to remove many of Japan's nontarriff barriers, such as the government's complex system for setting standards and certifying products that can be sold in the country.

Whatever the causes of the trade deficit, and they are obviously multiple, there is evidence of rising frustration in the United States. So far, leaders on both sides have prevented the trade difficulties from overflowing into the strategic arena and poisoning the U.S.-Japanese alliance. But unless the trade issue is resolved, such a danger will continue to exist.

The situation in the post-Marcos Philippines poses another serious problem for the United States. There is growing sentiment in the Philippines for a removal of the U.S. military bases at Subic Bay and Clark Field after 1991, when the existing base agreement expires. The loss of the Subic and Clark bases would be a big plus for the Soviet Union and an enormous blow to U.S. credibility, particularly if the

Soviet fleet remained in Cam Ranh Bay while the U.S. fleet was forced to retreat from Subic.

The building Soviet pressure on Pakistan represents a third serious challenge to Western interests in Asia. When Pakistani president General Mohammed Zia ul-Haq went to Moscow in March 1985 to attend Konstantin Chernenko's funeral, the new Soviet leadership bluntly warned him: Cut off Pakistani aid to Afghan insurgents or face a new Soviet campaign to goad the disgruntled Baluch minority into breaking away from the Pakistani state.[17] According to one informed analyst, Pakistan's military leadership has led the country into peril by sharply restricting internal political activity and by neglecting the grievances of ethnic minorities. "Together, internal divisions and external pressures are pushing Pakistan to the point at which other Third World countries, such as Cyprus, Lebanon and Pakistan itself in 1971, have fallen apart."[18]

Pakistan's ethnic problems stem largely from the continuing struggle of its three smaller provinces—Baluchistan, the North-West Frontier Province, and Sind—to resist the domination of the far more populous Punjab. The Sind has become a hotbed of separatist feeling since the execution of its favorite son, Zulfikar Ali Bhutto, in 1979. Violence erupted in the province's small towns and rural areas in late 1983, and reports suggest that much of the Sinhi countryside, the most economically depressed part of the country, continues to seethe with resentment. A radical populist movement, the Sindhi Awami Tehrik (Sindhi Peoples Movement), which blends peasant radicalism and Sindhi nationalism, has become extremely powerful.

Baluchistan has been remarkably passive in recent years; but according to one Baluch leader, the reason is that the Baluch are husbanding their resources and waiting for the external environment to become favorable for striking a deathblow to Pakistan.[19]

Three million heavily armed Afghan refugees have streamed into the North-West Frontier Province. The Pushtun people of the province sympathize with their displaced Afghan cousins, but the Pakistani Pushtuns resent the new competition they now face for grazing land and jobs. Moreover, some leading local politicians have demanded autonomy for the province and negotiations with Kabul to find a political solution to the Afghanistan problem.

In sum, although the overall picture in Asia is positive, the region faces a variety of problems and challenges. The United States certainly cannot take Asia for granted. The Soviet military buildup in the Pacific, political instability, and continuing Soviet opportunism pose a number of serious difficulties.

Coping with Soviet Power in the Pacific

The problem with coping with Soviet power in Asia can be discussed under four headings: the need to balance Soviet power; the importance of maintaining an effective security coalition; the importance of dealing with the "weak links"; and, finally, the desirability of some limited cooperation with the Soviet Union both to manage and prevent crises and to reduce tensions.

As already indicated, during the past decade or more, the Soviets have made impressive efforts to build up their military power in the Asia-Pacific region. Between 35 and 45 percent of Moscow's ICBM forces and ballistic-missile-firing submarines, as well as more than 30 percent of its strategic bombers, are now deployed east of the Urals. In the Far East, the Soviets have begun to deploy a substantial number of SS-20 intermediate-range nuclear missiles capable of covering the entire East Asian archipelago from positions in Siberia. The Soviets are modernizing and expanding their Pacific Fleet, which is now the largest of their four fleets. They have acquired significant support facilities for this fleet in South Yemen, Ethiopia, and Vietnam. Moreover, the Soviet Union has a large naval construction program under way that, according to *Jane's Fighting Ships,* will provide "formidable reinforcement." That program includes at least eight different classes of surface ships and seven different types of submarines. The Soviet submarine force is already the largest in the world. The Soviet naval aircraft program has kept pace with the ship-building program, and more than 100 Backfire bombers are now in service with Soviet Naval Aviation. In addition, about 325 long- and medium-range aircraft, some of which are now stationed in Vietnam, have been tasked for reconnaissance and ASW against U.S. Navy ships. The Soviet Union is also adding to the already large number of anti-ship cruise missiles deployed throughout the Soviet fleet.[20]

Whatever the intentions of this huge Soviet military buildup in the Pacific, the very fact of its existence poses severe challenges to the United States and its allies. As the head of a global maritime alliance, and as the world's largest trading nation, the United States has a vital interest in command of the Pacific. Its present strategy there is based on a forward deployment of ground and air forces and on a substantial naval presence. To carry out this forward strategy, maritime superiority is indispensable. Differences may exist among U.S. military strategists as to what kind of forward strategy and force projection capabilities best serve U.S. interests, but all schools accept the need for such naval superiority.[21]

Although the United States still maintains naval superiority in the Pacific, the margin of that superiority is declining. Both the quantity and quality of Soviet surface ships, submarines, and naval aviation are increasing. U.S. naval forces continue to be "stretched so thin that very little surge capability exists for rapid responses to additional crises."[22]

It has been estimated that approximately 80 percent of the U.S. sealift fleet would be needed to support a continuing military presence in the Gulf region.[23] Moreover, as Admiral Crowe said, "the Pacific and Indian Ocean basins present a different military challenge than any other theater because the vast distances influence everything we do and because our facilities and our allies are widely spread over islands and around the littoral."[24]

There is also the chronic problem of credibility. Although the Reagan administration's military buildup has gone a long way toward dispelling doubts among U.S. allies as to the reliability of the United States in the event of crisis, such doubts continue to exist. Recent polls among the Japanese indicate a basic lack of confidence that the United States would honor its commitments under the security treaty signed by the two countries in 1960. "Suspicions that the United States may be a muscle-bound giant set in during the hostage crisis in Iran five years ago, and they have not been dispelled by American immobility during more recent episodes."[25]

To meet the Soviet military challenge in the Pacific and elsewhere, the United States is engaged in a long-overdue effort to build a 600-ship navy that would include a level of 15 deployed aircraft carriers by 1990. The number of deployable naval vessels will reach 545 in 1985. These programs will have to be sustained in the face of rising criticism among the U.S. public of allegedly excessive defense spending. But this will not be an easy task in a nation where the public mood on defense is highly volatile.

It will also be important for Japan to continue the quantitative and qualitative improvements of its fleet and to sustain the higher level of cooperation with the U.S. fleet that has developed in recent years.

Finally, more thought needs to be given to the role in Pacific defense of other interested parties, including South Korea, Australia, the ASEAN states, France, Great Britain, and China. It is possible, for example, to imagine cooperative efforts between the United States and a number of Pacific countries on air defense, intelligence gathering, and so on. Japan could play a key role in guarding the exits from the Sea of Japan, thereby greatly complicating Soviet defense planning. So long as the Soviet Union continues to build up its military power in the Pacific at such an impressive rate, the need for greater efforts and greater burden sharing on the part of the Western alliance will remain.

Building and maintaining an effective coalition to contain Soviet power is the second challenge facing the United States in the Pacific.

At a time when relative U.S. economic and military power is declining, when Soviet military power is growing, and when nuclear stalemate reduces the credibility of extended deterrence, the United States needs the help of its allies more than ever before. "Indeed, the single greatest remaining U.S. strategic advantage over the USSR is that we are blessed with many rich allies while the Soviets have only a handful of poor ones. Most of theirs are a strain on the Soviet exchequer whereas most of ours pay their own way. They also fear their own forced allies while we fear *for* ours."[26]

The United States has to maintain the Pacific coalition in the face of substantial Soviet efforts to break it up and in spite of equally substantial divergences of interest among the members of this coalition. Soviet efforts to intimidate Japan will likely grow to the extent that Japan increases its security cooperation with the United States and adds to its own military forces. Efforts to intimidate may be coupled with efforts to woo. Similar tactics will be employed against China.

The United States will also be faced with the need to try to reconcile divergent perspectives and interests among its Pacific partners. The present conflict with New Zealand over port calls by U.S. nuclear warships is an example of the difficulties inherent in such a task. Dealing too harshly with New Zealand runs the risk of jeopardizing the ANZUS alliance. Dealing too leniently runs the risk of encouraging other U.S. allies in the region to follow in New Zealand's path.

Other contradictions abound. The United States requires Japanese naval assistance in keeping open the Pacific sea-lanes of communication. Yet other Asian allies are extremely wary of the Japanese. Similarly, the United States intends to help China defend itself against the Soviet Union, but other Asian countries are fearful that the United States may go too far in developing China's military power. It will be the continuing task of U.S. diplomacy to be sensitive to these differences and to prevent them from disrupting the security coalition.

Plugging the "weak links" in the U.S. position in the Pacific will also be difficult. There will be no easy or quick solutions to the U.S.-Japan trade competition, to the base problem in the Philippines, or to Soviet pressure on Pakistan. Nor can anyone be sure that China's new "open door" will remain as open in the post-Deng era as it has been during the past ten years. Dealing with these issues will require great skill and patience.

With regard to the U.S.-Japan trade issue, one can only hope that Japan's efforts to open domestic markets and the United States' efforts to lower the budgetary deficit, accompanied by continuing economic progress in both countries, will gradually defuse the present inflammatory situation. It is encouraging that, despite the trade issue, the overwhelming majority of Americans and Japanese continue to regard the other country as friendly. In a recent survey involving 1,569 adult Americans, 88 percent viewed relations with Japan as friendly, and 23 percent of those described them as *very* friendly. Similarly, a solid majority (73 percent) of 1,428 Japanese adults surveyed described the ties between the two countries as amicable.[27]

The task for U.S. and Japanese leaders is to make sure that these overwhelmingly positive attitudes do not erode in the years ahead as a result of continuing trade frictions.

In contrast to the first two or three years of the Reagan administration, when U.S. relations with China were erratic and tense, these relations have now become much more stable. This relationship should be able to weather minor changes in China's "open-door" policy. Technology transfer from the United States to China has grown rapidly in the past several years. Scientific, educational, and cultural exchanges have proliferated. Trade has increased rapidly. And the United States is now exploring ways of assisting the Chinese in upgrading their anti-tank and anti-air defenses as well as in their capacity to wage anti-submarine warfare.[28]

Given the Soviet military buildup in Siberia, the long and disputed border between the Soviet Union and China, the continuing geopolitical competition between the two countries in Korea, Indochina, and southern Asia, and the past history of relations, it seems likely that China will continue to regard the Soviet Union as its main enemy and to welcome U.S. efforts to balance Soviet power, particularly in Asia. A stable and cooperative Sino-American relationship is as much in China's interest as in that of the United States.

In Pakistan, as in the Philippines, there will be no quick or easy solutions to the problem of potential political instability. The United States should continue to increase military assistance to Pakistan as a token of support against Soviet efforts to intimidate. But it should also encourage President Zia to give greater autonomy to the provinces in order to defuse ethnic unrest. In addition, the United States should seek to enlist India's efforts in lessening Soviet pressure on Pakistan. It surely could not be in India's interests for Pakistan to be dismembered again.

Finally, there is the problem of dealing with the Soviet Union directly as an Asian power. It is time to engage the Soviets in a broad dialogue on Asian security issues and to offer them a role in helping to maintain regional security.

It cannot be reasonably denied that the Soviet Union, though an adversary, is also an Asian power with legitimate interests in the region. Moreover, in Asia, the United States and the Soviet Union share some significant common interests. Neither wants a new Korean war. Neither wants incidents at sea that could lead to confrontation. Neither wants to see the proliferation of nuclear weapons to non-nuclear states. Neither wants to see an escalation of the conflict in Cambodia. In short, the Soviet Union is as concerned as is the United States about the dangers of confrontation and escalation and the threat of war. Moreover, the Soviet Union now has a stake in the status quo in certain parts of Asia, such as Vietnam, Laos, Cambodia, and Afghanistan.

The new Soviet leader Mikhail Gorbachev has recently offered to undertake a wide-ranging discussion of Asian security issues with interested Asian powers. It is time for the United States, *after* very careful consultation with its Asian allies and friends, to explore this offer.

The Korean peninsula may be the place to begin. In the past, Moscow has been extremely prudent with regard to this region. Until quite recently, it had refused to sell advanced fighter planes to North Korea, and on a number of occasions in the 1960s and 1970s, it made clear its disapproval of provocative North Korean actions against the United States and South Korea. As noted, the Soviet Union does not want a new Korean war. It cannot afford to let Pyongyang win or lose a new Korean war. A North Korean loss in a new war would have profound political and psychological repercussions on the Soviet Union's other allies and treaty partners. A North Korean victory would run the risk of a U.S.-Soviet military confrontation on Soviet borders, end whatever chances now exist for improving U.S.-Soviet relations, carry the risk of Chinese intervention, and lead to great pressure within Japan for Japanese remilitarization—all of which would be severely detrimental to Soviet interests.

The Soviets have probably warned Kim Il-Sung privately that the price of increased military and economic assistance is greater obeisance to Soviet foreign policy positions. And there are signs that these warnings have been relatively successful.

This warming trend in Soviet–North Korean relations comes at a time when both Moscow and Pyongyang want to improve relations with the West. Pyongyang, for its part, is losing the economic and diplomatic race with South Korea, and if present trends continue, there will also come a time when it will fall behind in the military competition as well. At the same time, China has been acting as an intermediary between Pyongyang and Washington.

Even more recently, a direct North-South Korean dialogue has begun. There have been Red Cross and economic talks, negotiations for an interparliamentary meeting, and even some talk of a summit meeting.

All in all, the present moment is the most propitious time for a reduction of tension in the Korean peninsula since the early 1970s. The

United States, after careful consultation with Japan, China, and South Korea, could begin to probe the Soviets on the Korean issue. The Soviets, if they so choose, could lend their weight to a substantial reduction of tensions in Korea. And if the two superpowers could lend their respective weights to an easing of tensions in the Korean peninsula, the effect on their relationship more generally would be extremely beneficial.

To sum up, if the West wants to reduce tensions with the Soviet Union in East Asia, it will have to adopt a policy that combines the important but limited insights of both "hawks" and "doves." On the one hand, it must continue to build up its strength to balance Soviet power. On the other, it must seek, whenever common interests dictate, to probe for ways to reduce tensions.

Notes

1. John Erickson, "The Soviet Strategic Implacement in Asia," *Asian Affairs*.
2. *Izvestiya* (April 30, 1985), in FBIS, Soviet Union (May 3, 1985), p. C1.
3. Ibid.
4. *Red Star* (June 5, 1985), in FBIS, Soviet Union (June 7, 1985), p. C1.
5. Erickson, "The Soviet Strategic Implacement."
6. *Red Star* (May 28, 1985), in FBIS, Soviet Union (May 30, 1985), pp. C2, C3.
7. See the Bovin interview of March 15, 1985 with the Prague *Mlada Fronta*, in FBIS, Soviet Union (March 22, 1985), pp. B1–2.
8. Hisahiko Okazaki, "U.S.-Japan Relations in International Politics," *Japan Society Forum* (June 25, 1980).
9. Arnold Horelick, "U.S.-Soviet Relations: The Return of Arms Control," *Foreign Affairs*, Vol. 63, No. 3 (1985).
10. Ernst Kux, "Contradictions in Soviet Socialism," *Problems of Communism* (November-December 1984).
11. For the full text of this remarkable statement, see "Gorbachev Report at December Ideology Conference," in FBIS, Soviet Union, Annex (February 19, 1985).
12. O. Vladimirov, "Veduschchii factor mirovogo revolyutsionnogo protesessa," *Pravda* (June 21, 1985), pp. 3–4.
13. For further details, see John Stephan's article in Donald S. Zagoria, ed., *Soviet Policy in East Asia* (New Haven, Conn.: Yale University Press, 1982).
14. See *Asian Security* (1984), p. 34. A respected journal published annually in Tokyo by the Research Institute on Peace and Security.
15. This point has been made by Robert Scalapino and others.
16. *Wall Street Journal* (July 30, 1985), p. 35.
17. Mohammed Ayoob, "Dateline Pakistan: A Passage to Anarchy?" *Foreign Policy* (Summer 1985).
18. Ibid.
19. Ayoob, "Dateline Pakistan."

20. For details, see *Soviet Military Power* (Washington, D.C.: Department of Defense, 1985).

21. Robert W. Komer, *Maritime Strategy or Coalition Defense* (Cambridge, Mass.: Abt Books, 1984), p. 36.

22. See the testimony of Admiral Wesley McDonald, Commander in Chief, Atlantic Command, before Senate Armed Services Committee in *Hearings: Department of Defense Authorization for Appropriations for Fiscal Year 1984-1985*, Part 2, p. 115; cited in "Can America Catch Up? The U.S.-Soviet Military Balance," *Committee on Present Danger* (undated), p. 50.

23. Hearing of House Subcommittee on Merchant Marine (April 30, 1984); cited in *Committee on Present Danger*, p. 50.

24. Statement by Admiral William J. Crowe, Commander in Chief, U.S. Pacific Command, before Senate Armed Services Committee (1985), mimeo.

25. *New York Times* (August 6, 1985), p. A8.

26. Komer, *Maritime Strategy*, p. 27.

27. *New York Times* (August 6, 1985), p. A8.

28. See the speech by Michael H. Armacost, Undersecretary for Political Affairs (July 9, 1985), Current Policy No. 725.

11

Soviet Policies Toward Korea

Young C. Kim

The present chapter is an interpretative essay on Soviet policies toward Korea. Following a brief identification of the conception of Soviet interest, if first specifies the major factors that appear to have shaped Soviet policies in recent years and then discusses the selected policies that the Soviet Union has pursued vis-à-vis North and South Korea for the past ten years or so.

The Soviet Conception of Soviet National Interest

Abstractly speaking, the Soviet conception is that Soviet national interest dictates the prevention of the establishment of an external power's hegemonic influence over Korea, and that the Soviet Union itself will become the ultimate hegemonic influence in Korea. More specifically, the Soviets want at a minimum to ensure the existence of a friendly Korean regime—in the North at least—amenable to Soviet influence, and to use it as a base for projecting Soviet power elsewhere in Asia and in the Pacific whenever the opportunities are available. The Soviets see the geostrategic location of Korea to be of particular significance for their security interests.

Major Factors Shaping Soviet Policy Toward Korea

A review of Soviet policies indicates that the following considerations have been operative:

1. *Past and present policy programs, commitments, and guidelines regarding Korea that the Soviet government considers pertinent:* Unless an external development calls for reevaluation of Soviet policy, it is safe to assume that existing guidelines will continue to govern Soviet relations with Korea. For example, the Soviets will continue to use existing policy

guidelines to determine whether or not Soviet scholars are allowed to participate in Korean- (as distinguished from international-) sponsored conferences in Seoul. Barring new and significant events, Soviet policy forbids such participation. The inertia of the past precedents (political and bureaucratic) is thus a weighty factor in shaping Soviet policy toward Korea.

2. *The probable future policies that North and South Korea will pursue toward the Soviet Union:* The Soviets will most likely alter their North Korean policy if the North Koreans prove willing to support the Soviet position on the Vietnam and Kampuchea issue. Similarly, the Soviets might show considerable policy flexibility toward South Korea if that country were to recognize Vietnam.

3. *Internal developments in North and South Korea that more or less directly affect Soviet interests:* For instance, the rise of a clearly pro-Soviet leadership in Pyongyang might alter the Soviets' North Korean policy.

4. *Trends in relations between North and South Korea:* Soviet flexibility toward the South would be likely to increase if North-South dialogues were to move forward significantly.

5. *Developments indirectly affecting Soviet interests—especially those affecting Soviet relations with other principal actors in Asia such as the United States, the PRC, and Japan:* The Soviets are sensitive to any developments in or around Korea that might seriously worsen U.S.-Soviet relations and/or induce U.S.-Soviet military conflict. In addition, the Soviets are sensitive to how developments in Korea would affect Japanese policy making, and they often attempt to discourage developments that threaten to aggravate Japan's "militaristic tendencies." Greater tensions or military hostilities in the Korean peninsula would almost certainly provoke a Japanese response unfavorable to Soviet interests. Finally, the Soviets are highly wary of any Korean developments that might present the PRC with a chance to enhance Chinese influence on the Korean peninsula.

6. *The present and anticipated policies of the United States, the PRC, and Japan toward North and South Korea:* A flexible U.S. attitude toward the North would almost certainly prompt a similar Soviet attitude toward the South. Likewise, any Chinese efforts to promote greater exchanges with the South would prompt comparable moves by the Soviets. Moreover, if the United States were to make a significant departure from the present policy of supporting the Chun government in the South, Soviet policy toward Korea would change.

7. *Trends in relations between any two or among all three of the following countries—the United States, the PRC, and Japan:* The Soviets would perceive any improvements in the relations among these countries as

a serious threat and would be inclined to attempt to impede further improvements in these relations. (For an authoritative statement on this point, one need only recall both the speech made by the late Chernenko last year at a banquet honoring President Kim and Gorbachev's speech given this summer.) For example, a dramatic—albeit unlikely—increase in U.S.-PRC military cooperation might dispose the Soviets toward fostering a military conflict on the peninsula, with the expectation that China's support for the North and the United States' support for the South would effectively end any U.S.-PRC military collaboration.

Stated in abstract terms, considerations 2 through 7 above signify that the Soviets are sensitive to any external developments regarding Korea that might significantly affect the existing distribution of power, and that their Korean policies are in part conditioned by their perceptions of the existing state of and future trends in what they call the correlation of forces. The question of the extent and manner in which the domestic situation affects Soviet policy toward Korea is not dealt with in this chapter.

A brief review of Soviet policies toward Korea during the past decade is called for here. The Soviet government has been consistent in publicly declaring its support for North Korea's official position on reunification and other foreign policy programs. However, in its actual conduct of foreign policy, the Soviet Union often implicitly acknowledges the fact of the two Koreas. For the Soviets, the existence of two distinct governments in Korea is an immediate reality, whereas a reunified Korea is still only a distant and theoretical possibility.

Since 1973, the Soviets have with fair consistency allowed South Korean nationals to participate in numerous internationally sponsored conferences held in the Soviet Union. Those South Koreans allowed to participate have included both private citizens and government officials. With only a few exceptions, however, the Soviet Union has not permitted its own citizens to travel to South Korea for international conferences or any other occasion.

There was a remarkable development in the fall of 1982, when the Soviet government permitted a few Soviet officials (two officials of the *Tass* news agency and an official of the Ministry of Culture) to attend an international conference in Seoul. (Shortly thereafter, the North Koreans authorized a pro–North Korean Japanese newspaper to publicly convey North Korea's outrage at the Soviet betrayal.) The Soviet decision appears to have been related to the following developments and considerations:

1. The Soviets were dissatisfied with North Korea's stance on the Vietnam-Kampuchea issue.

2. President Kim's highly publicized visit to Beijing had just occurred—and this was an occasion that augured well for improvements in North Korean–PRC relations.

It is probable that these two considerations prompted the Soviets to display their displeasure as well as their power to influence developments in Korea and thus to affect North Korean interests. The timing of the Soviet decision is highly suggestive.

3. The Soviets knew that a Chinese scholar had attended a fall 1981 conference in Seoul and therefore felt fairly invulnerable to possible PRC or North Korean charges of betrayal.
4. The Soviets may have felt that the time was propitious for a re-demonstration of their interest in and goodwill toward South Korea. Contemplating an expansion of contacts with South Korea and mindful of the above-mentioned developments, the Soviets began to exhibit significant flexibility toward the South—until the KAL tragedy occurred. If this incident had never taken place, the Soviet Union would probably have been represented at the IPU meeting in Seoul in the fall of 1983. A subsequent decline in U.S.-Soviet relations then contributed to closer relations between the Soviet Union and North Korea. Soviet comments on the Rangoon incident of October 10, 1983, reflected considerable sensitivity to North Korea's position. When the Soviets declined to attend the IPU conference in Seoul, North Korea announced its full support for the Soviet version of the incident.

The attitude of the Soviet Union toward South Korea is not limited to a desire to maintain nonpolitical contacts. In fact, Soviet specialists seem prepared to witness a simultaneous admission of the two Koreas into the United Nations. Some go so far as to support a cross-recognition of the two Koreas by the major powers. Although the Soviets believe such developments to be possible, they will hesitate in pursuing them to avoid antagonizing North Korea and risking a strengthening of the bonds between th PRC and North Korea. More fundamentally, the Soviets display great caution in their relations with South Korea because they believe U.S. influence in South Korea to be overwhelming—so overwhelming as to probably render ineffective any Soviet gestures of goodwill toward the South. According to the Soviets, then, amicable advances toward South Korea would be a serious gamble: They would certainly provoke the North Koreans and possibly push them toward the PRC; at the same time, any positive results in terms of increasing Soviet influence with the South would be unlikely to occur.

Regarding Soviet policy toward North Korea, the following observations are in order:

1. Generally speaking, the Soviet Union has been willing to use its influence to support North Korea's foreign policy undertakings. On the issue of reunification, however, the Soviet Union has not gone beyond declaring its support for the peaceful reunification of Korea and for the withdrawal of U.S. forces from Korea.

2. The Soviets have recently expressed their support for ongoing North-South dialogues on all fronts—including economic interchanges, the issue of separated families, and interparliamentary talks. Yet the Soviets have been noticeably unresponsive to the North's proposal for a tripartite conference. The most fundamental explanation for their unwillingness to embrace the tripartite formula is that they believe that the Soviets must participate in any settlement of the Korea problem. The prospect of a four-party conference including the PRC, the United States, and the two Koreas is intolerable to them. However, the Soviet Union might acquiesce to a five- or six-nation conference—provided, of course, it was one of the participants.

3. In addition to any direct support that the Soviet Union provides North Korea, the former nation frequently, albeit indirectly, promotes the latter's interest through a Soviet media denunciation of South Korea's domestic and foreign policy programs.

Soviet media and publications occasionally comment on how extensive Soviet economic assistance to North Korea has been. Possibly, they offer such comments out of annoyance with the North Koreans, whose references to and acknowledgments of Soviet aid are scarce indeed. The Soviets are doing more than chastising North Korean ingratitude, though—they are reminding the world as well as North Korea of the considerable influence they wield over North Korea. In the past, it should be noted, the Soviets were compelled to roll over North Korean debts. Their general hesitance to assist North Korea since then has provoked the North Korean charge that the Soviets have not been forthcoming with meaningful assistance.

The North Koreans have been particularly dissatisfied with the Soviet transfer of advanced weapons systems. Despite the recent Soviet transfer of MIG-23s to North Korea, the Soviets have been generally hesitant about providing North Korea with advanced weapons systems. Apparently, the primary Soviet consideration is that arms transfers must not effect a drastic alteration of the existing peninsular balance. A North Korea with a decisive advantage might set off a chain of events that would pose a significant threat to peace and Soviet interests.

The recent transfer of MIG-23s to North Korea was a predictable, parallel development to President Kim's trip to the Soviet Union in

1984. That the Soviets welcomed Kim in Moscow signaled the fact that they were favorably inclined to follow through on other measures designed to demonstrate sensitivity to North Korea's needs and desires. Weapons systems such as the MIG-23s had long symbolized both the militant bond between the two countries and Soviet responsiveness to North Korean needs. The MIG-23 issue, therefore, must be examined in the context of an overall improvement in Soviet–North Korean relations, an improvement firmly grounded on the needs and expectations of each country.

It will be helpful in this connection to review last summer's decision to hold a Soviet–North Korean summit. From the Korean leaders' perspective, the trip promised to promote at least several of North Korea's foreign policy objectives. It provided Kim a high-level summit meeting in which he could directly solicit Soviet political, economic, and military aid. It also gave the North Korean leader a chance to seek a firm pledge from the Soviets to support his country's policy toward the South and to oppose any movement toward a policy recognizing two Koreas on the peninsula. In terms of Korean domestic politics, the trip provided Kim the opportunity to seek Soviet tolerance—if not understanding and support—concerning the issue of North Korea's political succession. At a minimum, Kim hoped to persuade the Soviet Union to abstain from interfering in North Korea's domestic affairs. At best, the North Koreans hoped to receive Soviet acknowledgment of Kim Chong-il's unique position as successor-designate to his father as head of the party and government.

The meetings also enabled Kim to convey North Korea's perception of the threat posed by U.S. and Japanese actions in and around Korea, and presented to the rest of the world a convincing demonstration of Soviet–North Korean solidarity, which, the North Koreans hoped, would constrain the actions of the United States, Japan, and South Korea and induce China to adopt a more positive attitude toward North Korea's interests. Actually, the fact that Kim's visit even occurred is significant. Although Moscow had been considering such a visit for a number of years, it never materialized. That the trip finally took place attests to the coincidence of the two nations' interests at the time.

Three additional factors expedited Kim's trip to the Soviet Union: the resumption of negotiations between the Soviet Union and China, the profound strengthening of North Korean relations with China, and the worsening of U.S.-Soviet relations. Thus, North Korean leaders may have thought the timing of Kim's trip appropriate, as they judged the friction between China and the USSR to be low and Soviet sensitivity and amenability to North Korea's requests to be high.

For their part, when pondering the implications of U.S. military activities in Asia and the evolving cooperative relationship among the United States, China, Japan, and South Korea, the Soviets undoubtedly recognized how closely Korean views and interests approximated their own. The Soviets clearly saw the necessity of exerting anew their influence over North Korea, an action that would afford them both the opportunity to prevent the North from drifting toward better relations with the United States and Japan under Chinese tutelage, and the chance to prevent a closer cooperation between China and North Korea. Thus, the Soviet Union sought to reassert itself as a dominant and interested force in Korean affairs, emphasizing that no political settlement, whatever the format of negotiations, was to take place without Soviet approval.

The Soviet decision to transfer MIG-23s to North Korea may not have been only a passive, delayed response to North Korea's persistent requests. Conceivably, the Soviet action was intended as a prelude to a Soviet offensive strategy involving substantial politico-military collaboration with North Korea. It is still unclear as to what the Soviets expect in return—whether it be greater North Korean deference to Soviet interests and policies and/or more concrete benefits.

This line of interpretation presupposes a heightened Soviet concern over the evolving relationship among the United States, Japan, the PRC, and South Korea as well as some degree of Soviet compulsion toward power projection.

Looking to the future, we may venture to guess that Soviet policy toward Korea will be more active and assertive than it was during the 1970s. One assumes that the probable nature and speed of future developments in Korea—as well as the attendant policy shifts of other major powers toward Korea—will compel the Soviets, conservative and cautious as they may be, to adapt their policies to this rapid change. This much is certain: that during the next several years, extraordinary and dynamic developments in and over Korea will pose a great challenge to Soviet foreign policy makers.

12

Japan and the Development of Siberia

Kazuyuki Kinbara

Economic interest and need were the primary bases for Japanese determination to participate in the development of Siberia. When the USSR started inducing the Japanese business community to participate in that development in the early 1960s, Japan was preoccupied with its rapid economic growth, and the volume of raw materials and energy resources needed for its economy to maintain its industrial activities was expected to grow larger and larger. The Japanese economy depends upon a steady influx of imports, and with rapid economic growth, Japanese exports were also increasing at a high tempo. To this must be added the fact that the majority of Japan's total exports are manufactured goods (the share of machinery and vehicle exports in the total turnover of export trade rose dramatically from 12.3 percent in 1955 to 46.3 percent in 1970). Hence Siberia was perceived as a promising export market.

Economic concern led the Japanese business community to embark upon cooperation with the USSR for Siberian development in response to the Soviet rapprochement, despite the chilly relationship between the two states and the traditional Japanese antipathy toward the USSR.

For the Soviet part, as the development of natural resources in Siberia became increasingly important for its domestic economy, Japanese credit and technology became essential for speeding up the development. As a consequence, several large-scale and long-term collaborative projects between Japan and the USSR, known as the Japan-Soviet Siberian Development Projects (JSSDPs), were realized after years of negotiations.

The aims of this chapter are to examine the evolution of Japanese-Soviet economic cooperation in Siberia over the past two and a half decades and to discuss its future prospects. Cooperation on the development of Siberia turned out to be a major element of the international relationship between Japan and the USSR during the period in question, and it took on the unique character of economic interchange between the countries. There are three primary reasons for this. First, even though Japan and the USSR had restored diplomatic relations through the Japanese-Soviet Joint Declaration in October 1956, political coolness has remained, and the last three decades have witnessed very little positive development on the political front of Soviet-Japanese relations. There has been no peace treaty between the two countries during this period, and, from the Japanese point of view, the major hindrance to the conclusion of such a treaty is the territorial issue of the Northern Islands—a matter that seems to hold no prospect of quick resolution. High-level dialogue between the two governments has been infrequent. Under these political conditions, economic cooperation over Siberian development has proved to be one of the very few areas within the relationship in which mutually advantageous intercourse could be identified.

Second, the institutional manner in which Japan has conducted economic cooperation over Siberian development with the USSR differs markedly from its trade relations with any other country. The Japan-Soviet Economic Committee (JSEC), set up by the Japanese business community in 1965, was exclusively responsible for conducting negotiations for Japanese participation in Siberian development, and it functioned as the only official channel with the Soviets. Such a national-level centralization of business activities is very unusual in the case of market economies such as that in Japan, where, needless to say, both domestic and overseas commercial activities are heavily influenced by the initiatives of individual corporations through free competition.

Third, although economic cooperation on Siberian development has not necessarily represented the whole picture of Japanese-Soviet economic relations, there can be little doubt that the emergence of the JSSDPs gave considerable impetus to the trade relations overall; certain new elements also came to the fore, particularly in the financial area. Moreover, because of their central importance, negotiations concerning economic cooperation in Siberia have sometimes served as a barometer of the state of Japanese-Soviet economic relations as a whole.

In a broader sense, any Japanese trade with the USSR may have a bearing on its contribution to Siberian development. It is reasonable to assume that a substantial portion of the Japanese industrial goods exported to the USSR outside the JSSDPs have been utilized in that region. Nevertheless, Japanese economic cooperation with respect to Siberian development is defined here in terms of the JSSDPs handled by the JSEC because the focus of this chapter is not the economic consequence or efficacy of the Japanese contribution to the Soviet economy but Japanese efforts to draw economic interest from its participation in Siberian development and the political and international implications of this effort.

Achievements of the Past: The Historical Dimension

Phase One (1961–1965)

Viewed in the general context of Japanese-Soviet economic cooperation in Siberia, the significance of the first phase is that it paved the way for the emergence of the JSSDPs in later stages. Although no concrete negotiations for collaborative projects took place between the two countries during this period, several important developments did occur. In June 1965 these developments culminated in the establishment of the JSEC. A noteworthy point is that most of the major developments in this period took the form of economic missions led by Japanese business leaders to the USSR on the one hand and visits by key Soviet figures to Japan on the other. These missions break down as follows:

August 1961	Visit by Mikoyan to Japan
August 1962	Japanese economic mission to the USSR led by Kawai
September 1962	Japanese civil-engineering delegation
September 1962	Japanese petrochemical delegation
October 1962	Japanese chemical-textile-industrial delegation
May 1963	Japanese machine-tool delegation
June 1963	Japanese trade mission to the USSR led by Kitamura, chairman of the Japan-Soviet and East European Trade Association
May 1964	Soviet parliamentary delegation led by Mikoyan
June 1965	Japanese steel mission led by Nagano
August 1965	Japanese economic mission led by Uemura

Among these Japanese missions and delegations, the Kawai, Nagano, and Uemura missions were particularly important for two reasons. First, these three missions more or less represented the Japanese business community and were headed by some of the most influential business leaders in Japan at the time. Second, because the Soviet side also recognized these missions as highly representative, the leaders of the missions were accorded opportunities for talks with Soviet national leaders, including Party Leader Khrushchev, Premier Kosygin, and Foreign Minister Gromyko. During these meetings, both sides exchanged views about future economic relations in general and the prospects of cooperation for Siberian development in particular. The two visits to Japan by Mikoyan, the first deputy chairman of the Council of Ministers of the USSR,[1] had a considerable impact on Japanese-Soviet economic relations in the sense that his speeches and proposals aroused the high expectations of the Japanese business community with regard to the possibility of the rapid expansion of bilateral trade related to Siberian development.

Phase Two (1965–1969)

With the establishment of the JSEC in 1965, economic cooperation between the two states entered into a new stage based upon the achievements of the exchanges mentioned above. Whereas Phase One was largely attributable to personalities such as Kawai, Nagano, Uemura, and Mikoyan, the developments of Phase Two were institutionalized under the JSEC and its counterpart on the Soviet side, the Soviet-Japan Economic Committee (SJEC), which is under the control of the Ministry of Foreign Trade. As it turned out, the committees and the joint conference were of central importance as the official negotiating channel for the JSSDPs throughout the period up to the present.

Consequently, the first three JSSDPs (i.e., the earlier-stage projects) emerged toward the end of the 1960s. The outline of these projects is as follows.

1. The Soviet–Far East Forest Resources Development Project was the first JSSDP to be realized between Japan and the USSR. After the proposal of this project was formally taken up in the second session of the joint conference, commercial negotiations were carried out at the subcommittee level. The General Agreement for this project was signed by the committees in July 1968. The outline of the agreement was that Japan had to supply the machinery and equipment needed for developing forest resources in the Soviet Far East with a $133 million credit extended to the USSR. In return, the USSR was to supply a total of 7.5 million cubic meters of timber to Japan between 1969 and 1973. Among the capital goods exported to the USSR under this project were road-building machinery, timber-felling chain saws, wire rope, mobile cranes, and powerful tractor-trailers. Their supply was the main component of the rise in Japanese exports to the USSR between 1969 and 1970.

2. The Vrangel Port Construction Project was initiated in the first session of the joint conference when the USSR disclosed a plan to expand the capacities of ports in the Soviet Far East and suggested the possibility of purchasing related equipment from Japan; a number of technical and commercial negotiations and field investigations took place

throughout the rest of the 1960s. As a result, a contract concerning the design of a new port (18 kilometers east of Nakhodka) was concluded in April 1970, and the General Agreement was signed in December. Japan was responsible for the design of a coal pier and a comprehensive freight-loading facility. Machinery and equipment were exported from Japan with an $80 million credit. Although this project did not include imports of raw materials by Japan, it was considered a natural-resources-oriented project because the improvement of the transportation system in the Soviet Far East would contribute to the smooth and prompt supply of Siberian natural resources to Japan.

3. The Chip and Pulp Development Project was originally intended to be a part of the Forest Resources Development Project, but during the process of negotiations it became a separate, though similar, project. Negotiations on this project intensified after both committees agreed to realize the project in the third session, but the final agreement was delayed until December 1971 due to the disagreement between the two committees concerning the amount of delivery of chip and pulp. The amount of credit provided to the USSR under the agreement was $45 million, and the chip and pulp delivered to Japan between 1972 and 1981 totaled around 12 million cubic meters.

Phase Three (1970–1975)

Phase Three witnessed a new development that brought Japanese-Soviet economic cooperation over Siberian development to a peak by the close of the period. This period may be differentiated from the periods preceding it in three respects.

1. Highly-intensive negotiations took place between the JSEC and its Soviet counterpart for the JSSDPs during this period. Three "executive sessions" were held between the meetings of the full Joint Committee: in August 1973 (Tokyo), in March 1974 (Moscow), and in June 1975 (Tokyo). Although the scale of delegations for the executive sessions was much smaller than that for the joint conference, more intensive and more detailed negotiations were conducted at executive sessions.

2. A marked difference in both quality and scale can be identified between the JSSDPs of Phase Two and the JSSDPs that were taken up and negotiated in Phase Three. The energy-related projects proposed during this period were the South Yakutian Coking Coal Project, the Yakutian Natural Gas Project, the Sakhalin Continental Shelf Oil and Gas Project, and the Tyumen Oil Development Project. All required or would have required an enormous financial input to develop. Both their size and the fact that they were energy related made these projects conspicuous; thus they sometimes caused controversy and repercussions.

3. In contrast to Phase Two, when the JSSDPs were strictly bilateral matters conducted entirely within the JSEC, issues relating to economic cooperation for Siberian development sometimes spilled over outside the committee during Phase Three. From the Japanese point of view, this outcome had two dimensions. One was that the Japanese government, although it had not associated itself with the JSSDPs throughout Phase Two, found itself involved in them to some extent during Phase Three, primarily with regard to finances. It must be pointed out that the summit meeting between Japanese Prime Minister Tanaka and Soviet Party Leader Brezhnev in Moscow in October 1973 had a considerable impact on economic cooperation between the two states; but this is not to say that the Japanese government had decided to become a direct party to negotiations on projects. The reality was that the government continued to stay outside actual negotiations with the USSR throughout the 1970s.

The second dimension concerned third-party countries, namely the United States and China. Some attempts were made by the JSEC to bring the United States in as a third partner in two of the JSSDPs (Tyumen oil and Yakutian natural gas), for political and economic reasons. The military implications of the Tyumen oil project was believed to cause serious concern in China, particularly when the possibility of a Japanese contribution to building the Baikal-Amur-Magistral railway (BAM), as an aspect of the cooperation with the USSR on the Tyumen oil project, emerged in the course of negotiations.

The following is an outline of the four JSSDPs that materialized as a result of the negotiations in Phase Three. Although these projects were undertaken as part of Phase Three, they were executed in the later 1970s and are still in operation.

1. Regarding the South Yakutian Coking Coal Development Project, under the General Agreement signed in June 1974, Japanese exports of $450 million of equipment covered facilities for coal extraction, freight vehicles, crane parts, and other machinery intended for use in the development of a coalfield (Neriungri) in southern Yakutia. In return, Japan was to receive coking coal totaling 105 million tons between 1979 and 1998, with the annual rate of supply to increase gradually up to 6.5 million tons after 1985.

2. The second stage of the Soviet Far East Forest Resources Development Project was based on the successful fulfillment of the first stage. It was a continuation of the first stage rather than a new one, but on a much larger scale. Under the General Agreement signed in June 1974, Japan provided the USSR with a $550 million bank loan for timber exploitation facilities, ship building, and related machinery and equipment. In return, Japan received a total of 18.4 million cubic meters of

timber between 1975 and 1979. The third stage of the project started with the signing of a General Agreement in March 1981.

3. The Yakutian Natural Gas Project was the only project that involved U.S. corporate participation.[2] According to the terms of the plan, Japan and the United States were each to provide $1.7 billion worth of credit to the USSR, and in return the USSR would supply 10 billion cubic meters of gas annually to both countries over twenty years. For the initial exploratory stage of this vast plan, the General Agreement signed in December 1974 envisaged a $50 million bank loan, half to come from the EXIM Bank of Japan and half from the Bank of America; the USSR was to purchase the machinery and equipment necessary for a prospecting operation to confirm at least 1 trillion cubic meters of gas reserves. When the operation had confirmed the existence of this quantity, Japan and the United States were to begin negotiations on another General Agreement for the next stage—namely, development of Soviet gas reserves. Neither Japan nor the United States, however, had received any report from the USSR to confirm 1 trillion cubic meters by the end of 1984, and it appears unlikely that this project will be realized in the near future.

4. The Sakhalin Continental Shelf Oil and Natural Gas Project is divided into two stages: exploration, and development and supply. The General Agreement signed in January 1975 covered the operation of the first stage. Under the agreement, Japan provided the USSR with $170 million worth of credit for purchase and lease of machinery and equipment from Japan to prospect for oil and gas on the continental shelf off Sakhalin. If the prospecting operation proved successful, Japan, under the second stage, was to extend a bank loan for the USSR to import machinery and equipment from Japan to develop its oil and gas over ten years. The prospecting operation, still partly in progress as of the end of 1984, found that gas has more promise than oil.

Phase Four (1976–1985)

Japanese-Soviet economic cooperation in Siberian development during Phase Four was at a low ebb. In contrast with Phase Three, no materialization of new JSSDPs occurred during the fourth phase except for the third stage of the Soviet Far East Forest Resources Development Project. The JSEC and its Soviet counterpart held only three joint conferences and no executive sessions during this period. It was after an interval of more than five years that the most recent session of the joint conference was held in Tokyo in December 1984.

As far as large-scale projects are concerned, economic cooperation between the two states seems to have peaked at the end of Phase Three.

But this was not necessarily the consequence of Japanese hesitation or reluctance to embark on new large-scale projects. The simple fact was that the USSR failed—probably for domestic economic reasons—to put forward any concrete ideas for new projects that would attract the attention of Japanese businessmen. But it would be misleading to connect this Soviet failure with a deterioration of the political relationship between the two states.

In this respect, it is crucial to remember that since the conclusion of the Japanese-Soviet Treaty of Commerce in 1957, the USSR has always been more eager than Japan to strengthen economic ties, regardless of the stage of its political relations with Japan. In most cases it was the Soviets who took the initiative; the Japanese tended to show a very cautious attitude. In light of these factors, it is safe to speculate that the USSR failed to propose a new large-scale project in Phase Four not because it did not wish to do so but because it could not afford to do so given its lack of capital and labor.

On the other hand, from time to time during this period the USSR emphasized the necessity of a framework designed for even longer-term economic cooperation. This can be understood in the same context as the Soviet attempts to make the Japanese government a direct party to economic cooperation, as was strongly demonstrated at the fifth session of the joint conference held in Tokyo in February 1972. In fact, the Soviet demand for the Japanese government's more active participation was intensified during this period.

The Soviet call for economic cooperation on a longer-term basis was first made in August 1976, when a Keidanren mission headed by its chairman, Toshio Doko,[3] visited the USSR at Brezhnev's invitation. Most recently, an appeal to the same effect was repeated by Deputy Minister of Foreign Trade Sushkov on the occasion of the ninth session of the joint conference in Tokyo in December 1984.[4]

The Difficulties of Forming New JSSDPs

In considering the prospects of Japanese-Soviet economic cooperation in Siberia for the next decade or so, the following points merit careful examination.

Despite the achievements of the Japanese business community, one cannot escape the impression that the net result of more than two decades of Japanese economic cooperation in Siberia has been unspectacular, given the time, cost, and efforts involved.[5]

The reasons for the rather modest degree of Japanese involvement in Siberian development since the establishment of the JSEC are primarily economic in nature. In fact, there are a number of economic, technical, and institutional problems that tend to decrease the likelihood that any new Siberian collaborative projects will be realized in the next decade.

The Siberian natural resources in which Japan has an interest are for the most part situated in remote areas to which access is costly. Therefore, prior to the actual development of the natural resources, a huge amount of investment is needed for improving the infrastructure of the area. But Japanese participation has been discouraged not only by Soviet proposals that Japan contribute to such costs but also by the preclusion of Japanese operational involvement.[6]

Another important factor is the gap in geographical priorities between Japan and the USSR. In the overall strategy of Siberian development, the USSR has laid emphasis on West Siberia, an area close to Soviet industrial centers, whereas Japan had wanted to obtain the natural resources located east of Lake Baykal, an area close to Japan. Much of the potential of Siberia did not in itself justify massive Japanese investment. This difference in priorities created a barrier to the realization of any new JSSDPs, particularly as Soviet economic difficulties (capital and labor shortages) worsened. The low-key relationship in Phase Four may largely be attributed to this factor.

"Energy Link" as Political Pressure?

Viewed in the broader context of East-West trade as a whole, arguments concerned with Japan's dependence on the USSR for natural resources and security considerations are related to a common issue in the West regarding the wisdom of increasing trade relations with the USSR in energy. One could argue that Japanese dependence on the USSR for energy resources allows the USSR to "point a knife at her throat."[7] In more moderate terms, Japan is unusually susceptible to political influence from the USSR.

On the other hand, one could also argue that Japan is able to restrain Soviet behavior by creating a web of economically interdependent relationships. This argument justified the promotion of détente in the early 1970s. Given the decline in Japanese-Soviet economic cooperation over Siberian development during Phase Four, and given the fact that there is little likelihood that new large-scale JSSDPs will emerge in the foreseeable future, the two arguments are highly problematic. Indeed, they are both based on the dubious assumption that the magnitude of economic cooperation between the two countries in Siberia could be large enough to exert a substantial impact on Japan's national security.

Thus we are led to question the likelihood that the USSR will use economic leverage vis-à-vis Japan for political purposes. From the Western point of view, the threat of politically motivated supply stoppages of strategic raw materials and energy resources from the USSR cannot be totally ruled out. However, several reasons support the conjecture that the USSR is unlikely to use economic leverage over Japan as a political weapon in the foreseeable future.

In the first place, the amount of energy that Japan imports from the USSR is very small. A research report by the Office of Technology Assessment (OTA) of the U.S. Congress[8] calculates that the share of Japanese energy imports from the USSR relative to its total energy demand consistently fell below 1 percent throughout the 1970s. According to a Japanese government forecast, the possible maximum rate of dependency upon the USSR for LNG could rise in the 1980s to 24.3 percent, and for coking coal to 9.2 percent. However, this forecast is questionable because it assumes that the supply of energy resources from Siberia based upon the current JSSDPs will start without delay according to original plans. Bearing in mind that the Yakutian Natural Gas Project has virtually been shelved, with no prospect of future action, the forecast for LNG should be corrected. The recalculated figure would be 7.7 percent[9] instead of 24.3 percent. If this is the case, it is estimated that Japanese dependence upon the USSR for energy resources throughout the rest of the 1980s will still be just over 1 percent. The amount of oil imported from the USSR, on the other hand, has been and will continue to be negligible. It is safe to argue, therefore, that a sudden all-out cutoff of energy from the USSR would not be a serious problem for Japan.

Hence an embargo on the sale of natural resources to Japan may not be an effective weapon for the USSR. Certainly the cost of such a measure for the USSR would be enormous. Not only would such action preclude further Japanese participation in Siberian development, but it would also undercut Soviet reliability as a trade partner in the eyes of the Western business community. Furthermore, the USSR would lose its largest export market in the Far East for natural resources. It is obvious that the USSR would be unable to find an alternative export market in the Far East that is as large as Japan.

As a political tool, a Soviet embargo of imports of Japanese goods would be even more counterproductive for the USSR. It should be remembered that what the USSR is importing from Japan, mainly machinery and steel equipment, is essential to the Soviet economy—particularly for Siberian development, whose economic significance is growing.

It should also be noted that Japan's level of trade with the USSR has persistently been low—less than 3 percent of aggregate foreign trade over the last two decades.

In sum, any Soviet attempt to achieve political goals vis-à-vis Japan by manipulating bilateral trade would be not only ineffective but also damaging for the USSR. At the same time, Japan would suffer no national security problems as a consequence of economic cooperation with the USSR in Siberian development for the foreseeable future.

The Lessons of the Tyumen Oil Development Project

Among the JSSDPs negotiated during Phase Three (1970–1975), the Tyumen Oil Development Project was perhaps the only case in which noneconomic obstacles arose at both the bilateral and international levels. After years of very intensive negotiations in Tokyo and Moscow, this project was eventually abandoned. The project's negotiation process is too complex to be dealt with here. But the implications of the abandonment of the project need to be discussed because they provide valuable insights into an assessment of the noneconomic variables involved in Japanese-Soviet relations.

Although it is difficult to answer definitively the question as to why the Tyumen project alone failed to reach an agreement,[10] we can identify the factors that politicized its negotiations and substantially distinguished the project from the others.

First, the project was perceived to have a strong military color, thus arousing Chinese concerns and prompting the Japanese to seek U.S. involvement. The important point here is that the special strategic value of oil per se constituted a serious problem.

Second, the Japanese government was required by the JSEC to take an active part in the project from the outset. Such an outspoken request by the JSEC for the government's support was not made in the negotiations surrounding projects that involved government participation only at the financial level. In any event, despite repeated requests by the JSEC, the government did not treat the Tyumen project as a special case.

Third, there is some evidence that arguments in favor of a strategy to link the Tyumen project to pending political issues (e.g., the Northern Territories question) erupted within the Japanese government. (These arguments, however, were never more than just exchanges of ideas and were never reflected in the actual policies.)[11] The intention was to draw Soviet concessions on the Northern Islands by rendering assistance to the Tyumen oil development. The crucial matter of relevance here is that the Tyumen project caused controversies over a linkage strategy. A linkage strategy regarding economic cooperation over Siberian development was not at issue in the case of other JSSDPs. Imazato (the chairman of the Petroleum Subcommittee on the Japanese side) never obtained either his own government's full support or that of the U.S.

corporations—a clear indication that the realization of the Tyumen project was beyond the capability of the JSEC alone.

Imazato's failure also implies that in the present political and international environment there is a maximum permissible limit to Japanese involvement in Siberian development. The limit in this case reflects neither the amount of Japanese credit to the USSR nor the volume of the Soviets' supply of natural resources to Japan, although both are important indicators. Rather, the issue is political and psychological. It seems clear that the Tyumen project would have gone beyond those latter limits, whereas the projects that were realized stayed within them. The factors related to the setting of such limits include Japan's suspicion toward the USSR, the political antipathy amplified by the Northern Territories problem, Japan's constant and firm loyalty to the United States, and the steady Sino-Japanese rapprochement since the early 1970s.

Therefore, as long as Japanese economic cooperation over Siberian development remained within these limits, the Japanese business community, acting through the JSEC, could manage to proceed with negotiations for cooperation with the USSR without any direct support from the government. In short, the policy of "Seikei Bunri" (separation of politics from economics) worked well.

Such limits may distinguish Japanese-Soviet economic cooperation from the general pattern of East-West trade. In the global context, it is true that the expansion of Japanese-Soviet economic relations coincided with the era of détente, and the détente generally encouraged East-West trade. When the Tyumen project was abandoned, however, the period of détente was in full swing and East-West trade was rapidly growing.[12]

Apart from détente, the fact that Japan's only potential enemy has been the USSR and its only ally has been the United States remains a constant concern in Japanese international relations. One may argue that Western European states have also perceived the USSR as their biggest potential threat and that they, too, have been U.S. allies. Yet the historical Japanese experience with the USSR (Russia) is unique, and its unilateral and heavy dependence upon the United States in political and military areas[13] has set the features of the U.S.-Japanese relationship apart from those of the U.S.–Western European relationship. The alliance aspect revealed itself when Japan obediently followed the United States' economic sanctions following the Afghanistan incident while Western Europe did not.[14] Thus, Japan's policy toward the USSR was essentially governed by its special relationship with the United States—a relationship that left little room for Japanese maneuvering vis-à-vis the USSR.

Toward a New Direction? The Ninth Session of the Joint Conference

The ninth session of the joint conference between the JSEC and its counterpart on the Soviet side was held under very heavy security in Tokyo in December 1984. The Soviet delegation, headed by Deputy Minister of Foreign Trade Sushkov, was composed of more than seventy high officials and specialists. According to Hiroshi Anzai, the head of the Japanese delegation and the chairman of the JSEC, "the very fact that the dialogue between the JSEC and the Soviets concerned was resumed through the joint conference was a big step forward for Japanese-Soviet economic relations."[15] In actuality, the communications channel of the joint conference had been closed somewhat in line with the policy of the Japanese government to protest against the December 1979 Soviet invasion of Afghanistan.

With regard to prospects for Japanese-Soviet economic cooperation in Siberia, four important indications were identified in the ninth session of the joint conference.

First, it was eventually confirmed that the era of huge energy-related projects is over. No serious discussion of new large-scale projects took place during the session, although some reviews were made concerning the fulfillment of existing JSSDPs. The reasons are to be found on both the Soviet and the Japanese sides. The domestic economic situations of the Soviets (capital and labor shortages as well as a difference of priorities within Siberia) prevented the USSR from presenting blueprints for new projects to the JSEC. On the other hand, the incentive for the Japanese side to get involved in new large-scale projects in Siberia diminished as a result of structural changes in the Japanese economy. During the two oil crises of the 1970s, Japan managed to adapt to the new international economic situation by reshaping its main sectors into energy-efficient and intelligence-intensive industries. Thus it substantially altered domestic demand for energy and other natural resources.

These factors lead to the conjecture that, even with the removal of all existing political obstacles, there would be very little likelihood of a revival of the "Siberian boom" in natural resources within the Japanese business community. But does this mean the end of Japanese economic cooperation for Siberian development? Or will Phase Five (1986–?) bring about any new developments? The answer to the first question is probably negative, and to the second one, probably affirmative.

Second, the possibility of diversifying forms of economic interchanges between the two states was seriously discussed in an attempt to break the present stalemate. Among the new forms of economic interchange discussed during the session were the following: Japanese cooperation in the modernization of Soviet light industries and electrical industries, including power stations, to attain higher efficiency; Soviet purchases of petrochemical and agricultural machinery plants from Japan on a turnkey basis; Soviet purchases of Japanese equipment and technology for automatization or robotization; Japanese management and marketing in the USSR; legitimation of joint ventures in the USSR; and establishment of a free trade zone in the Soviet Far East.[16] Although most of these ideas are still just that, further investigation by its JSEC and its Soviet counterpart might indicate a new direction for Japanese-Soviet economic cooperation in Siberia; it might also change the definition of JSSDPs.

Third, for the first time the JSEC responded in a somewhat positive manner to the repeated Soviet proposals for government-level economic cooperation agreements on a long-term basis. In the joint communiqué adopted at the closing of the ninth session, it was stated that "the Japanese side took note of the Soviet proposal," whereas the Japanese government has continued to deny flatly the need for such agreements with the USSR on the grounds that there is no evidence to suggest that lack of agreements between the two governments has affected the volume of Japanese-Soviet trade.

In the past, the JSEC has taken virtually no notice of the various forms of Soviet pressure for a framework for long-term economic cooperation and the conclusion of related government-level agreements; nor has it ever made any official response to the Soviet side. The fact that the JSEC cautiously shifted its stance from "no notice" to "take note" on this matter may imply that the JSEC has begun to consider government-level arrangements of this kind to be a catalyst for Japanese-Soviet trade relations.

Fourth, for the first time in the history of the joint conference since the establishment of the JSEC in 1965, the Japanese side made direct references to the sensitive political issue of the Northern Territories. In his guest speech, Foreign Minister Abe called attention to the fact that because of this fundamental political issue, no peace treaty has existed between the two states throughout the postwar period. He stated that resolution of this pending political problem would open the possibility of promoting positive bilateral relations, including economic relations over the long term.[17] In his keynote speech, JSEC Chairman Anzai stressed that the conclusion of a peace treaty with the USSR through the resolution of the territorial issue, a strong wish of all Japanese people, would expedite economic interchanges between the two states.[18] The Soviets responded to such outspoken references to political problems with displeasure. In his closing remarks Sushkov expressed his regret that the long-observed practice of avoiding references to political matters on the occasion of the joint conference was undermined by the Japanese side, and added that he hoped it would not be repeated in future.[19]

Such remarks by Foreign Minister Abe and Chairman Anzai clearly suggested a substantial departure from the traditional Japanese policy of "Seikei Bunri" (separation of politics from economics) vis-à-vis the USSR, which used to justify expanding trade relations with politically difficult countries (particularly with the communist states). During his official visit to the USSR in October 1973, then Prime Minister Tanaka made plain that the Japanese government would support "Seikei Bunri" regarding Japanese cooperation for Siberian development.[20] Viewed in this context, the establishment of the JSEC was in itself a clear indication of the practice of "Seikei Bunri" in relation to the USSR, given that the JSEC was a purely private organization comprising leading Japanese firms in various sectors.

It may be misleading to assume, however, that the departure from "Seikei Bunri" by the Japanese side that was demonstrated in the ninth session of the joint conference will immediately affect Japanese-Soviet economic cooperation over Siberian development; after all, the emergence of such large-scale and conspicuous projects as the Tyumen Oil Development Project seems unlikely for the next decade or so. The new forms of cooperation mentioned earlier, if realized, appear to be rather modest and will have little opportunity to cause political repercussions. All one can safely predict at present is that the JSEC will continue its efforts to maintain the balance between political considerations and economic interests into the foreseeable future.

Notes

1. Mikoyan was the first Soviet cabinet-level figure to visit Japan since the normalization of diplomatic relations in 1956.

2. Occidental Petroleum Corporation and El Paso Natural Gas Company.

3. Toshio Doko took over the chairmanship of Keidanren when Uemura retired in 1975.

4. See section "'Energy Link' as Political Pressure?" in this chapter.

5. It is said that more than twenty would-be JSSDPs, or ideas for such projects, were abandoned since the establishment of the JSEC, while only eight JSSDPs were realized.

6. Because the Soviet government continues to emphasize that "enterprises belong wholly to our state," it does not seem to envisage forms of joint venture that involve foreign equity participation (as in Bulgaria, Hungary, Romania, and even Poland, with certain restrictions).

7. This statement was made by Joseph Nye at a Shimoda conference in September 1981. See *Report of the Fourth Conference on Soviet and East European Problems* (Tokyo: Soren Too Boeki Kai, 1981), p. 6.

8. OTA Research Reports, "Soviet-Japanese Energy Relations," in *Technology and Soviet Energy Availability* (November 1981).

9. In this case, it is assumed that the delivery of LNG within the framework of the Sokhalin Continental Shelf Oil and Natural Gas Project alone (3.5 million tonnes per year) will be carried out by the end of the 1980s.

10. Incidentally, no official statement was ever made by the JSEC as to why the Tyumen oil project was abandoned.

11. Interministry differences in this regard are discussed in several newspaper articles. See especially *Nihon Keizai Shimbun* (March 1 and October 11, 1973); and *Asahi Shimbun* (March 7, August 23, and October 11, 1973).

12. According to statistics provided by the OECD, the total volume of East-West trade in 1975 reached US$44 billion.

13. Japanese economic dependence upon the U.S. has also been heavy, but in this area the dependence is somewhat more mutual.

14. At a Japan-Soviet symposium sponsored by *Sankei* in Sapporo, Japan, in November 1981, a Soviet representative of the Ministry of Foreign Trade attributed Japan's decline as a Western trading partner with the USSR, from second in 1979 to fifth in 1980, to differences in policy on trade with the USSR between Japan and Western Europe following the Afghanistan incident. See *Sankei Shimbun* (November 23, 1981).

15. See the *Report on the Ninth Session of the Japan-Soviet Joint Conference [Dai 9 Kai Godo Kaigi Hokokusho]*, Tokyo JSEC.

16. Ibid., pp. 57, 73–78.

17. Ibid., p. 36.

18. Ibid., p. 41.

19. Ibid., p. 96.

20. Keisuke Suzuki, *Siberia Kaihatsu to Nisso Keizai Kyoryoku* (Tokyo: Nikkan Kogyo, 1977), p. 233.

Appendix A

SUMMARY OF CONFERENCE PROCEEDINGS

The symposium opened on October 2, 1985, with a special lecture by Mr. Iichiro Hatoyama, former foreign minister. He spoke on Japan's international role from now until the year 2000 and beyond. Two prominent Soviet studies specialists, Dr. Seweryn Bialer, director of the Research Institute on International Change at Columbia University in New York, and Admiral Sir James Eberle, director of the Royal Institute of International Affairs in London, gave the conference's keynote speeches.

Professor Bialer's presentation, "The Soviet Union in a Changing World," focused on the change in the correlation of forces due to the revolution in the communications, information, and service sectors that is currently under way. In this connection, he explained that although the U.S.-USSR military balance has not changed much—even after the U.S. military buildup—in nonmilitary fields such as the economy, culture, and society, Soviet leaders face a crisis. Specifically, they are confronted with a dilemma stemming from the decline of their power within their own territory and "empire" and their ambition for external expansion. Moreover, Professor Bialer stressed that the Soviet economy is unable to adapt to the technological revolution.

He warned, however, that the present Soviet crisis has not yet reached a stage that would make structural reform unavoidable. He predicted that the type of reform initiated under the present leadership will be aimed at "structural reorganization," emphasizing more effective functioning of the status quo.

Turning to Soviet foreign policy, he stressed four major policy objectives held by the Soviet leaders: to restore the image of Soviet power, to damage the image of U.S. invincibility, to launch a peace offensive toward Europe and Japan, and to try to reach an arms control agreement with the United States.

Last, Professor Bialer recommended the following as long-term U.S. policies toward the Soviet Union: to recognize that confrontation is still the primary feature of the two superpowers' relationship, to continue to rely on the effectiveness of nuclear deterrence, to maintain the understanding that minimization of the risk of direct conflict is a mutual interest, and finally to conduct policy based on a long-term perspective rather than succumbing to pressures to exploit the other's short-term weaknesses.

Sir James Eberle gave the second keynote speech, entitled "East-West Relations: A European Perspective." He warned against mutual suspicion and mistrust in U.S.-USSR relations caused by the isolation of both countries from each other and by a lack of communications. He then pointed out that perceptions of the Soviet Union and its behavior differ among the Western countries. He explained that most Europeans still believe in the effectiveness of nuclear deterrence, and that they do not recognize the Soviet Union to be an immediate threat to their security to the same degree as the Americans do. He also explained that the Europeans prefer a policy stemming from a more subtle combination of national interests—in other words, from more comprehensive security policies.

Regarding the Gorbachev regime, Director Eberle expressed his view that Gorbachev is not only a new type of Soviet leader in terms of style but, also, that he has a more positive attitude toward improving Soviet relations with the United States and Europe. To explain this, Director Eberle mentioned the changes taking place inside the Soviet bloc—namely, the fact that Moscow has begun to allow the Eastern Europeans to develop their economies in a way best suited to their own historical, geographical, and economic needs. Although there is a naturally imposed limit to such changes, Moscow recognizes the need for the Soviet and Eastern European countries to enhance cooperation with Western countries in order not to drop further behind the economic progress of the West. On the future perspective of Soviet behavior, he suggested that it seems very unlikely the Soviets will have anything to offer to the world in terms of ideology and economic management, although the Soviet Union is likely to remain a global power by virtue of its military strength.

As for the policy alternatives, Director Eberle mentioned the following two options while insisting that such changes inside the Soviet Union should take place gradually and peaceably: (1) a policy of forcing changes upon the Soviet Union by maintaining pressures in every field, and (2) a policy of encouraging changes in the Soviet society with constructive dialogues and exchanges with the outside world. He concluded his speech by saying that it would be desirable for Western policy makers to place an emphasis upon the latter policy.

On the second and third days of the symposium, four sessions were held among participants to review the domestic, economic, and foreign policy aspects of the Soviet Union. In the first session, the domestic policies of the Soviet Union were discussed. In this connection, papers were presented by Professor Hiroshi Kimura, director of the Slavic Research Center of Hokkaido University, and by Professor Boris Meissner, Institute of Soviet and East European Law, University of Köln (West Germany).

Professor Kimura explained his views on the Gorbachev regime in his presentation entitled "'Gorbachevism'—Simply Old Wine in a New Bottle?" and posed a question: Does the change in leadership make a difference in Soviet domestic and foreign policies? He then analyzed the changes in economic policies and foreign policies brought about following Gorbachev's inauguration. To start with, he noted three major factors that Gorbachev must take into account in his attempt to initiate policy changes—namely, "human environment," "the Soviet system," and "the international environment." He then pointed out that unless we define the meaning of the changes and ascertain the areas in which these changes are taking place (such areas as style, personnel, approach, policy, system, and political objectives), the discussion will be fruitless.

According to his analysis, certain changes in both style and personnel have occurred since Gorbachev became general secretary. Kimura then proceeded with an analysis of the concrete changes that have occurred in other areas. First, he reviewed the extent to which Gorbachev intends to carry out economic reform and explained that what Gorbachev has in mind is a mere reform within the framework of the present system and not a "systemic" change. Second, he contrasted the "United States–first" policy of the Gromyko era with the more indirect approach to the U.S.-Soviet relationship that aims at undermining the solidarity of the West through maintaining closer ties with Western Europe and Japan. Professor Kimura recognized signs in the Soviet foreign policy that the country is inclined toward the latter. In the context of Soviet policy toward Asia, Professor Kimura reviewed the Soviet proposal for the Pan-Asia Forum (the collective security system), improvement of Sino-Soviet relations at the practical level, and the ever-growing tendency toward a buildup of military power. He suggested that the former Soviet perception, or slighting, of Japan as a militarily inferior nation may gradually undergo a change because of the increased Soviet interest and growing importance of Japan in the economic relations within the Asia-Pacific basin regions. He pointed out that a shift of weight toward Japan can be recognized in certain changes in policy that have taken place since Gorbachev appeared on the scene. According to Professor Kimura, the replacement of Foreign Minister Gromyko, who had held a strict stance toward Japan, helped remove one obstacle that has been hindering improvement of Japan-USSR relations. He viewed the change as a more promising and challenging opportunity for Japan to improve its relations with the USSR.

Professor Boris Meissner's presentation, entitled "Implications of Leadership and Social Change for Soviet Policies," revealed the changes in Soviet leadership in Brezhnev's latter period and during the regimes of Andropov, Chernenko, and Gorbachev in terms of the social changes involved. The significance of the power change after Brezhnev was reviewed first. Professor Meissner explained that the distinct nature of the Soviet Union lies in its organization as a one-party as well as an oligarchic state. One problem confronting the leadership changes under such a system is the fact that no formal arrangement exists for the succession of power. Moreover, in a system in which no one is able to acquire his dominant position as he likes, there is a limit for an individual to exert a monolithic and solid leadership. Gorbachev is no exception. Election of Gorbachev as general secretary was not unanimous, and he must still act within the framework of the collective leadership inasmuch as he has been unable thus far to form his own faction within the party.

Despite his efforts to rejuvenate the leading cadres to overcome this problem, Gorbachev is in a difficult position in his relationship with the military, which has an influential power over policy making. Next, Professor Meissner reviewed the domestic reforms that have taken place since the Brezhnev era. Due to changes in the constellation of power among the leaders, coupled with the diversification of the social structure in the Soviet Union, its rise to a superpower, and the increasing interdependence of domestic and foreign policies, the Soviet policy inevitably oscillated as early as the Brezhnev era. Gorbachev is presently promoting an intensification of the entire economy within the formula of "completion of developed socialism." It is difficult to speculate on the form the system of economic management will take in the future. What also remains unclear is how the contradiction between comprehensive central control and planning (given the greater part being played by the party) and the envisaged increased autonomy of factories will be resolved. These changes are not irrespective of the effects of the far-reaching social changes that are undermining the Soviet Union. The increasing number of discrepancies within the bureaucratic system, and the fact that the scientific/cultural intelligentsia is at a much greater disadvantage than the technical intelligentsia, have been fostering social transformation, instability, and diversification. Gorbachev is tackling the task of extensive reforms that entail fundamental changes in the superstructure as well as in the social consciousness. If Gorbachev is to succeed, he will need a firmer and more solidified basis of power. However, as Professor Meissner warned, social reforms may unleash certain forces seeking reorganization of the existing social structure. The Communist party itself may also be forced into self-restraint.

Following the two presentations, the participants sized up the new Soviet leadership under Gorbachev and attempted to assess the possibility of changes in the Soviet Union during his administration. Many participants commented on Gorbachev's forceful personality and potential as a strong leader. Gorbachev was described as "a quite remarkable leader," "a great manipulator," "one of the most powerful leaders in Soviet history," and "a leader for emergency." Many panelists also made reference to the remarkable swiftness with which Gorbachev is consolidating his power base and boldly replacing aging officials in the party, the government, and the military with younger personnel of his own choosing.

One Japanese participant suggested the following objectives of Gorbachev's personnel policy: placing the right men in the right places of the highest organs in the party and government; seeking broader support among middle-level cadres, particularly party officials; recruiting specialists who are in a position to express their views on paper or indirectly through policy (i.e., specialists working in academic research institutes, advisers to the general secretary, and consultants attached to party and state organs). Noting that Gorbachev has thus far appointed a somewhat irregular group of associates, each with his own power base, the participant characterized Gorbachev's personnel policy to date as a "personal alliance system."

An American panelist observed that, in every succession of power in Soviet history since the days of Lenin and Stalin, each new leader has responded in his own way to "the Soviet public opinions" of his era. Gorbachev, he said, is responding to the expectations of those elites who want change and movement. This orientation, the panelist predicted, makes it very probable that Gorbachev will make sweeping changes in the ranks of the major organs at the coming 27th Party Congress. These changes, he said, may be the most extensive since the bloody purge of Stalin's day.

The same panelist noted that oligarchic rule is rarely conducive to change. He speculated that Gorbachev, himself a member of the oligarchy of the Soviet leadership, might try to bring about power beyond the oligarchy, aiming at something similar to the activism of the Khrushchev era but lacking that era's "hare-brained schemes" and constant reorganizations.

Responding to a question of whether Gorbachev intends to bring about systemic change or simply "within-system" change, a Japanese scholar argued that Gorbachev's plans for reform are limited not only to the economy. Rather, he said, Gorbachev hopes to reform the whole of Soviet society and envisions a new "revolution." He added, however, that the ultimate success of that revolution is another question entirely.

Another Japanese participant in the discussion postulated that limited economic and organizational reforms could potentially spill over into other areas and eventually lead to a change in the Soviet system itself. Then an American panelist questioned the notion of classifying change as either "change in the system" or "change of the system." No one really anticipates a fundamental change in the Soviet system in the near future, he argued. Rather, he said, the reforms conceivable in the Soviet system amount to only "the adjustment of practices." The panelist reminded us that one of the most striking features of Soviet history has been that almost every economic change in the past has been minimal and nonaccumulative, and has eventually been absorbed by the system itself. That system, he maintained, has remained Stalinist to the present day. He then expressed the belief that significant economic reform will be very difficult for Gorbachev to accomplish.

The majority of the participants on the panel shared this skeptical view. Some noted that all leaders face the difficulty of overcoming innate passivity and resistance to change by people at all levels who do not want to lose any of the functions or prerogatives associated with the existing system. An American panelist was skeptical about the impact that Gorbachev's rising political power would ultimately have on the Soviet economy. He stressed that the Soviet economy has become much bigger and more complicated than most powerful leaders have ever experienced.

Turning to the overall situation in the Soviet Union, one panelist cautioned against the tendency to underestimate the inherent stability of the Soviet system. That system has been operating for nearly three-quarters of a century, he said. In contrast to Eastern European systems, which have been transplanted from outside, the Soviet system has acquired a great deal of legitimacy. Moreover, he noted, that system is based on both Russian tradition and the experience of the Soviet people since the Revolution. Its legitimacy has also been upheld through repression, fear, and apathy. Furthermore, he argued, inadequate opportunities for upward mobility, coupled with the relatively low expectations of the Soviet people, reinforce that basic stability. The Soviet intelligentsia is firmly entrenched, and the dissidents are passive and unable to offer an alternative to the existing system. And although the nationalities problem remains unsolvable, the non-Russians in the Soviet Union tend to be calm and stable as a result of successful national policies. The panelist acknowledged that these forces are gradually weakening, but he concluded that social conditions within Soviet Russia are a long way from being "unstable."

That argument was challenged by two European scholars. One stressed that the Soviet social structure is presently undergoing a number of potentially destabilizing changes, and the other insisted that the Soviet Union is confronting a series of grave problems.

An American participant called the panel's attention to two views prevailing in the United States with regard to the influence of domestic conditions on the Soviet Union's external behavior. Some, he said, maintain that the Soviet Union will resort to further foreign expansion as a means of diverting the popular tension that will result from domestic decline. Others, he said, think that economic decline will ultimately constrain Soviet expansionism.

Another American panelist expanded on this point with the observation that events since the death of Stalin clearly demonstrate the fact that the legitimacy of their foreign policy has become an increasingly important priority for the Soviet leadership. For instance, he said, the détente of the early 1970s was a boost for Soviet stability because it enabled the Soviets to project the image that the Soviet Union was considered equal to the United States. On the other hand, he asserted, legitimacy was supported by the cold war, which created a "siege mentality" and an atmosphere of imminent crisis among the people.

The same panelist added that it is important to distinguish between Soviet activities that reinforce legitimacy of the regime and those that do not. As an example, he cited the harsh policy of the government toward Poland during the Solidarity movement. That policy was supported by the Soviet people. On the other hand, he said, the Soviet's expansionist policy toward the Third World (Afghanistan and elsewhere) is not popular. The worst situation for the leadership, he concluded, is a period in which there is neither détente, nor recognition of foreign dangers, nor a "siege mentality."

The panel also discussed the role and influence of the military under Gorbachev's leadership. A European panelist pointed out that, although the Soviet military has been very successful in getting a fairly big share of Soviet resources to build up a remarkable defense establishment, there has been no indication of any increase in the role of the military in terms of influence on the political leadership. The panelist added that the relationship between the military and political leadership might be considered somewhat similar to that in the West.

Another European participant argued that the Soviet military, though under party control, exerts more influence on policy making than do its Western counterparts. He conceded, however, that Gorbachev's relationship with the military has not been as close as that of former Soviet leaders such as Brezhnev, Andropov, and even Chernenko.

A Japanese panelist cautioned against assuming too much antagonism in the relations between the military and the party. The Politburo, as the nation's central decision-making body, acts as a kind of coalition of ruling institutions, he said. He suggested that it might be more useful for panelists to pose the question in this way: Has the voice of the military become stronger in relation to other ruling institutions?

All panelists agreed that the military, in principle, does not oppose economic reform. They concurred that the military is worried about the poor performance of the Soviet economy and is interested in raising the economy's technological standard.

Toward the end of the session, a Japanese panelist wondered what changes might be expected in the Soviet Union in the near future: Will the new leadership be strong (or desperate) enough to embark on a major reform of the stagnating Soviet society, or will it continue to "muddle through" the years ahead, leaving the major difficulties unresolved?

An American panelist concluded that although Gorbachev is a strong leader presiding over a militarily strong nation, his country remains quite weak in many other respects, especially in technology. Therefore, he said, the Soviets must be quite worried by the challenges that will face them in the years to come.

The economic policies of the Soviet Union were discussed during the second session, during which the following three presentations were made. The first presentation was given by Professor Marshall I. Goldman, associate director of the Russian Research Center at Harvard University. In his report entitled "Soviet Economic Trends, with Special Emphasis on Investment and Energy Policies," he reviewed recent trends in energy production in the Soviet Union and called attention to the shortfall between planned and actual output in coal and oil production. He then explained the importance attached by the Soviets to energy as a source of hard-currency earnings and for export to Eastern Europe. He also touched upon the Soviets' recent efforts to prevent further drops in production and to improve energy conservation. Professor Goldman predicted, however, that systemic flaws in the Soviet economy will impede the success of such measures. He concluded that the Soviet system will remain inefficient as long as the bureaucracy resists meaningful structural economic reform.

The second presentation was given by Professor Tsuneaki Sato, professor of economics at Yokohama City University. In his report entitled "Economic Reforms in China in Light of Soviet and Eastern European Experiences," Professor Sato explained that the economic reform in China has certain features in common with that of the CMEA countries. In particular, he introduced the policies to raise the living standard and to open the door to the outside world. But Professor Sato emphasized certain differences as well: (1) The level of industrial development in China is low, and competent cadres are lacking although the pressure on employment is enormous; (2) the problems that occurred in the CMEA countries during the first wave of economic reforms were appearing also in China and overlapped with the features observed during the second wave in a more compressed manner. He then suggested that the following points be taken into consideration in a comparative analysis of the economic reform in China with that in other countries: First, although the industrial reforms in China resemble those in the Eastern European countries, there is a difference in the policies on agriculture and external economic relations, which are more radical in China. Second, China aims at breaking away from the "slack centralized system of the Mao era" and not from the "tight centralized system" of the Soviet Union. Third, the economic reforms in the CMEA countries are diversified. Last, the

Chinese economy has undergone various changes as a result of the reform: (1) Different types of ownership and management now coexist; (2) the market has increased in importance; (3) economic decision making has been decentralized and has shifted more toward enterprises; and (4) material incentives have been introduced. These changes can be summarized as the manifestation of the "economic pragmatism" of China, in reaction against the predominant role of politics. The same phenomenon was observed in the CMEA countries in the 1960s, when the economic efficiency and autonomy of economic units were more strongly advocated.

Finally, Professor Sato pointed out the characteristic problems facing China during its economic reform: (1) the "slack centralized system" itself may hinder the reform; (2) development of the commodity economy is running into difficulties, and (3) enterprises are burdened with the social task of absorbing unemployed people. Hence the economic system of China is only at the initial stage of institutionalization, and the "slackness in the centralized system" has been rather enhanced by the reform. Although the economic reform of China will certainly bear an impact on the CMEA countries, the country still faces such political issues as abandonment of the paternalistic attitude of the state toward enterprises and the need for enterprises to tighten their budget restrictions. The enormous pressure for employment has aggravated the problem. However, with the advancement of its reform, China will be redefining its limits in terms of both planning and market, but without recapitulating the sequence of reform measures experienced in Hungary.

The next presentation was given by Professor Peter Knirsch, Free University of Berlin (West Germany). In his report entitled "Economic Relations Between the Soviet Union and Eastern Europe and Their Implications for East-West Relations" Professor Knirsch explained the foreign economic relations among the CMEA countries in terms of the following factors: (1) the central governments' control of the impact of their foreign economic relations on national economy by means of planning and restrictive measures; (2) the indirect reflection of world market prices of import goods on domestic prices; and (3) the dominant influence of political decisions on intra-CMEA trade as well as trade with the Western industrialized countries. Another general characteristic of the foreign trade of the CMEA countries is that it accounts for a larger share of national income among Eastern European members of CMEA than in the Soviet Union. A fairly high dependence on the Soviet Union also exists in these smaller CMEA countries. Although this has an institutional advantage given that the Eastern European countries have much in common with the Soviet Union, it is disadvantageous because it perpetuates their inability to compete on the world market.

Professor Knirsch then pointed out that economic integration within the CMEA has been hindered by the distrust of the Soviet Union felt among the smaller member countries and by their insistence on national sovereignty aroused by the following historical developments: (1) the economic growth of the smaller countries, which declined because they had to procure the funds necessary to explore natural resources in the Soviet Union; (2) increased deficits in their national economy due to the revision of price agreements and the oil price rise;

and (3) cancellation of the bilateral delivery agreements regarding Polish products as a result of the crisis in Poland.

Turning to the subject of East-West economic relations, Professor Knirsch explained that smaller percentages of total exports from the Soviet Union and the United States are accounted for by East-West trade, relative to that of the smaller member countries. This difference has sowed seeds of discord among the member countries of each bloc. The East is more dependent on trade with the West than the other way around. So long as the East imports commodities from the West in order to fill the shortage of domestic daily goods, the economic growth rate of the East cannot be improved and thus presents an obstacle to invigoration of East-West trade. Economic factors such as stagnation of the CMEA economy, accumulated debts, and recession of the Western economy have slowed East-West trade. As a result, the significance of intra-CMEA trade has increased. However, intra-CMEA economic relations will not be in a position to replace East-West trade. In a sense, as East-West economic relations supplement intra-CMEA relations, they may contribute to a reduction of the dependence of Eastern European countries on the Soviet Union. In other words, the CMEA countries can find an advantage in extension of the East-West trade relations.

The panelists followed these presentations with a discussion of the energy problem as a case study of the Soviet economy. They subsequently turned their attention to the problem of technological development and the prospects for economic reform under Gorbachev.

Commenting on the energy problem, a Japanese panelist drew attention to the Soviets' notoriously inefficient use of energy. In the Soviet Union, he observed, energy is consumed at 50–100 percent more per unit of GNP in every category than it is in the United States, the European Community, and in Japan. The Soviets might more profitably concern themselves with promoting energy conservation than increasing energy production, he said. Soviet leaders and economists acknowledge this need for a shift in emphasis, he added. The question now, he pointed out, is whether the Soviet leaders will change their energy policy to favor conservation, or whether they will pursue a two-front policy aimed at expanding production *and* enhancing conservation.

Gas production in the Soviet Union is forecast to continue to increase steadily, offsetting the decline of oil production. But gas cannot be exported to the West as easily as oil because of the nature of gas consumption patterns and the lack of sufficient pipelines. So, unless exports to Eastern European countries and/or domestic consumption are rolled back, the Soviets' energy exports to hard-currency countries will gradually decline. The problem now, the panelist said, is implementing conservation programs that will create an oil surplus.

An American economist advanced the opinion that, thus far, Gorbachev seems to have pursued simultaneously expanded production and increased conservation, and noted that Gorbachev emphasized these two goals on his recent trip to Tyumen. The economist stated that he has grave doubts as to whether Gorbachev can succeed in accomplishing both of these objectives.

On the subject of Soviet technology, a Japanese economist commented that in recent years, the Soviet economy suffered from a lack of continuity in the field of technological development. Soviet influence in the international realm, he observed, has been predicated on its vast natural resources, its extraordinary military power, and its high economic growth rate. But the Soviet economy has performed poorly of late, and if it remains as it is, each of the other factors will inevitably suffer. The problem facing Soviet leadership now, he said, is whether they can revive the nation's weak economy in such a way that it will be able to hold its own in an era of technological innovation.

Acknowledging some gains in production in the Soviet economy, the same panelist called attention to declining efficiency in the manufacturing, agriculture, and energy sectors. The Soviet economy seems to be having difficulty shifting from an agricultural economy to an industrial economy, he said, and has particular trouble making the transition to a service economy.

When measured in terms of input per unit of GNP, output, and productivity, Soviet R&D endeavors stack up fairly well, he said. But, he added, the evidence suggests that the Soviets' will have a difficult time matching international standards for high technology. Rapid technological development presupposes at least four preconditions, he said: mass-production of hardware, orientation to mass participation, technological literacy throughout the nation, and innovation from below. In other words, the new technology demands that programmers and systems engineers be able to act freely and that the circulation of information be unrestricted. Lacking these preconditions, he concluded, the Soviet Union's command economy is ill-suited to promotion of new technology.

The same economist forecast three policy options for the Soviet economy in the future: (1) to ease international tension as a means of obtaining new technology on credit from the West; (2) to restrict military expenditures and avoid increased investment in the military sector; and (3) to embark on reform from above. However, the top-down nature of the Soviet economy will have to be dramatically restructured if entrepreneurship from below is to flourish. Can Gorbachev succeed in making such revisions in the old system? The Japanese economist answered in the negative.

A European scholar remarked that the Soviets' main problem in the high-technology field is not invention but implementation. Under the centralized socialist system it is very difficult to make use of new technology, he said, whether it is developed within the Soviet Union or imported from abroad.

Another Japanese panelist expressed disappointment in Gorbachev's programs for economic reform on the grounds that they lack fresh ideas and are too narrow in scope. Although Gorbachev can correctly be described a reformer, he seems to have disappointed Western hopes that he might be a promoter of market socialism. The panelist was hesitant to categorically label Gorbachev's programs as conservative and did not rule out the possibility that he might introduce a quasi-market socialism similar to the economies of Hungary or China. The panelist also pointed out, however, that the Soviet leaders seem unmoved by the potential advantages of market socialism. Their starting point for economic reform, he said, is not market socialism but adjustment of the present centrally planned economy.

Acknowledging Gorbachev as a strong leader—far stronger than Deng Xiaoping of China—an American participant expressed doubt as to whether Gorbachev is in a position to move as effectively as Deng in revitalizing the economy. The panelist suggested that the Soviets' critical response to China's economic reforms gives some indication of the problems Gorbachev is worried about in carrying out economic reform in the Soviet Union. Generally speaking, Gorbachev's problem is that the Soviet economic system is far stronger and far more deeply entrenched than that of China. Thus, the Soviet Union would face severe problems if it were to embark on a program of reform as ambitious as that undertaken in China.

In assessing economic reforms in China, the Soviets have focused on inflation and the potential for anarchy, the panelist said. They have shown particular disdain for the expanding role of China's private sector, fearing that as private activities come to play a more important role in the economy, that of the central planners becomes less significant. Any departure from a system of central planning, they fear, might ultimately lead to disruption and anarchy in the whole economy.

There are many other aspects of the Chinese economy, the panelist added, that disturb the Soviets inasmuch as they are contrary to the notion of socialism as they understand it. Chinese socialism has allowed the introduction of foreign capital on a wide scale. It has also spawned increasing unemployment and engendered the growth of corruption within Chinese society.

As in China, the strongest opposition to reform in the Soviet Union comes from within the bureaucracy. The bureaucrats fear that reform will result in a downgrading of their power and prerogatives. In addition, radical economic change would require the Soviet leaders to break the implicit social contract to provide law and order without inflation or unemployment.

Coming to grips with his nation's high-technology problem will be Mikhail Gorbachev's greatest challenge, the American panelist said. To date, the nation's greatest strength has been the Soviet system's ability to mobilize large amounts of capital for expanding the scale of production and promoting technological development. Those policies worked well while the rate of technological development was relatively stable, but, he said, the pace of high-technology improvements is much more rapid today. At present, the life cycle for high-technology products is only two to three years. In this situation, what matters is not centralized mobilization and allocation of capital but flexible performance and quick response time. The essentials today are much different: diversity of invention, unrestricted movement of people, the free flow of information, decentralized financing, and so on. In fact, he asserted, the central planning system of the Soviet Union is "exactly an antithesis" of what functions most effectively in the high-technology age. The panelist drew the conclusion that the meaningful reforms desired by Gorbachev will inevitably affect so many segments off the Soviet society that their success seems unlikely.

A Japanese economist, by contrast, said that he is "slightly optimistic" about the prospects for change in the Soviet economy. Agreeing with other participants' contentions that Gorbachev's reform will encounter a good deal of resistance, he stressed that Gorbachev has clearly started off in a new direction that must be considered a distinct departure from the Brezhnev course. He said he foresees two possible types of change in the Soviet economy: reform of management and administrative structure, and market-oriented reforms. He conceded that the latter cannot be expected to be carried out in the latter half of the 1980s. But some reorganization of economic administration (e.g., "integration" of certain branch ministries, founding of new "big" ministries, and reorganization of the State Planning Committee) might prove "not at all unimportant," for these changes, he said, would improve the coordination of activities among the Soviet Union's economic organizations. However, he too was pessimistic about the possibility of legalization of "the second economy."

Citing panelist Marshall Goldman's recent article in *Foreign Affairs,* one American said that sheer "desperation" would play a key role in the course of economic reforms. The Chinese decided to embark on economic reform only after they had undergone severe political and economic convulsions following the Cultural Revolution. The Soviet Union, however, has not yet reached such a desperate situation. Nevertheless, he said, Soviet intellectuals have begun talking about contradictions between the basis and the superstructure of the Soviet society, feared to be on the verge of exploding sooner or later if nothing is done. The problem of reform in the Soviet Union, he said, should therefore be viewed in a wider political context. The pressure within the Soviet system will continue to increase, he said, and if the reforms in China should prove successful and the technological gap between the Soviet Union and the rest of the world continues to grow, the need for reform might be so acute that even the military might turn reformist.

According to an American economist, the Soviet economy could sustain a certain degree of growth without reform, but it would be the wrong kind of growth. It would be growth limited to old technology. In any case, he said, the Soviet Union will continue to be a strong military and political power, even if it cannot reach world levels in economic development because economic power and military capability do not always coincide. The cases of Japan and China clearly illustrate this fact, he added.

A European participant noted the possibility of better use of resources under the existing system, and observed that the Soviet economy might do even better in the next five or ten years if that system could be rationalized. He cited the Soviet Union's poor infrastructure as the primary bottleneck of the economy.

The comment of a Japanese panelist summed up what seems to have been the consensus of those present at the session. The panelist remarked that it was unlikely that economic reforms would bear fruit under the Gorbachev regime, and that the Soviet Union will continue to "muddle through" in years to come just as it has in the past. There were slight differences in the panelists' views on this point, of course, ranging from "most pessimistic" to "slightly optimistic."

The same Japanese panelist raised the following questions in conclusion: Could the Soviets possibly find a middle road between a central planning system and a market economy? Could these two contradicting systems coexist, or even supplement each other?

An American economist answered in the negative, pointing out again that the Soviets were unlikely to permit either expansion of the private sector or legalization of "the second economy"—primarily because they feared that these measures would bring about dispersion of resources, infringe on the powers of those in the public sector, and eventually lead to anarchy in the economy.

If the Soviets embark on economic reform, the American panelist said, it will be easier for them to begin with agricultural reform. Changes in this area, he offered, will have the least impact on the country as a whole. The economist noted, however, that Gorbachev has initiated certain agricultural measures, such as more irrigation, more productivity, harder work, and so on; but he has made no mention of allowing more private plots or implementing the "collective contract system based on family" that academician T. Zaslavskaya has proposed. In other words, Gorbachev has been talking about the amelioration of a bad situation, not about fundamental reform.

Expressing a view of the majority of the panelists, the American concluded that "the experiences of the '60s left me very skeptical" about the prospect of economic reform under the Gorbachev leadership.

The theme of the third session of the symposium was Soviet foreign policy in general. Professor Kenichi Ito, Aoyama-Gakuin University, presented his views on "Continuity in the Pattern of Russo-Soviet External Behavior." He discussed the external behavior of the present-day Soviet Union at three levels—grand strategy, military strategy, and diplomatic negotiating tactics—and attempted to find a continuity between current sociocultural factors and those of Tsarist Russia. At the grand strategy level, he pointed out that the external behavior of the Russo-Soviet nation can be regarded as falling into the "hunter" category. This "hunter" type exercises power prudently against strong opponents but aggressively against weaker opponents. At the military strategy level, the Soviets' external behavior is characterized by the disparity between their defensive strength and their offensive fragility and by their inherent tendency to try to compensate their qualitative weaknesses with quantitative superiority. At the level of diplomatic negotiating tactics, their behavior exhibits such features as (1) lack of consistency, (2) reliance on the "rule of force" rather than the "rule of law" (a contractual concept), and (3) coexistence of righteous language with aggressive actions based on adoption of "fait accompli."

These characteristics of the Soviets' external behavior are attributable to two factors harking back to Tsarist Russia—the geopolitical/natural factor and the historical/human factor—and to three factors of disruption—Marxism, technological progress, and higher international status. The "hunter" trait of the Russians was formed as a result of the fact that the steppes could not be used as natural barriers against foreign invasions; in addition, the forests of Russia offered a shelter from invaders. The historical influence of the Byzantine and Mongolian empires increased the tolerance of the Russians toward the State's interference in the activities of individuals; it also made them indifferent to human rights and alienated them from Western individualism. The disruptive nature of Marxism, which has been Russianized, should not be overestimated. Although the Soviet Union's technology has advanced to the extent that the buffer zones have lost their classic military significance, and although the Soviet

Union has achieved an unprecedentedly high international status, it is still unlikely to modify its "hunter"-type behavior. In this context, it may be said that the external behavior of the Soviet Union has inherited much from Tsarist Russia. This approach is positioned halfway between the "essentialist" and "contextualist" approaches.

Professor Tsuyoshi Hasegawa, Slavic Research Center of Hokkaido University, made his presentation on "The Military Factor in Soviet Foreign Policy." He reviewed the differences between the "essentialist" and "contextualist" approaches in terms of historical factors, ideological factors, military power, and military doctrine. The "essentialist" approach represented by Richard Pipes asserts that Soviet expansionism is historically attributable to the innate nature of the Russian nation. But according to Professor Hasegawa, such expansionism should instead be regarded as motivated by national security, nationalism, and imperialism, as the nation has had to depend heavily on military power in order to defend the socialist system from both internal class enemies and external imperialist nations. The Soviet political and social systems were militarized as a function of this ideology; more particularly, Leninism inherently incorporates the militaristic mentality. The role of ideology in diplomacy declined drastically as (1) national interest was emphasized as a political object, (2) China emerged, (3) the attraction of the Soviet model of industrialization was diminished, and (4) nuclear weapons were developed. (Despite such changes, ideology continues to function as an international political theory of power politics, which asserts the right of the strongest.) Military power has thus become important as a diplomatic means. Indeed, the Soviet Union has become a global superpower as a result of its enormous military buildup. But it has had to pay the costs for this as well: (1) The response of adversaries (e.g., SDI) has been provoked; (2) the means of assistance for the Third World has been relegated to the area of military power; and (3) the nation has been forced to sacrifice economic well-being. That the Soviet Union is beset by these problems while maintaining military superiority indicates that it is inherently motivated by the need to exert military power.

The "essentialists" assert that the Soviet Union aims at acquiring first-strike capability because of its war-fighting philosophy but, in reality, it reached parity with the United States in the 1970s and shifted to mutual deterrence. If the Western countries react with military expansion alone, overlooking the fact that Soviet military doctrine has been changing to meet new situations, and if they do not pursue military management concurrently, Soviet military doctrine will be changed in such a way as to disturb the safety and security of the Western countries. In reviewing such factors newly involved in this issue, we should reject the rigid theory of confrontation against the Soviet Union based upon the essentialistic view; at the same time we should pay attention to the fact that the history and ideology unique to Soviet Russia causes it to behave differently from the Western countries in response to foreign countries. We should refuse to accept those two illusions and, instead, approach the issue on the premises of long-term competitive and conflicting relations with the USSR.

Discussion during the third session naturally centered on the basic characteristics of Soviet foreign policy. Issues considered under this heading included domestic and foreign policy connections in Soviet decision making, the military role in the formation of Soviet foreign policy, and possible diplomatic options open to the Gorbachev regime.

The panelists opened the discussion by taking up the question of methodology. Which analytical framework, they asked, best suits the task of assessing Soviet foreign policy? The responses to this question can broadly be summarized as follows: Soviet foreign policy is partly motivated by immutable factors such as geography, and partly by contextual factors such as U.S.-Soviet relations in a given period or the impact of a particular foreign policy on internal Soviet affairs.

Russo-Soviet nationalism was also mentioned as a factor affecting the formation of Soviet foreign policy. A European panelist noted the discontinuity inherent in Russo-Soviet nationalism, which, he said, has been heavily influenced by Orthodox Christianity, whereas Soviet nationalism is predicated on Leninism and the influence of Stalin.

Turning to the "nuts and bolts" of regular Soviet foreign policy planning, some panelists expressed the view that Soviet foreign policy planners have a tendency to think that their foreign policy can be implemented in a vacuum and seldom consider what possible reaction their policy might bring about in the other superpower's policy.

A second focus of discussion during this session was the role of the military in Soviet foreign policy. An American participant warned that, to avoid confusion, it was essential that the panelists first clarify what aspect of "military role" they intended to explore. He cautioned against the tendency to confuse the role of the military *factor* in Soviet policy making with the role of the military *sector* in Soviet policy making.

The Soviets have always depended on a strong military as the primary means of realizing their foreign policy objectives, he said. That dependence has prevailed as a central feature of Soviet foreign policy design since the Revolution, and will remain a dominant factor in domestic and international policy making in the future. That dependence, he explained, derives not only from the Soviets' belief that power grows from the end of a gun barrel but also from the scarcity of ideological, economic, cultural, and political resources available to them as foreign policy tools. He cautioned, however, that it would be wrong to infer from these observations that the role of the Soviet military establishment has expanded in Soviet decision making. On the contrary, he said, his observations have led him to the conclusion that, under the present leadership, the influence of the military sector is on the decline. In support of this contention he cited the following factors: There is no full Politburo member from the military; the influence of the present military leader is weaker than that of his predecessors; and leaders from the younger generation seem to have fewer ties with the military than do their elders.

The third major point of discussion in this session concerned Soviet military technology and its implications for security. Many participants expressed interest in the present level of military technology in the Soviet Union and the attitude toward economic reform in the military sector. Agreeing with an observation made in the presentation of a Japanese panelist that the Soviets tend to compensate technical inferiority with numerical superiority, a European scholar pointed out that the Soviets are inclined to use obsolete and outdated weapons. But he warned that, in wartime, the sophisticated weapons recently introduced in the West may not be utilized as efficiently as in peacetime; thus we should not underestimate the number of obsolete weapons being stocked by the Soviets.

A Japanese participant described as a misconception the notion that the Soviets are behind in every technological field. In some fields, notably those of production and deployment of military hardware, the Soviets have demonstrated an excellent capacity to investigate the R&D of other nations and, with a lag-time of only about five years, have been catching up to the technological superiority of the West. The Soviets might also develop a north-south overland transportation capability in the future, he said, and could eventually develop a year-round transpolar transportation capability, both of which will have a major impact on the security interests of the West. He also argued that the West should not underestimate the Soviets' appetite for new technology. That appetite might compel them to seek a sort of neo-détente similar to that of the early 1970s, but such an agreement would be aimed only at introducing and catching up to the Western level of technology.

The panelists also took up the question of military balance in Asia and attempted to assess Soviet perceptions of both military balance and "equal security" in that region. A Japanese panelist recalled that an influential and prominent Soviet specialist had responded to the same question by saying that, because of geographical asymmetries, the Soviets will not be satisfied with mere quantitative equality in weapons, missiles, and so on. He asserted that the Soviets are convinced of their right to have more weapons, and that this attitude was clearly demonstrated in the European INF talks. The notion of regional parity is much harder to define in Asia, the Japanese panelist said, as it is an area involving more complicated political, diplomatic, and geographical circumstances.

Extending on this idea, an American participant recalled a somewhat sarcastic observation made by one U.S. general that, to the Soviets, "near-parity" is a numerical superiority of 6 to 1, and "parity" is a ratio of 10 to 1.

On the topic of allocation of resources to the military, one scholar expressed the opinion that the Soviets' primary problem is no longer a matter of what percentage of the nation's resources should be allotted to the military, as it was in the post-Brezhnev era, but, rather, a question of how that fixed percentage should be allocated within the military. Should it go to "direct military expenditure for weapon systems," or should it be earmarked for investment to the military industrial complex? The scholar noted a difference of views between Ustinov and Ogarkov on this issue.

With respect to the attitude of the military sector toward economic reform, the general consensus was that the military per se does not oppose reforms as it opposed détente in the early 1970s. At the same time, however, an American participant expressed the view that real reform in the Soviet system will be implemented only when the military might of the Soviet Union is truly in danger.

A fourth area of discussion during this session was the rather broad topic of prospects of foreign policy under Gorbachev. According to one American participant, the Gorbachev administration has four medium-range foreign policy objectives: bolstering the image of the Soviet Union as a world power; denigrating the notion of U.S. invincibility through propaganda campaigns and skillful exploitation of Western weaknesses; encouraging détente and developing closer relations with Europe and Japan; and proceeding with efforts to reach an arms control agreement with the United States.

The scholar doubted, however, that all of these objectives could be sustained in the long term. He ruled out near-isolationism and détente with the United States as viable prospects for U.S.-Soviet relations. The best possible option available for the Gorbachev regime is to conclude an arms control agreement with the United States, without détente. After presenting these observations, the American scholar remarked that the policy options left for Gorbachev are very limited.

The fifth major issue for discussion was the prospect of an arms control agreement between the two superpowers. Such an agreement was considered by the panelists as the minimum prerequisite to a significant improvement in U.S.-Soviet relations. Most of the scholars expressed concern that the deployment of SDI by the United States would undoubtedly result in a massive arms race between the two countries; they also agreed that the United States should handle the SDI issue with extreme caution.

A European panelist warned that the pace of arms development is already so rapid that there might be less chance to restrain it at lower levels in the future. An American panelist, noting the present bilateral climate in U.S.-Soviet relations, worried about the presence of a "vicious circle" in the two superpowers' relations: Stymied political relations bar progress in military negotiations, and vice versa. He said that a spirit of accommodation was essential in order to resolve the miliary questions, but that the present political situation makes it difficult for either side to develop or foster such a spirit.

In the fourth session, the panel discussed the Soviet Union's foreign policy in Asia, following three presentations. Professor Donald S. Zagoria, in his presentation entitled "The U.S.-Soviet Rivalry in East Asia," expressed the view that the overall situation in the Pacific and Asian area is favorable for the West for the foreseeable future, despite its many vulnerabilities in the region. He said that the foreign policy options for Gorbachev are particularly slight in this region. He also stressed that in terms of the military balance in the region, the United States retains a naval and air superiority that seems unlikely to change.

In addition, he maintained that the long-range danger for the Soviet Union in this region is growing. He cited the formation of a U.S.-led security and economic coalition as one possible example of such a danger. The Soviet Union, he said, is deeply concerned about the existing correlation of forces, and trends for the future are moving against their aspirations.

Professor Zagoria then explained the present situation in the Asia-Pacific region and its future perspective, focusing especially on the economic trends in the region, U.S.-Japan-China relations, and the strategic situation. He concluded that the overall correlation of forces is generally unfavorable to the Soviet Union. Regarding the Asian Security proposal, Professor Zagoria said that the purpose of the plan is to get the Soviets into the security game in this region, from which they are now almost isolated. He stressed that military expansion by the Soviets in the region is aimed at enhancing their ability of power projection. He then summed up by observing that there are many obstacles hindering the Soviets from improving the situation in their favor, and he doubted the possibility of their making any major breakthrough.

Professor Young C. Kim, Institute for Sino-Soviet Studies at George Washington University, made three major points in his presentation entitled "Soviet Policies Toward Korea." First, he tried to clarify the concept of Soviet interest in the Korean peninsula, arguing that Soviet policy is directed toward the prevention of the establishment of hegemonic influence over Korea by an external power. He said that the Soviet Union itself aims to exercise the ultimate hegemonic influence over Korea.

Next, he touched upon the major factors shaping Soviet policy toward Korea, including the present and probable future policies being pursued by North and South Korea toward the Soviet Union, internal developments in both countries, and the international political environment on the peninsula as influenced by the major actors in the area—the United States, China, Japan, and the Soviet Union. He pointed out that the Soviets are sensitive to any external developments regarding Korea that might significantly affect the existing distribution of power.

Finally, Professor Kim singled out some of the policies being pursued by the Soviets during the past decade. He pointed out that the Soviet government has been consistent in publicly declaring its support for North Korea's official position on reunification and other foreign policy programs. He noted, however, that the Soviet Union often implicitly acknowledges the existence of two Koreas in its actual foreign policy. The Soviet attitude toward South Korea is not limited to a desire to maintain nonpolitical contacts. The Soviets display great caution in their relations with South Korea because they believe the U.S. influence there to be overwhelming and want to avoid antagonizing North Korea, thereby risking a strengthening of the bonds between China and North Korea.

With regard to Soviet policy toward North Korea, Professor Kim explained that the Soviets have recently expressed their support for an ongoing North-South dialogue on all fronts; moreover, in addition to direct support, the Soviet Union frequently—albeit indirectly—promotes North Korea's interests through a Soviet media denunciation of South Korea's domestic and foreign policy programs. In this connection, he emphasized the recent transfer of the MIG-23 to North Korea. At the end of his presentation, Professor Kim concluded that during the next several years, extraordinary and dynamic developments in and concerning Korea will pose a great challenge to Soviet foreign policy makers.

Mr. Kazuyuki Kinbara, staff economist, Japan Federation of Economic Organizations (Keidanren), made his presentation on "Japan and the Development of Siberia." He explained that Japan's interest in Siberia, because of its resources and potential as a market, coupled with the Soviet Union's interest in seeking credit and technology from Japan, have given rise to the Japan-Soviet Siberian Development Projects (JSSDPs). Mr. Kinbara explained that the economic cooperation over Siberian development has taken on a unique character for three major reasons: (1) It is one of the very few areas in which the interests of both countries meet, despite their chilly relationship overall; (2) the Japan-Soviet Economic Committee (JSEC) is the only official channel for negotiations on this matter, and no individual cooperation takes part in the actual negotiations; and (3) it has served as a barometer of the state of Japan-Soviet economic relations as a whole. He then reviewed the political and international implications of this economic cooperation over Siberian development by dividing its history into four phases. The First Phase (1961–1965) witnessed the establishment of the JSEC and the initiation of economic missions, led by such individuals as Kawai, Nagano, Uemura, and Mikoyan, that paved the way for mutual cooperation. The development projects were institutionalized during Phase Two (1965–1969) through the efforts of the Japan-Soviet Economic Committee and the Soviet counterpart, the Soviet-Japan Economic Committee (SJEC). Three JSSDPs were established during this period. The Japan-Soviet cooperation over Siberian development reached its peak in Phase Three (1970–1975). This period may be differentiated from Phase Two in four respects: (1) Joint "executive sessions" of the two committees were held; (2) the energy-related projects were expanded in terms of both quality and scale; (3) the Japanese government was involved, primarily with respect to finances; and (4) certain projects, such as the Yakutian Natural Gas Development Project, in this phase had impacts strong enough to oblige the JSEC to seek U.S. participation and to cause serious concern on the part of China. Economic cooperation during Phase Four (1976–1985) fell to a low ebb when no new projects materialized (except for the "Third Stage of the Soviet Far East Forest Resources Development Project," which was a continuation of the preceding phases). This was primarily due to a failure on the Soviet side to propose new projects, which it could not afford to do because of capital and labor shortages.

On the other hand, the Soviet Union emphasized the necessity of a framework for even longer-term economic cooperation and attempted more strongly to make the Japanese government a direct party. But a number of problems decrease the likelihood of the realization of new Siberian collaborative projects. These problems include (1) the discontent felt by the Japanese side as to its contribution to costs in the projects and its preclusion from the operation, (2) the gap between the two nations in geographical priorities for the Siberian development, and (3) the Soviet Union's economic difficulties. Japan's dependence on the Soviet Union for natural resources is not significant, and cooperation is unlikely to have much impact, so that the Soviet Union would not exert political pressure on Japan by threatening supply stoppage of the resources developed by these projects. Because of its strong military character, the Tyumen Oil Development Project failed to obtain effective support from the Japanese government and the United States. The Japanese government, on the other hand, linked the project with the Northern Territories issue. The implication is that a maximum permissible limit to Japanese involvement exists with regard to Siberian development.

Another factor restricting Japan-Soviet economic cooperation is Japan's constant and firm loyalty to the United States. The era of huge energy-related projects is over, and because of the economic problems in the USSR and the structural changes in the Japanese economy, the cooperation will steer toward the modernization of Soviet industry and establishment of joint venture businesses. Government-level basic economic cooperation agreements are also likely. In any case, the political issues must be weighed against economic matters for the time being.

During the fourth session, discussion focused on Japan-Soviet relations, Sino-Soviet relations, and Soviet policy in the Korean peninsula. A Japanese panelist, reflecting on past and present economic relations between Japan and the Soviet Union, speculated that the Japanese business community might remain cool to the notion of moving ahead with bilateral trade even if the political dialogue between the two nations improves. This is so, he said, because Japan's industrial structure has undergone a transformation that has rendered it less dependent on the type of natural resources available through Siberian development.

Following some further discussion of the prospects of improvement in the Japan-Soviet economic relationship, the panel discussed the two nations' political relationship. A Japanese commentator emphasized the need to analyse Soviet-Japanese relations in a broader context—in the framework of international politics in East Asia and the global power confrontation between the Soviet Union and the United States. He argued that the Northern Territories issue is not the sole barrier to improved Japan-Soviet relations. Rather, he said, that issue may be a symbol of a more important confrontation between the two nations. In a departure from the sometimes strident stances taken by foreign policy under the direction of Gromyko, the Gorbachev administration seems to be trying to pursue a softer line in its relationship with Japan; but the Japanese scholar said that he doubted the possibility of a substantial change in policy. The Soviet Union's policy options with regard to its relationship with Japan in East Asia, he noted, are severely limited. He surmised that Foreign Minister Schevardnadze's visit to Japan will be aimed at improving Japan's image of the Soviet Union: He will try to demonstrate the new administration's difference from the old leaders.

As for possible Japanese reactions to such overtures, the panelist recommended that Japan overestimate rather than underestimate Gorbachev's abilities. He advised Japan to cautiously take stock of his leadership by assessing how effectively Gorbachev manages to change domestic and foreign policy.

Another panelist expressed a slighly more optimistic assessment of the possibilities for Soviet-Japanese trade. The Gorbachev administration may realize, he speculated, that it can ill-afford to channel resources to the development of Siberia if it hopes to deal adequately with domestic economic priorities. Consequently, its desire for foreign capital assistance may grow to the point that it becomes willing to re-approach Japan with a more attractive offer in return for financial assistance.

A European panelist noted the similarity in trade relations between Japan and the Soviet Union and those between Eastern and Western Europe. In both relationships, he said, political constraints emerged during the 1970s as trade volumes increased. Also in both cases, he added, trade relations were complicated by the fear of overdependency on the part of the nations in the Western bloc.

Turning to the subject of Sino-Soviet relations, a Japanese participant raised three points of disagreement with the conclusions of an American scholar on the panel, arguing that the present situation in Asia does not permit much room for optimism. First, he warned, careful analysis of the policy orientation does not warrant the conclusion that China can be considered a quasi-ally of the West. He admitted that Chinese foreign policy is still more pro-Western than it is pro-Soviet, but he insisted that, after 1982, Chinese foreign policy became "multidimensional." China's policy, he argued, should not be interpreted as exclusively pro-Western, for it differs issue by issue (the Chinese, he noted, call it "independent foreign policy"). He acknowledged that there is probably no possibility of any major breakthrough in Sino-Soviet relations, but he cited Vice Prime Minister Arkhipov's visit to China, Vice-Premier Yao Yilin's visit to Moscow, the conclusion of the long-term trade agreement, and a series of improvements in emotional climate as indications that the Sino-Soviet relationship is improving. The present Chinese policy direction, he concluded, strongly resembles that of the nonaligned countries.

Some panelists expressed the idea that a reliable means of predicting the future development of Sino-Soviet relations is to determine whose technology China needs more—that of an advanced Western nation or that of the Soviet Union. The panelists were divided on this question; some emphasized China's need to introduce Western technology, and others argued, first, that in order to modernize machines and equipment purchased from the Soviet Union in the 1950s, China will need Soviet technology, and, second, that Soviet technology more closely corresponds to the Chinese economy in its present stage of development.

A Japanese panelist warned against an overly optimistic assessment of the situation in East Asia. He noted that many pro-Western nations in Asia perceive China as a threat and are staunchly opposed to the idea of expanded cooperation between the West and China. He cited the fear of certain Asian countries that expanded cooperation from the West might unduly strengthen China and noted that this attitude is particularly evident in the Indonesian move for rapprochement with Vietnam.

An American panelist rebutted this argument by saying that China has many interests relating to the West, and noted that this attitude is reflected in some of the political problems in Asia, including the Cambodian issue and the geopolitical problems relating to Pakistan. Moreover, he said, China needs the United States to counterbalance the Soviet Union. Perception of China as a threat has also undergone a transformation in some of the Asian countries such as Singapore, he said.

There seemed to be a divergence in the assessments of the American and Japanese panelists in terms of the overall East Asian situation and their interpretations of China's status vis-à-vis the West. The panelists agreed, however, that neither present trends in East Asia nor recent changes in China's attitude toward the West are necessarily at odds with Western interests.

With regard to China's influence in the Korean peninsula, an American specialist expressed the opinion that the Chinese influence is not as strong as the Chinese think it is. The relevance of Chinese economic modernization is allowing the North Koreans to implement similar programs more easily by using China's modernization as a justification for such policies. As to the implications of the 1988 Olympics regarding the political situation in the Korean peninsula, the American panelist noted that it will challenge the legitimacy of the North Korean regime. He also said that an arrangement of some means by which North Koreans can participate in the Olympics would be highly desirable.

Turning to the subject of recent Soviet–North Korea relations, the panelists noted the transfer of the MIG-23 and wondered what the Soviets had requested from North Korea in return. One panelist asked if there was any truth to a Japanese news report that the Soviets had received rights to fly military aircraft over North Korean territory. An American panelist responded that the Soviet part of the bargain is not yet totally clear, but he acknowledged that the Soviets regularly exercise fly-over rights as well as the right of port call at Najin for commercial purposes. He cautioned that this right of port call might take on military significance in the event of an emergency.

With respect to the idea of cross-recognition between the two Koreas, the American panelist said that because of the strong opposition of the North Korean leader, the prospect for acceptance of this idea by all concerned parties is not very promising. This same panelist proposed that the six countries concerned with the recognition issue—North Korea, South Korea, the Soviet Union, China, the United States, and Japan—must establish trade or liaison offices in each other's capitals. Although this proposal stops short of reaching cross-recognition, it would be a first step, he said, toward promoting a dialogue among the countries involved.

Kinya Niiseki

Appendix B

PROGRAM AND CONFERENCE PARTICIPANTS

PROGRAM

October 2, 1985

KEYNOTE LECTURES

Japan's Role in the International Community for the Twenty-first Century
Iichiro Hatoyama, Member of the House of Councillors, former Minister for Foreign Affairs

The Soviet Union in a Changing World
Seweryn Bialer, Director, Research Institute on International Change, Columbia University, New York

East-West Relations: A European Perspective
James Eberle, Director, Royal Institute of International Affairs, London

October 3, 1985

SESSION I: SOVIET DOMESTIC POLICY

"Gorbachevism"—Simply Old Wine in a New Bottle?
Hiroshi Kimura, Director, Slavic Research Center, University of Hokkaido

Implications of Leadership and Social Change for Soviet Policies
Boris Meissner, Professor of Law, Institute of Soviet and East European Law, University of Köln

Discussion
Discussants: Prof. Seweryn Bialer
Prof. Shugo Minagawa
Prof. Akio Kimura

SESSION II: ECONOMIC POLICIES

Soviet Economic Trends, with Special Emphasis on Investment and Energy Policies
Marshall I. Goldman, Professor of Economics, Wellesley College, and Associate Director, Russian Research Center, Harvard University

Economic Reforms in China in Light of Soviet and Eastern European Experiences
Tsuneaki Sato, Professor of Economics, Yokohama City University

Economic Relations Between the Soviet Union and Eastern Europe and Their Implications for East-West Relations

Peter Knirsch, Professor of Economics, Osteuropa Institut, Free University of Berlin

Discussion

Discussants: Mr. Tatsuo Kaneda
Prof. Kimio Uno

October 4, 1985

SESSION III: SOVIET FOREIGN POLICY IN GENERAL

Continuity in the Pattern of Russo-Soviet External Behavior

Kenichi Ito, Professor, Aoyama-Gakuin University, Tokyo

The Military Factor in Soviet Foreign Policy

Tsuyoshi Hasegawa, Professor, Slavic Research Center, Hokkaido University

Discussion

Discussants: Sir James Eberle
Prof. Seweryn Bialer
Prof. Tomoyoshi Hirai
Mr. Makoto Momoi

SESSION IV: THE SOVIET UNION AND ASIA

The U.S.-Soviet Rivalry in East Asia

Donald Zagoria, Professor of Government, Graduate Center, City University of New York

Soviet Policies Toward Korea

Young C. Kim, Professor of Political Science and International Affairs, Institute for Sino-Soviet Studies, George Washington University

Japan and the Development of Siberia

Kazuyuki Kinbara, Staff Economist, Japan Federation of Economic Organization (Keidanren)

Discussion

Discussants: Prof. Hiroshi Kimura
Tatsumi Okabe

PARTICIPANTS

Rapporteurs

Seweryn Bialer, Director, Research Institute on International Change, Columbia University (U.S.A.)

James Eberle, Director, Royal Institute on International Affairs (U.K.)

Marshall Goldman, Professor, Wellesley College, and Associate Director, Russian Research Center, Harvard University (U.S.A.)

Tsuyoshi Hasegawa, Professor, Slavic Research Center, Hokkaido University (Japan)
Kenichi Ito, Professor, Aoyama-Gakuin University (Japan)
Young C. Kim, Professor, Institut for Sino-Soviet Studies, George Washington University (U.S.A.)
Hiroshi Kimura, Director, Slavic Research Institute, Hokkaido University (Japan)
Kazuyuki Kinbara, Staff Economist, Japan Federation of Economic Organizations (Japan)
Peter Knirsch, Professor, Osteuropa Institut, Free University of Berlin (F.R.G.)
Boris Meissner, Professor, Institute of Soviet and East European Law, University of Köln (F.R.G.)
Tsuneaki Sato, Professor, Yokohama City University (Japan)
Donald Zagoria, Professor, Graduate Center of the City University of New York (U.S.A.)

Commentators

Tomoyoshi Hirai, Professor, Osaka City University (Japan)
Tatsuo Kaneda, Director, Agriculture Division, Asian Productivity Organization (Japan)
Akio Kimura, Professor, Aoyama-Gakuin University (Japan)
Shugo Minagawa, Professor, Nanzan University (Japan)
Makoto Momoi, Guest Research Fellow, Yomiuri Research Institute, Yomiuri Shimbun (Japan)
Tatsumi Okabe, Professor, Tokyo Metropolitan University (Japan)
Kimio Uno, Associate Professor, Tsukuba University (Japan)

Conference Organizers

Kinya Niiseki, Chairman and Director, JIIA
Masatada Higaki, Executive Director, JIIA
Kumao Kaneko, Director of Research, JIIA
Jin'ichi Otsuki, Research Fellow, JIIA
Masao Takahashi, Research Fellow, JIIA

Appendix C

PROFILES OF THE RAPPORTEURS

Seweryn Bialer has been Ruggles Professor of Political Science and director of the Research Institute on International Change at Columbia University. He is a specialist in Soviet domestic and foreign policies, contemporary Soviet elites, and U.S.-USSR relations. He is author and coeditor of numerous publications including *Russia at the Crossroads, The 26th Congress of the CPSU, The Domestic Context of Soviet Foreign Policy,* and *After Brezhnev: Sources of Soviet Conduct in the 1980s.*

Sir James Eberle has been director of the Royal Institute on International Affairs since 1984. He was formerly a major NATO commander and U.K. commander-in-chief. He is the author of many articles on maritime strategy and international affairs. He is coauthor of a book entitled *Management in the Armed Services.*

Marshall I. Goldman has been professor of economics at Wellesley College and associate director of the Russian Research Center at Harvard University. He is a specialist in Soviet economy. His books include *U.S.S.R. in Crisis: The Failure of an Economic System, The Soviet Economy: Myth and Reality,* and *The Enigma of Soviet Petroleum.*

Tsuyoshi Hasegawa has been a professor at the Slavic Research Center at Hokkaido University. He received a Ph.D. from Washington University. The main focus of his recent research has been on the military aspect of the Soviet Union. He is the author of *February Revolution: Petrograd 1917.*

Kenichi Ito is professor of International Relations at Aoyama-Gakuin University and overseas representative in Japan of the Center for Strategic and International Studies at Georgetown University. He is a specialist on Japanese, U.S., and Soviet foreign policy. He is the author of *State and Strategy.*

Young C. Kim is professor of political science and international affairs at the Institute for Sino-Soviet Studies at George Washington University. He is coeditor of the *Journal of Northeast Asian Studies.* He has written extensively on international politics. His recent publications include *Japanese-Soviet Relations: Politics, Eco-*

nomics and National Security, Soviet Strategy Toward Japan and U.S., and *Japanese Policies in Asia* (as coauthor and coeditor).

Hiroshi Kimura is director and professor of Political Science at the Slavic Research Center at Hokkaido University. He has a Ph.D. from Columbia University and has been engaging in research on Soviet-Japanese relations with a special emphasis on security. He is the author of numerous books and has contributed many articles on Soviet policy. His titles include *The Soviet Union and the Russians* and *The Soviet Union in Paradox.*

Kazuyuki Kinbara is staff economist at the Japan Federation of Economic Organizations. He spent two years at St. Anthony College at Oxford University, and he participated in the Soviet Study Group of the Chatham House as an academic member. He wrote about Japanese-Soviet economic relations during this period, and his article appeared in a book entitled *The Soviet Union in East Asia.*

Peter Knirsch is professor of the Osteuropa Institut at the Free University of Berlin. He is a specialist on comparative economics, especially comparative planning systems, East-West economic relations, and economy and technology in Eastern Europe. He is the author of many books and articles, including *Structure and Form of Central Economic Planning* and *Development of Technology and Central Planning Economy.*

Boris Meissner has been professor of the Institute of Soviet and East European Law. He is coeditor of several books devoted to the foreign policy, international law, and law of Eastern countries. He is also the author of many books concerning the Soviet Union, Eastern Europe, and East-West relations, including *Russia in Upheaval* and *Russia and Khrushchev.*

Tsuneaki Sato is professor of Economics at Yokohama City University. He has written extensively on the socialist economy, especially that of the Soviet Union. His major publications are *Contemporary Socialist Economy* and *The Economic Reforms in Soviet and East European Countries.*

Donald S. Zagoria teaches international relations at the Graduate Center of the City University of New York and is a fellow of the Harriman Institute and the Research Institute on International Change, both at Columbia University. Professor Zagoria has written several books and more than one hundred articles on Sino-Soviet relations. His recent works on Sino-Soviet relations appear in *Foreign Affairs.* His books include *Soviet Policy in East Asia.* During the Carter administration, he was a consultant to the National Security Council and to the East Asia Bureau of the Department of State.